Teaching Evidence-Based Academic Writing for ESL Educators

This resource helps teachers prepare ESL students for the demands of academic writing that they will encounter in tertiary institutions when they undertake study in English. With over thirty ready-to-use but adaptable lesson plans, this book uses a scaffolded, sequenced approach to instruction so that students are able to progress through their development and practice of academic writing with each iterative lesson through the three distinct writing categories of planning, generating, and reviewing.

The book includes writing exercises for students to practice evidence-based writing and provide justification for their claims, along with examples and answers with explanations for teachers. The lessons themselves will cover a range of writing strategies, including critical reading and analysis, note-taking, organisational strategies, using academic language, critiquing and evaluating texts, constructing and organising an argument, brainstorming, and many more.

This is a practical text, perfect for tertiary and secondary-level teachers of EAL/ESL students, as well as educators working with students in bridging programs for first language speakers of English, tutors, and academic advisors.

Pat Strauss is Senior Research Associate at the University of Johannesburg. Her teaching and research interests include academic writing, student and teacher identity, language teacher education, and English for research and publication purposes.

Teaching Evidence-Based Academic Writing for ESL Educators

Resources and Lesson Plans

Pat Strauss

Routledge
Taylor & Francis Group
NEW YORK AND LONDON

Designed cover image: © Getty Images

First published 2026
by Routledge
605 Third Avenue, New York, NY 10158

and by Routledge
4 Park Square, Milton Park, Abingdon, Oxon, OX14 4RN

Routledge is an imprint of the Taylor & Francis Group, an informa business

© 2026 Taylor & Francis

The right of Pat Strauss to be identified as author of this work has been asserted in accordance with sections 77 and 78 of the Copyright, Designs and Patents Act 1988.

All rights reserved. No part of this book may be reprinted or reproduced or utilised in any form or by any electronic, mechanical, or other means, now known or hereafter invented, including photocopying and recording, or in any information storage or retrieval system, without permission in writing from the publishers.

For Product Safety Concerns and Information please contact our EU representative GPSR@taylorandfrancis.com. Taylor & Francis Verlag GmbH, Kaufingerstraße 24, 80331 München, Germany.

Trademark notice: Product or corporate names may be trademarks or registered trademarks, and are used only for identification and explanation without intent to infringe.

Library of Congress Cataloging-in-Publication Data
Names: Strauss, Pat author
Title: Teaching evidence-based academic writing for ESL educators : resources and lesson plans / Pat Strauss.
Description: New York, NY: Routledge, 2026. | Includes bibliographical references.
Identifiers: LCCN 2025036843 (print) | LCCN 2025036844 (ebook) | ISBN 9781032889818 hardback | ISBN 9781032889801 paperback | ISBN 9781003541691 ebook
Subjects: LCSH: Academic writing--Study and teaching | English language–Study and teaching--Foreign speakers | English language–Rhetoric--Study and teaching
Classification: LCC P301.5.A27 S77 2026 (print) | LCC P301.5.A27 (ebook)
LC record available at https://lccn.loc.gov/2025036843
LC ebook record available at https://lccn.loc.gov/2025036844

ISBN: 978-1-032-88981-8 (hbk)
ISBN: 978-1-032-88980-1 (pbk)
ISBN: 978-1-003-54169-1 (ebk)

DOI: 10.4324/9781003541691

Typeset in Palatino
by SPi Technologies India Pvt Ltd (Straive)

Access the Support Material: www.routledge.com/9781032889801

Contents

Acknowledgements vi

1 Introduction 1

2 Cycle 1: Food in the 21st Century 28

3 Cycle 2: Technology in the Modern World 85

4 Cycle 3: Using Social Media........................... 160

5 Cycle 4: Fast Fashion 221

6 Cycle 5: Artificial Intelligence (AI).................... 271

7 Conclusion... 333

Acknowledgements

My heartfelt thanks go to the teachers and tutors whose questions, insights, and concerns inspired the writing of this book. I am especially grateful to Paula Ollewagen, whose help with the technical aspects was invaluable. Finally, thank you to Johann for his constant support and encouragement.

1

Introduction

Why This Book

English is recognised as the international language of research and scholarship (Hyland, 2013) in line with its rise as the global *lingua franca*. This has led to English for Academic Purposes (EAP) being taught around the world. Bruce (2022) claims the emergence of EAP is "possibly the most academically and economically important development in global teaching" (p. 9). One would expect that given the importance of EAP those involved in its teaching would be valued. Sadly, this is not the case. All too often these teachers are overworked and given few, if any, opportunities for professional development (Joubert & Clarence, 2024).

Their work is not easy. Often, they have not had specific training in the teaching of EAP, and teaching students who need English for their studies is very different from teaching English to those who are learning for general purposes (Hamp-Lyons, 2011). To exacerbate matters, many EAP teachers are employed on non-permanent or sessional contracts. Student ability in the same class often varies widely and class numbers can be high. Staff are often only paid for teaching and marking and not paid for developmental work or undertaking research (Joubert & Clarence, 2024).

I speak from experience in this regard. I specialised in teaching English as a second language (ESL), and when I found myself employed as an EAP teacher I had a great deal of work to do to equip myself to help the students who came to our student centre. Although the experience fired my interest in EAP, it was only when I became a permanent staff member in a university department that I was able to pursue this interest, researching EAP teaching practice and materials development. In this role I taught students who were employed to teach EAP. The complaint voiced repeatedly over the years was that they had no time to develop the kinds of lessons they knew were needed and that they wanted to teach. I hope that this book can in some way alleviate the pressure under which many EAP practitioners work. It has been designed to be a practical aid, but it is not intended to be prescriptive.

Often aids can be used by teachers to stimulate their own thinking (Harwood, 2005), leading them to adapt, improvise and reconfigure the materials on offer (Li and Xu (2020). How teachers "bridge the gap between materials and the students lies at the heart of effective materials use" (Li & Xu, 2020, p. 11). Teachers should use this book in ways that they believe will best help their students. This will probably mean altering and discarding some of the material on offer and that is exactly how it should be. I hope that the book can serve as a springboard for more innovative and interesting material.

Later in the chapter I will lay out how I propose the book could best help practitioners but I would like to explore some of the issues that are central to EAP teaching.

What Is EAP?

English for Academic Purposes (EAP) is defined by "its focus on teaching English specifically to facilitate learners' study or research through the medium of English" (Hamp-Lyons, 2011, p. 89). EAP programmes range from English for General Academic Purposes (EGAP) to English for Specific Academic Purposes (ESAP). The difference between EGAP and ESAP courses is that the latter aims at teaching the kind of English required in a specific discipline area while EGAP courses teach skills that are applicable across a range of disciplines (James, 2010). These skills include note taking, paraphrasing, summarising, plagiarism avoiding skills, citations etc (Flowerdew, 2016).

The gold standard for teaching academic writing is generally considered to be ESAP. Wette (2019) points out that discipline lecturers are experts who can speak with authority about the writing requirements of their areas of expertise. In addition, the question of the transfer of writing skills from a generic approach to a specific discipline area can be problematic.

However, there are serious drawbacks to leaving the teaching of academic writing to discipline staff. These lecturers are often unwilling to take time from content teaching to focus on writing skills. Teaching writing skills is often viewed as a distraction to the content they believe should be their main focus, and they argue that these skills can and should be taught elsewhere (Sun & Soden, 2021; Wette, 2019). Some do not believe that they have the necessary expertise or time for such instruction (Flowerdew, 2016) and feedback on the writing aspect of assignments is not an area that enjoys the attention of many discipline lecturers (Sun & Soden, 2021). In addition, as Wette notes, ESAP programs tend to have "a precarious existence" (p.37) subject as they are to budgeting constraints, staff changes and shifting curricula priorities. In defence of the more generic approach Ferris (2017) argues that activities that promote awareness about writing and language use "increase the likelihood that students will transfer and extend knowledge to new learning situations in academic contexts" (p. 147).

What Are the Challenges Students Face in Academic Writing?

The problems are complex and often difficult to address. Students struggle to:

- Produce essays written in a suitable academic register (Matikainen, 2024).
- Find and use sources (Kocatepe, 2021; Matikainen, 2024; Sun & Soden, 2021). Students find it difficult to interweave different sources with their own ideas, Kocatepe notes that many students simply incorporate information into essays at sentence level. Little attempt is made to draw links between the cited material and their own ideas.

- Demonstrate critical thinking (Haider & Tahira, 2019).
- Avoid plagiarism. Obviously, difficulty communicating in English is an important factor but a lack of training in the use of sources is another important element (Li et al., 2024). In this book the concept of plagiarism is discussed and students are shown how to avoid accusations of plagiarising. They are also given opportunities to put this knowledge into practice.
- Improve organisation and coherence (Matikainen, 2024).
- Enlarge their academic vocabulary (Matikainen, 2024).
- Adopt academic voice (Matikainen, 2024; Sun & Soden, 2021). Voice (or the writer's presence) is regarded as an important component of successful English academic writing (Street 2009; Wingate, 2012).
- Write at length. Sun & Soden (2021) point out that students are often expected to move from courses where they have only practised writing short passages to writing much longer assignments. Chinese undergraduate students in a recent study (Zhu & Strauss, 2025) told researchers that the writing task in their school leaving English exam only required them to write a passage of around 200 words.

These broad areas of concern cannot be seen in isolation from the rest of the student experience. Often ESL students struggle with assignments because they do not understand what is required of them. The types of assignments might well be unfamiliar to them. Matters are exacerbated as these students are often reluctant to ask questions in class because of their cultural backgrounds and/or concern about their spoken English.

This book attempts to address these issues using exercises that allow students to practise the required skills. To achieve the desired outcome, it is important that the lessons are scaffolded and sequenced. These lessons also need to be interesting and enjoyable as students respond better to material they find engaging. Finally, social interaction during class has a very important role to play. Classroom dialogue is regarded as essential for student learning (Tong & Ding, 2024). Students are provided with multiple opportunities to engage in class, group and pair discussions, some led by the teacher and others guided by the students themselves.

The Role of Technology

The rapid advance of technology has affected all sectors of society, and the education sector is no exception (Oates & Johnson, 2025). Therefore we need to consider the role that technology plays in education. On the whole, there appears to be optimism about the role of artificial intelligence (AI) in education, although it is also widely recognised that the use of AI can have serious disadvantages (Farrokhnia et al., 2024; Oates & Johnson, 2025). In this book students are provided with opportunities to explore the benefits of using chatbots in their writing, but they are also afforded opportunities to explore the drawbacks of an over reliance on the technology. The use of technology in providing feedback on students' writing is another area that deserves attention.

Feedback

As indicated earlier, EAP teachers very often have heavy work schedules that make extensive preparation difficult. This is not the only demand on their time as it is essential that they provide written feedback to their students. Providing good feedback is time-consuming. In addition, teachers are justifiably concerned that the effort they put into giving feedback is often wasted. Research indicates that students do not always read the feedback, nor do they act on the advice given (Alisoy, 2024; Lee, 2017. At the same time students expect feedback and are annoyed if it is not provided promptly (Zhang & Hyland, 2022). Many of the exercises in the lesson plans can be marked by the students themselves, but obviously a certain amount of written feedback from the teacher is indispensable.

Ultimately, the aim should be to improve the feedback literacy of students. Molloy et al. (2000) define feedback literacy as the "students' ability to understand, utilise and benefit from feedback processes" (p.528). The authors see feedback-literate students as those who:

- ◆ View feedback as a way to improve their work.
- ◆ View feedback as an active process. They understand that they should not just wait passively for teacher

feedback but should reach out to others – e.g. their peers – for input.
- Seek out feedback on particular aspects of their work e.g. the linking of different sections of an essay.
- Understand that it is natural to feel hurt or disappointed at times when feedback is given, but that this is part of the learning process.
- Acknowledge that as well as getting feedback they should be prepared to provide it.
- Are prepared to put the feedback they receive into practice.

As noted earlier, providing comprehensive feedback for students is time-consuming and many teachers are simply not able to provide detailed feedback for each piece of writing. Using automated writing evaluation (AWE) systems would appear to offer a solution to this dilemma. These systems correct grammar errors, improve clarity and guide students to improve the readability of their texts (Gozali et al., 2024; Zhang & Hyland, 2022). The feedback is very prompt, offering real-time support. Zhang and Hyland believe that because there is no delay students are more willing to engage in revisions. If students take this feedback on board, it should mean that when they are marking teachers do not have to spend time correcting basic errors and can focus on the more cognitive aspects of essay writing such as organisation and development (Gozali et al., 2024).

The development of ChatGPT, however, has added a new dimension to the debate. ChatGPT's ability to understand the content of essays and suggest appropriate changes seems to position it as a more powerful tool than other AWE systems. In addition, ChatGPT's feedback provides the rationale behind suggested changes, an approach which is likely to prove helpful to students (Guo & Wang, 2024). The system's frequent use of praise and encouragement is seen as a bonus.

Although the advantages of ChatGPT are widely recognised, there are concerns that the feedback is often lengthy and not always easy to follow. In addition, the system has no knowledge of the students, and some comments might be inappropriate.

Zhang and Hyland (2022) suggest a compromise. They propose that teachers make use of AWE but also use peer and teacher feedback.

Peer review (which is covered in detail in Chapter 5) is important because its use often leads to exchanges of ideas. In addition, students value the social engagement and support. It is clear though that any AWE feedback, including ChatGPT, cannot and should not replace teacher feedback. Research (Karatay & Karatay, 2024) indicates that though AWE provides speedy feedback, students perceive teacher comments as vital because they are tailored to their specific needs. Students can request that their work is scrutinised for a particular challenge such as the linking of sections. The teacher could then provide detailed feedback on this particular aspect of the student's writing. This not only reduces the teacher's workload but also empowers the students, and they are more likely to pay attention to feedback that they have specifically requested.

The Guiding Principles for the Book

There were many factors to consider in the writing of this book, but these are the six principles that I regarded as key:

1. *Literacy is a social practice rather than a set of skills that need to be learnt* (Hyland, 2013). Hyland explains that texts do not exist in isolation but are "part of the communicative routines of social communities" (p. 7). The communities of EAP are the disciplines in which students and academics research and study. Successful communication is, of course, the result of dialogue. So, dialogue is an essential part of the learning process. In this book extensive use is made of class discussions and group and pair work. Such interactions between students, and students and teachers leads to negotiation of meaning. Each student brings to the discussion the repertoires they have built up during their engagement in other discourses (Kocatepe, 2021). Students are able to test concepts and make adjustments

to their writing plans when they receive feedback from peers (Soltani & Zhang, 2024). In addition, Kocatepe points out the importance of allowing students to interrogate meaning-making practices and develop their own interpretations. In this book students are provided with opportunities to challenge material given to them and make improvements.

2. *The book is evidence-based.* The materials and exercises in this book are based on the research of experts around the world.

3. *The exercises in this book are scaffolded.* Scaffolding refers to the support offered by a teacher or, in some cases, a peer, which enables learners to perform at a higher level than they would have been able to do on their own (Heinonen & Lennartson-Hokkanen, 2015; Tabari et al., 2024). Early activities in the book are heavily scaffolded. As learners grow in their understanding of what is required of them, less support is offered. Scaffolding can be both oral and written. In terms of oral support, the teacher makes space for dialogues to develop which enable students to participate in mutual meaning-making. Discussing and reflecting on material allows students to develop a greater and deeper understanding than they would if they simply listened to an explanation provided by the teacher. Sun and Soden (2021) emphasise the importance of scaffolding activities to guide students through the process of translating source material into their writing.

4. *The exercises in this book are sequenced.* Sequencing is very important in the development of L2 writing. Research (Tabari et al., 2024) indicates that if exercises are sequenced from simple to complex, students are less anxious about the writing process. In addition, if there is a repetition of the same kinds of exercises this also serves to lower student anxiety as they become more familiar with the type of tasks that will be required of them. The book is built on the concept of starting with easy exercises and then moving to more complex tasks. In addition, the same types of exercises are repeated in all cycles allowing students to become familiar with the skills essential for good writing.

5. *The exercises are designed to ensure student interest and enjoyment.* There is a recent move to encourage positive emotions in the learning process (Hu & Zhang, 2025; Tabari et al., 2024). Education enjoyment is seen as the satisfaction a student experiences when participating in an activity. This feeling with regard to L2 writing has been defined as the "learner's experience of joy and pleasure while writing in a second language" (Papi et al., 2022, p. 383). This enjoyment has been linked to an increase in student confidence and willingness to cope with challenges. It is also important as positive emotions towards writing encourage students to take ownership of the process (Hu & Zhang, 2025). Alzubi and Nazim (2024) point out that interested students are more likely to be motivated to write. To encourage this enjoyment students are exposed to a variety of texts. The bulk of these texts are versions of academic articles that have been summarised in such a way that they are more accessible. In addition, other material such as newspaper and online articles, blogs, TED talks and video clips have been used to stimulate student interest and increase enjoyment. These less traditional materials also help with the sequencing of materials as these inputs are often written in more easily understandable English, and as such can help students progress to more demanding writing tasks (Kocatepe, 2021).
6. *The lesson plans should be detailed and explicit.* The lesson plans in this book are very detailed. All the material needed for the teaching is provided and prompts for discussion and suggestions for teaching strategies are included. Answers are given for all questions and models for student responses are provided. As indicated earlier, teachers should feel free to make any changes to the lessons they feel would be an improvement. The suggested models and answers are supplied to free up time teachers could put to better use engaging with students. In addition, advice about the marking of exercises is provided. Many of the exercises can be marked by students themselves, working individually or in pairs or groups.

Before I move onto discussing how the book has been structured I would like to say a brief word about the use of citations and references and pronouns in the book.

Citations and References

To summarise briefly – a citation is a way of giving individuals credit for their work so a citation style is a set of rules explaining how someone else's work needs to be referred to in an academic text. A reference list situated at the end of the text lists all the sources that have been cited (Pandey et al., 2020). There are three main types of citation:

- Parenthetical citations e.g. APA, where the details of the author are given in brackets in the text, usually with the date or the page number (e.g. Johnston, 2023).
- Numerical citations e.g. Vancouver, where each source is given a number which corresponds to an entry in the numbered reference list (e.g. [24]). In the Reference list this would be cited as:
  24. Johnston. R. *Student Writing in the Modern World.* Auckland (NZ): Bonson Press; 2023.
- Note citations, where the full citation is included in a footnote or endnote.

Practically, it would not be possible to represent all the various citing and referencing styles. Pandey et al. (2020) discuss 17 of the most used systems! Therefore, I have chosen to use APA 7. The APA style provides useful guidelines for academic writing regardless of the discipline area (Purdue University, n.d.) and it is the most frequently used style in social sciences (Pandey et al., 2020). However, it would not be difficult to employ another citation and referencing system if you feel that this would help your students.

Use of Pronouns

There are two issues that need to be covered here. The first is the use of "they" as a singular pronoun e.g. XX (2023) refers to epicene pronouns in *their* article on academic writing. In recent years, there has been a growing desire to avoid gender bias in language (Stormbom, 2019). Up until the second half of the 20th century it was customary to use "he" as a generic pronoun, but as researchers pointed out it was very difficult not to associate "he" with a male (Stormbom, 2019). In this book the pronoun "they" (with a plural verb) is used as the third-person singular pronoun. It might be an idea to point this out to students in case they believe that the use of "they" is a grammatical error.

The second issue has to do with the use of first-person pronouns to refer to the author. The use of "I" in academic writing has increased dramatically. Hyland and Jiang (2017) note that between 1965 and 2015 the use of first-person pronouns in academic writing had increased by 45%. Avoiding the first person to convey impartiality used to be "a hallowed principle" (Hyland & Jiang, 2017, p. 45), but that practice is changing. In the exercises in this book I have suggested that students be allowed to use "I" as this makes it easier for them to express their opinions. I suggest that you point out to them that the use of "I" differs from one discipline to another and that they should check with their discipline lecturers.

The Layout of the Book

The book consists of seven chapters. Chapter 1 is the introduction. Chapters 2–6 contain the lesson plans. Each of these chapters constitutes a cycle made up of 6 interrelated lessons. Over the 30 lessons it is envisaged that the students will develop growing competence in the areas outlined earlier. I have chosen to include 30 lessons as this should meet the needs of most institutions offering writing tuition for students planning to enter tertiary English-medium institutions. Often these courses are offered in blocks ranging in duration from a month to six months. The lessons can be taught on a weekly, biweekly or daily basis.

The final chapter discusses the role of classroom assessment in teaching academic writing. These assessments are informal and serve primarily to inform teachers and students of the latter's progress and where there appear to be challenges.

Suggestions are provided about the design and implementation of class assessments. The first assessment is analysed in detail in the final chapter. The other assessments can be accessed online. You can access them by visiting the book product page: www.routledge.com/9781032889801 (or search for the book title on routledge.com).

The strategies students need in order to produce successful academic writing must be practised. The students' first piece of writing is a 150-word paragraph (Cycle 2 Lesson 2). The length of the written work is gradually increased until students are equipped to write an essay of approximately 1500 words. In order to reach this goal an iterative approach is employed for the development of writing skills. For example students are introduced to the concept of paraphrasing in Cycle 1 Lesson 3. Initially, students simply choose what they believe to be the best paraphrase of a short extract, providing a reason for this choice. The next step is to paraphrase a sentence. Advice is provided to the teacher as to how paraphrasing can best be introduced. As students progress, they will be required to undertake more complex paraphrasing, and more advice will be provided. This is the approach that is adopted for all the strategies taught in the book. The aim is to increase the complexity once students have become familiar with the concept.

It is important that students find the context of the lessons interesting and relevant to their own lives. One of the advantages offered by ESAP courses is that the classwork is situated in the field of study in which students are, or plan to be, enrolled. This is not possible in an EGAP resource, so the chapter themes have been chosen for their broad appeal and relevance.

Themes

Chapter 2 Cycle 1: Food in the 21st Century.
Chapter 3 Cycle 2: Technology in the Modern World.
Chapter 4 Cycle 3: Social Media.
Chapter 5 Cycle 4: Fast Fashion.
Chapter 6 Cycle 5: AI and Education.
Chapters 2–6 (Cycles 1–5) cover the following:

	Cycle 1	Cycle 2	Cycle 3	Cycle 4	Cycle 5
Preparation for writing	Recording data Writing up data Taking notes Listening for information	Listening for information Reading to collect data	Reading data from figures Writing up notes Introducing literature reviews Finding reliable sources	Collecting data from different sources	Taking notes Tabling data from different sources Planning an essay
Language skills	Paraphrasing Academic register Linking words	Academic vocabulary Changing register Linking words Personal pronouns	Paraphrasing idiomatic language		Paraphrasing
Cognitive skills	Inferring Voicing opinion	Critical thinking Creative thinking Weighing pros and cons Exploring and comparing definitions Looking at different sides of an argument Inferring	Linking data Comparing and contrasting data Critical thinking Evaluating sources	Critical thinking Creative thinking Relating data to own observations Introduction to an academic theory Discussing plagiarism Peer reviewing Putting peer review into practice Critiquing peer review guidelines. Dialogue between writers and reviewers	Comparing and contrasting data Using AI in writing Critical thinking Creative thinking Using a thinking strategy Considering reliability of chatbots. Discussing opinions with peers for possible reconsideration

(*Continued*)

	Cycle 1	Cycle 2	Cycle 3	Cycle 4	Cycle 5
Writing skills	Evidence based writing Argumentative essay Writing up own ideas	Summarising Introductions Body paragraphs Conclusions Writing definition Structuring an essay Using examples	Description in academic writing Summarising similar results Evidence based writing Writing the discussion essay	Using collected data to write an essay Implementing changes after a review Planning an essay Writing an essay	Analysing data and giving opinions Recording changing opinions Implementing feedback Writing a peer review Writing an essay
Technical skills	Introduction to referencing Translating data into graphs Reading graphs for information Using graphic organisers	Identifying sources Using in-text citations Using direct quotes	Drawing up a graph Using in-text citations	Using data to draw a diagram Completing diagrams Reviewing in-text citations and references	Using direct quotes Using Google Scholar Checking citations and references

The Layout of Each Lesson

Each lesson has the following items:

- Time.
- Overview.
- Purpose and Strategies.
- Teacher Notes.

Time

Each lesson has been designed for two hours. However, this time is quite flexible. You might wish to shorten certain exercises or omit them altogether. Equally you might feel that some of the activities that students are enjoying could be extended. In the last two cycles it is unlikely that students will be able to complete the written work in class and the completion of these exercises should be done in the students' own time.

Overview

The overview is a very brief summary of the context of the lesson and the work students will be required to complete. Here is the overview from Cycle 1 Lesson 1:

> This lesson serves as the introduction to the course. The topic *Food in the 21st Century* was chosen for this lesson cycle because it is sure to have wide appeal! This lesson introduces the idea of register in writing and the importance of evidence-based writing. Students are asked to provide evidence for their answers. Finally, students are required to complete a brief questionnaire.

Purpose and Strategies

These tells you what the aims of lessons are and how these aims can be achieved. Here is an example from Cycle 1 Lesson 1:

Purpose	*Strategies*
Introducing academic register	Identifying formal and informal vocabulary
Finding evidence for claims	Using the reading to agree or disagree with claims

(Continued)

Purpose	Strategies
Recording data	Filling in a questionnaire
Writing up data	Using questionnaire to write a short paragraph

Teacher Notes

Each lesson has extensive teacher notes. They are indicated by

⇒ *Teacher Notes*

These notes cover every aspect of the lesson. They explain in detail what the lesson aims to achieve and suggest ways in which the teaching can be approached. The answers and models in the lesson plan are shown in capitals to make them easy to identify. Here is an example from Cycle 3 Lesson 5. Students are asked to write a very short essay about misrepresentation in research reporting. The necessary information has been supplied as has a model answer indicated in this way:

ACADEMIC MISREPRESENTATION: THE CASE OF DAVID HÄNIG

ACADEMIC MISREPRESENTATION MEANS THAT RESEARCH FINDINGS ARE NOT ACCURATELY PRESENTED. THE RESEARCH OF DAVID HÄNIG IS AN ILLUSTRATION OF ACADEMIC MISREPRESENTATION. THIS ESSAY WILL OUTLINE HÄNIG'S RESEARCH AND EXPLAIN HOW AND WHY IT WAS MISREPRESENTED. THE ESSAY WILL CONCLUDE WITH A BRIEF DISCUSSION OF THE SERIOUSNESS OF SUCH MISREPRESENTATION.

HÄNIG WAS A GERMAN SCIENTIST WHO WAS INTERESTED IN HOW HUMANS PERCEIVED THE DIFFERENT TASTE SENSATIONS OF SWEET, SALTY, BITTER AND SOUR. HE DISCOVERED THAT CERTAIN AREAS OF THE TONGUE WERE MORE RECEPTIVE TO THE DIFFERENT SENSATIONS THAN OTHERS. THE RECEPTORS AT THE TIP OF THE TONGUE WERE MORE SENSITIVE TO SWEET SENSATIONS, THE RECEPTORS AT THE BASE OF THE TONGUE RECORDED BITTERNESS THE BEST, WHILE THE SIDES OF THE TONGUE IDENTIFIED SWEET AND SALTY MORE EASILY. HOWEVER, HÄNIG MADE IT VERY CLEAR THAT EVERY SENSATION CAN BE TASTED ACROSS THE ENTIRE TONGUE, AND THE SENSATIONS ARE ONLY SLIGHTLY INCREASED IN THE AREAS INDICATED.

BECAUSE HÄNIG WAS GERMAN HE PUBLISHED HIS RESEARCH IN HIS NATIVE LANGUAGE. THIS MEANT THAT IT COULD ONLY BE READ BY PEOPLE WHO COULD READ GERMAN. ALSO, ONLY THOSE WITH EXPERTISE IN HIS RESEARCH AREA COULD REALLY UNDERSTAND HIS FINDINGS. IN ADDITION, HIS COMPLICATED DIAGRAMS WERE SIMPLIFIED TO MAKE THEM EASIER TO UNDERSTAND. THE SIMPLIFICATION IMPLIED THAT SENSATIONS COULD ONLY BE TASTED IN CERTAIN PARTS OF THE TONGUE. THIS IS WHAT PEOPLE CAME TO BELIEVE.

Student Worksheets

Student worksheets have been designed for each of the 30 lessons. These worksheets are all available on the webpage for this book:

www.routledge.com/9781032889801

Here is an example of the worksheet for Cycle 1 Lesson 1:

WORKSHEET
CYCLE 1: LESSON 1

NAME _____

Exercise 1
Read the passage and answer the questions that follow.

READING: THE GROWING POPULARITY OF STREET FOOD

Street food is defined as ready-to-eat food and beverages prepared and sold by vendors, especially in the streets. It is the people's food. Although street food stalls have been on the go for over 4000 years, they have all come into being for the same reason. They cater for the working classes who cannot afford expensive ingredients or restaurant meals. The popularity of street food was increased by urbanisation. People no longer live close to their workplaces and the long commute means that they cannot go home for a meal in the middle of the workday. In addition, overcrowding in cities means that many people live in small, cramped spaces without adequate kitchen facilities. Women's roles have also changed, and as more and more women work outside the home it becomes difficult for them to meet the nutritional needs of their families.

Street food is more prevalent in the countries of the southern hemisphere where they are an important source of cheap food and employment. About 2.6 billion people eat street food in some form every day.

However, street food has very much stepped into the 21st century. There are several TV series about street food, documenting its development and highlighting the role of vendors. Social media has become a very important marketing tool for these vendors. It provides free publicity and gives potential consumers all the necessary information they need about the products. It is also a recognised tourist drawcard. It offers tourists affordable food and entertainment at the same time. They have an opportunity to mix with the locals and experience the sense of togetherness that comes with people chatting and laughing over the meals.

There are, of course, a number of disadvantages. There are concerns about overcrowded streets presenting a traffic hazard. There is always a great deal of noise and litter where there are food stalls. Food storage can be a problem particularly in hot and humid climates where food can spoil quickly. Often people have to work without running water. Authorities might not be bothered about food standards and the quality of food might not be well regulated or it might not be regulated at all. Nonetheless, street food has much to offer in providing employment, inexpensive meals, a place for people to meet and mingle, and a growing way to attract tourist money.

REFERENCES

Bouafou, K. G. M., Beugré, G. F. C., & Amani, Y. C. (2021). Street food around the world: A review of the literature. *Journal of Service Science and Management, 14*, 557–575. https://doi.org/10.4236/jssm.2021.146035

Fusté-Forné, F. (2021). Street food in New York City: Perspectives from a holiday market. *International Journal of Gastronomy and Food Science, 24*. https://doi.org/10.1016/j.ijgfs.2021.100319

Henderson, J. (2019). Street food and tourism: A Southeast Asian perspective. In E. Park, S. Kim, & I. Yeoman (Eds.), *Food tourism in Asia* (pp. 45–57). Springer.

Wiatrowski, M., Czarniecka-Skubina, E., & Trafialik, J. (2021). Consumer eating behaviour and opinions about the food safety of street food in Poland. *Nutrients, 13*, 594. https://doi.org/10.3390/nu13020594

Exercise 1.1

In this exercise find the formal words in the text which mean the same as the phrases/words provided. The first answer has been filled in.

Column A	*Column B*
The movement of people from the country to cities	Urbanisation
People who sell items to the public	
A set distance that is travelled usually between work and home	
Necessary for good health	
Something that attracts people's attention	
Buyers	
Something that is dangerous	
Controlled by rules	
Providing sources of information	

Exercise 1.2

The text has given us information about street food. Read the statements below and decide whether they are true (T) or false (F) or whether there is no evidence (NE) in the text for you to make a decision. Based on the information contained in the text you need to provide evidence for your choice.

Statement	T/F/NE	Evidence
Street food's greatest contribution is that it attracts international tourists.		
There are concerns that people buying street food could be hurt by passing vehicles.		
According to the text street food is likely to be more popular in England than in South Africa.		
The rising employment of women has had an effect on the way many families eat.		
Eating street food is good for your health.		

Exercise 2: Recording data

Complete the questionnaire on your street food usage. Put a cross in the box to show your answer.

How often do you buy street food?

Every day	At least twice a week	Once a week	Two or three times a month	Once a month	Once every two or three months	Never

How important is price when you buy street food?

Very Important	Important	Neutral	Not Important	Not Important at All

How important is the location when you buy street food?

Very Important	Important	Neutral	Not Important	Not Important at All

How important is hygiene when you buy street food?

Very Important	Important	Neutral	Not Important	Not Important at All

How important is the menu when you buy street food?

Very Important	Important	Neutral	Not Important	Not Important at All

Exercise 2.1
Number the following statements with 1 being most important and 6 being least important for you.

I eat street food because it is convenient.	☐
I eat street food because I don't have time to prepare meals myself.	☐
I eat street food because I like to discover new flavours.	☐
I eat street food because I don't like cooking.	☐
I eat street food because I do it with my friends.	☐
I eat street food because it is cheap.	☐

What street food do you like the most? _____

(Adapted from: Wiatrowski, M., Czarniecka-Skubina, E., & Trafialik, J. (2021). Consumer eating behaviour and opinions about the food safety of street food in Poland. *Nutrients*, *13*, 594. https://doi.org/10.3390/nu13020594)

As discussed earlier, the demands in the lessons have been carefully sequenced. Initially, students write very short paragraphs starting in the second lesson. These texts increase in length as students progress. It is difficult to estimate how much space each student will require to complete the various paragraphs and essays, so no space has been allocated for exercises that require more than a few words or a short sentence. Students should complete these exercises online or on paper. It is important that students save their work as many of the exercises are based on students' own earlier work.

There are numerous tables for students to complete, and these have all been reproduced in the worksheets. Most of these tables contain prompts and reminders for students as they are working through the exercises. This is in keeping with the principle of scaffolded learning.

The Phases of the Lesson

Each lesson consists of three sections:

- Pre-class activities.
- Activities during class.
- Post-class activities.

The pre-class activities serve as an introduction to the lesson. They range from class discussions to quizzes to viewing short video clips. All the activities are designed to relate to the students' own lives and spark interest in the lesson content. Normally, these activities would be introduced to students at the beginning of the class. However, Yaylacı and Beauvais (2017) point out that students who lack confidence in their English might be hesitant to take part in discussions. If you feel that this might be the case with your own students, you might wish to give them prior warning of the topic so that they can come prepared to participate in the discussions.

The activities during class make up the bulk of the lesson plan.

The post-class activities are suggestions for extra work for students. This work can be given as homework or could be useful in a class where there are differing proficiency levels. More advanced students can explore the extension activities allowing time for you to focus on students who need more help.

References

Alisoy, H. (2024). The role of teacher feedback in enhancing ESL learners' writing proficiency. *Global Spectrum of Research and Humanities, 1*(2), 65–71. https://doi.org/10.69760/gsrh.01022024007

Alzubi, A.A.F., & Nazim, M. (2024). Students' intrinsic motivation in EFL academic writing: Topic-based interest in focus. *Heliyon, 10*, e24169. https://doi.org/10.1016/j.heliyon.2024.e24169

Bruce, I. (2022). Universities in the twenty-first century: Structures, funding, management and governance. In I. Bruce & B. Bond (Eds.), *Contextualizing English for academic purposes in higher education: Politics, policies and practices* (pp. 9–28). Bloomsbury Publishing.

Farrokhnia, M., Banihashem, S.K., Noroozi, O., & Wals, A. (2024). A SWOT analysis of ChatGPT: Implications for educational practice and research. *Innovations in Education and Teaching International, 61*(3), 460–474. https://doi.org/10.1080/14703297.2023.2195846

Ferris, D. (2017). Facilitating L2 writers' academic language development. In J. Bitchener, N. Storch, & R. Wette (Eds.), *Teaching writing for academic purposes to multilingual students* (pp. 145–167). Routledge.

Flowerdew, J. (2016). English for specific academic purposes (ESAP) writing: Making the case. *Writing & Pedagogy, 8*(1), 5–32. https://doi.org/10.1558/wap.v8i1.30051

Gozali, I., Wijaya, A. R. T., Lie, A., Cahyono, B. Y., & Suryati, N. (2024). ChatGPT as an automated writing evaluation (AWE) tool: Feedback literacy development and AWE tools' integration framework. https://doi.org/10.29140/jaltcall.v20n1.1200

Guo. K., & Wang, D. (2024). To resist it or to embrace it? Examining ChatGPT's potential to support teacher feedback in EFL writing. *Education and Information Technologies, 29*, 8435–8463. https://doi.org/10.1007/s10639-023-12146-0

Haider, G., & Tahira, M. (2019). The role of critical thinking in academic writing: An investigation of EFL students' perceptions and writing experiences. *International Online Journal of Primary Education, 8*(1), 1–30.

Hamp-Lyons, L. (2011). English for academic purposes. In E. Hinkel (Ed.), *Handbook of research in second language teaching and learning volume II* (pp. 89–105). Routledge.

Harwood, N. (2005). What do we want EAP teaching materials for? *Journal of English for Academic Purposes 4*, 149–161. https://doi.org/10.1016/j.jeap.2004.07.008

Heinonen, M. E., & Lennartson-Hokkanen, I. (2015). Scaffolding strategies: Enhancing L2 students' participation in discussions about academic texts. *Journal of Academic Writing, 1*(1), 42–51.

Hu, N., & Zhang, C. (2025). Effects of strategy-based instruction on Chinese EFL learners' writing enjoyment: A mixed-methods study. *SAGE Open*, 1–15. https://doi.org/10.1177/21582440251315221

Hyland, K. (2013). Writing in the university: education, knowledge and reputation. *Language Teaching, 46*(1), 1–18. https://doi.org/10.1017/S0261444811000036

Hyland, K., & Jiang, F. (2017). Is academic writing becoming more informal? *English for Specific Purposes, 45*, 40–51. https://doi.org/10.1016/j.esp.2016.09.001

James, M.A. (2010). An investigation of learning transfer in English-for-general academic-purposes writing instruction. *Journal of Second Language Writing, 19*, 183–206. https://doi.org/10.1016/j.jslw.2010.09.003

Joubert, M., & Clarence, S. (2024). "I just feel very dispensable": Exploring the connections between precarity and identity for academic literacy developers. *Journal of English for Academic Purposes, 71*, Article 101425. https://doi.org/10.1016/j.jeap.2024.101425

Karatay, Y., & Karatay, L. (2024). Automated writing evaluation use in second language classrooms: A research synthesis. *System, 123*, 103332. https://doi.org/10.1016/j.system.2024.103332

Kocatepe, M. (2021). Reconceptualising the notion of finding information: How undergraduate students construct information as they read-to-write in an academic writing class. *Journal of English for Academic Purposes, 54*, Article 101042. https://doi.org/10.1016/j.jeap.2021.101042

Lee, I. (2017). Working hard or working smart? Comprehensive versus focused written corrective feedback in L2 academic contexts. In J. Bitchener, N. Storch & R. Wette (Eds.), *Teaching writing for academic purposes to multilingual students* (pp. 168–180). Routledge.

Li, Y., & Ge, M., & Chen, Q. (2024). How English academic writing textbooks written by Chinese EFL teachers address the issue of plagiarism. *Journal of English for Academic Purposes, 69*, Article 101388. https://doi.org/10.1016/j.jeap.2024.101388

Li, Z., & Xu, Y. (2020). Unpacking the processes of materials use: An interdisciplinary perspective of language teachers' use of materials in China. *SAGE Open, 10*(4). https://doi.org/10.1177/2158244020977875

Matikainen, T. (2024). Academic writing in English: Lessons from an EMI-program in Japan. *Journal of English for Academic Purposes, 68* Article 101358. https://doi.org/10.1016/j.jeap.2024.101358

Molloy, E., Boud, D., & Henderson, M. (2000). Developing a learning-centred framework for feedback literacy. *Assessment & Evaluation in Higher Education, 45*(4), 527–540. https://doi.org/10.1080/02602938.2019.1667955

Oates, A., & Johnson, D. (2025). ChatGPT in the classroom: evaluating its role in fostering critical evaluation skills. *International Journal of Artificial Intelligence in Education.* https://doi.org/10.1007/s40593-024-00452-8

Pandey, S., Pandey, S., Dwivedi, S., Pandey, D., Mishra, H., & Mahapatra, S. (2020). Methods of various citing and referencing style: Fundamentals for early career researchers. *Publishing Research Quarterly, 36*, 243–253. https://doi.org/10.1007/s12109-020-09726-0

Papi, M., Vasylets, O., & Ahmadian, M. J. (2022). Individual difference factors for second language writing. In S. Li, P. Hiver, & M. Papi (Eds.), *The Routledge handbook of second language acquisition and individual differences* (pp. 381–395). Routledge. https://doi.org/10.4324/9781003270546-30

Purdue University (n.d.) *APA style workshop*. https://owl.purdue.edu/owl/research_and_citation/apa_style/apa_overview_and_workshop.html

Soltani, B., & Zhang, L. (2024). Implementing feedback literacy practices through self-assessment and peer feedback: A language socialization perspective. *Australian Review of Applied Linguistics*. https://doi.org/10.1075/aral.23053.sol

Stormbom, C. (2019). Language change in L2 academic writing: The case of epicene pronouns. *Journal of English for Academic Purposes, 38*, 95–105 https://doi.org/10.1016/j.jeap.2019.02.001

Street, B. (2009). "Hidden" features of academic paper writing. *Working Papers in Educational Linguistics (WPEL), 24*(1), 1–17. http://repository.upenn.edu/wpel/vol24/iss1/1

Sun, Q., & Soden, B. (2021). International students' engagement with support in developing source use abilities: A longitudinal case study. *Journal of English for Academic Purposes, 51* Article 100981. https://doi.org/10.1016/j.jeap.2021.100981

Tabari, M. A., Khajavy, G. H., & Goetze, J. (2024). Mapping the interactions between task sequencing, anxiety, and enjoyment in L2 writing development. *Journal of Second Language Writing, 65*, Article 101116. https://doi.org/10.1016/j.jslw.2024.101116

Tong, Y., & Ding, Y. (2024). Productive classroom dialogue and its association with student achievement in knowledge-building environments. *Language and Education, 39*(1), 232–251. https://doi.org/10.1080/09500782.2024.2323207

Wette, R. (2019). Embedded provision to develop source-based writing skills in a Year 1 health sciences course: How can the academic literacy developer contribute? *English for Specific Purposes, 56*, 35–49 https://doi.org/10.1016/j.esp.2019.07.002

Wingate, U. (2012). Argument! Helping students understand what essay writing is about. *Journal of English for Academic Purposes, 11*, 145–154. https://doi.org/10.1016/j.jeap.2011.11.001

Yaylacı, Ş., & Beauvais, E. (2017). The role of social group membership on classroom participation. *PS: Political Science & Politics*. https://doi.org/10.1017/S104909651600319X

Zhang, Z., & Hyland, K. (2022). Fostering student engagement with feedback: An integrated approach. *Assessing Writing*, *51*, 100586. https://doi.org/10.1016/j.asw.2021.100586

Zhu, Y., & Strauss, P. (2025). The perceptions of undergraduate Mainland Chinese students of the effect of English instruction on their ability to write academic English. *New Zealand Studies in Applied Linguistics*, *31*(1), 24–43 https://doi.org/10.59690/dh16304

Cycle 1

Food in the 21st Century

Lesson 1: Street Food

Time: 2 hours

Overview

This lesson serves as the introduction to the course. The topic *Food in the 21st century* was chosen for this lesson cycle because it is sure to have wide appeal! This lesson introduces the idea of register in writing and the importance of evidence-based writing. Students are asked to provide evidence for their answers. Finally, students are required to complete a brief questionnaire.

Purpose and Strategies

Purpose	*Strategies*
Introducing academic register	Identifying formal and informal vocabulary
Finding evidence for claims	Using the reading to agree or disagree with claims
Recording data	Filling in a questionnaire
Writing up data	Using questionnaire to write a short paragraph

⇒ *Teacher Notes*

It is often a good idea to start a lesson by drawing on students' prior knowledge. In this lesson the focus is on street food, which is sure to be something that almost all your students know about. Talking about simple familiar topics is a good way to get students to relax and take part in discussions in English.

Pre-Class Activities
Start a conversation with the class about street food. You might mention what you like and why. Here are a few questions you could ask:

- What is your favourite street food?
- Where is the best place to buy it?
- What are your favourite savoury/sweet/snack dishes?
- How often do you buy street food?
- What does it take to be a good street food vendor?
- What do you think about the prices?

During Class
Exercise 1

⇒ *Teacher Notes*

There are a number of ways in which you can approach reading this text. You might:

- Read it through with the class and discuss it as you go.
- Give it to students to read on their own in class.
- Ask students to read the text in preparation for the class.
- Ask students to read the text in groups.

Here are a few questions that you might want to give to students before the reading to help guide them through the passage:

- Why is street food popular with ordinary working people?
- How has urbanisation made street food even more popular?
- How have street food vendors being affected by social media in the 21st century?

Exercise 1
Read the following passage.

READING: THE GROWING POPULARITY OF STREET FOOD

Street food is defined as ready-to-eat food and beverages prepared and sold by vendors, especially in the streets. It is the people's food. Although street food stalls have been on the go for over 4000 years, they have all come into being for the same reason. They cater for the working classes, who cannot afford expensive ingredients or restaurant meals. The popularity of street food was increased by urbanisation. People no longer live close to their workplaces and the long commute means that they cannot go home for a meal in the middle of the workday. In addition, overcrowding in cities means that many people live in small, cramped spaces which lack adequate kitchen facilities. Women's roles have also changed; as more and more women work outside the home, it becomes difficult for them to meet the nutritional needs of their families.

Street food is more prevalent in the countries of the southern hemisphere, where they are an important source of cheap food and employment. About 2.6 billion people eat street food in some form every day.

However, street food has very much stepped into the 21st century. There are several TV series about street food, documenting its development and highlighting the role of vendors, for whom social media has become a particularly important marketing tool. It provides free publicity and gives potential consumers all the necessary information they need about the products. Street food is also a recognised tourist drawcard, simultaneously offering tourists affordable food and entertainment. They have an opportunity to mix with the locals and experience the sense of togetherness that comes with people chatting and laughing over meals.

There are, of course, a number of disadvantages, including the overcrowded streets presenting a traffic hazard. There is always a great deal of noise and litter where there are food stalls. Food storage can be a problem, particularly in hot and humid climates where perishable goods can spoil quickly. Often people have to work without running water. Authorities might not be bothered about food standards and the quality of food might either not be well regulated, or might even not be regulated at all. Nonetheless, street food has much to offer in terms of providing employment, inexpensive meals, a place for people to meet and mingle, and a growing way to attract tourist money.

REFERENCES

Bouafou, K. G. M., Beugré, G. F. C., & Amani, Y. C. (2021). Street food around the world: A review of the literature. *Journal of Service Science and Management, 14,* 557–575. https://doi.org/10.4236/jssm.2021.146035

Henderson, J. (2019). Street food and tourism: A Southeast Asian perspective. In E. Park, S. Kim, & I. Yeoman (Eds.), *Food tourism in Asia* (pp. 45–57). Springer.

Fusté-Forné, F. (2021). Street food in New York City: Perspectives from a holiday market. *International Journal of Gastronomy and Food Science, 24.* https://doi.org/10.1016/j.ijgfs.2021.100319

Wiatrowski, M., Czarniecka-Skubina, E., & Trafialik, J. (2021). Consumer eating behaviour and opinions about the food safety of street food in Poland. *Nutrients, 13,* 594. https://doi.org/10.3390/nu13020594

Exercise 1.1

⇒ *Teacher Notes*

REGISTER

This is an introductory vocabulary exercise that asks students to find the word in the text that links up with the definition provided. What is also important about this first exercise is that it introduces students to the concept of register – that is, the idea that texts are written in a certain style.

Register is important in academic writing. What we mean by register is the kind of grammar and words that are chosen for a piece of writing to ensure it is appropriate for its purpose. Academic writing is always formal. The rules of grammar are followed and vocabulary is carefully chosen. Slang and colloquialisms (the kind of word we use in ordinary conversation with friends) are usually avoided.

Here are two examples that you could use to explain this concept to students:

In the reading we find the sentence beginning:

> Although street food stalls have been *on the go* for over 4000 years…

The term on *the go* is colloquial language that doesn't belong in academic writing. It is better to say:

> Although street food stalls have been *in existence* for over 4000 years…

The second example from the reading:

> Authorities *might not be bothered* about food standards…

The term *might not be bothered* is colloquial language that doesn't belong in writing. It better to say:

> Authorities *might not regulate* food standards well.

In this exercise the first answer has been filled in for the students. Column A gives a description of formal words found in the text they have just read. They are asked to write these words in Column B next to their description.

This exercise could be marked by the students themselves; alternatively, they could mark each other's work. A good way to do this would be to discuss the exercise in class and allow the students to come up with the correct answers.

Exercise 1.1

In this exercise find the formal words in the text which mean the same as the phrases/words provided.

Column A	Column B
The movement of people from the country to cities	urbanisation
People who sell items to the public	VENDORS
A set distance that is travelled usually between work and home	COMMUTE
Necessary for good health	NUTRITIONAL
Something that attracts people's attention	DRAWCARD
Buyers	CONSUMERS
Something that is dangerous	HAZARD
Controlled by rules	REGULATED
Providing sources of information	REFERENCES

Exercise 1.2

⇒ *Teacher Notes*

READING CRITICALLY

Students need to read texts with understanding and insight. One of the most common criticisms that higher education teachers have of their students is that the students do not engage critically with the text they read. In other words, they don't think critically about what they are reading. In order to encourage students to think more analytically Exercise 3 asks them to find evidence for their answers from the text. The exercise also requires them to consider whether the text does provide an answer.

A good way to start this exercise is to do the examples with the class, and then allow them, either individually or in groups, to complete the rest of the exercise. Once this has been done, their responses can be discussed as a whole class exercise and students can mark their own work.

EXAMPLE 1

The text has given us information about street food. Read the statements below and decide whether they are True or False based on the information contained in the text. You may find there is No Evidence for the statement. For example, look at the statement:

> People move to cities so that they can sell the food they make in more densely populated areas.

This is not mentioned in the text so there is No Evidence for this statement. Where you respond with True or False you need to provide a reason for your answer.

EXAMPLE 2

> Food stalls do not usually inconvenience people living in the streets where food stalls are set up.

This is False as the text tells us that there is a great deal of litter and noise around food stalls.

Exercise 1.2

Statement	T/F/No evidence	Evidence
Street food's greatest contribution is that it attracts international tourists.	F	WHILE ATTRACTING TOURISTS IS AN UNDENIABLE BENEFIT, STREET FOOD'S MOST IMPORTANT SERVICE IS PROVIDING AFFORDABLE FOOD FOR RESIDENTS OF CITIES
There are concerns that people buying street food could be hurt by passing vehicles.	T	WE ARE TOLD THAT STREET FOOD STALLS ARE A TRAFFIC HAZARD. HAZARD IS ANOTHER WORD FOR DANGER.
According to the text, street food is likely to be more popular in England than in South Africa.	F	WE ARE TOLD THAT STREET FOOD IS MORE PREVALENT (WIDESPREAD) IN THE SOUTHERN HEMISPHERE. SOUTH AFRICA IS IN THE SOUTHERN PART OF THE WORLD AND ENGLAND IS IN THE NORTHERN PART OF THE WORLD.

(Continued)

Statement	T/F/No evidence	Evidence
The rising employment of women has had an effect on the way many families eat.	T	WOMEN ARE WORKING OUTSIDE THE HOME IN GREATER NUMBERS AND THIS HAS AFFECTED THEIR ABILITY TO PROVIDE FOOD FOR THEIR FAMILIES.
Eating street food is good for your health.	NO EVIDENCE	WE ARE TOLD THAT STREET FOOD IS CHEAP BUT NOT THAT IT IS GOOD FOR US. SOME STREET FOOD MIGHT NOT BE HEALTHY AT ALL.

Exercise 2

⇒ *Teacher Notes*

RECORDING DATA

One of the most important skills in academic writing is the ability to record data accurately. Exercise 4 asks students to complete a simple questionnaire and ranking question. This questionnaire is adapted from an academic research project. As well as providing material for the students to write up in Lesson 2, the exercise introduces them to the use of questionnaires, a data collection tool widely used in research. Students should each complete the questionnaire and then use this data as a basis for discussion. This could be a whole-class or a group discussion. For example, the responses of all students to the multiple-choice questions could be circulated to the whole group. (This could be done by a show of hands.) The students could work on their own or in groups. Students would then be able to compare and contrast preferences and choices.

Here is one easy way. Say you have a class of 30 students. Here are their responses to the first question *How often do you buy street food?*

Every day	At least twice a week	Once a week	Two or three times a month	Once a month	Once every two or three months	Never
4	10	6	7	1	2	1

Students could then look more closely at the figures. It could be noted that 20 students eat street food at least once a week. Another way that this could be recorded is that two-thirds of the class eat street food at least once a week. Taking it a step further the data reveals that 27 of the students (or 90%) eat street food at least two or three times a month. The discussion could then focus on why street food is so popular or the students could move on and look at the group's answers to the next question.

The second part of this exercise asks students to rank their preferences as far as street food is concerned. Weighing and evaluating options is an important part of academic writing and this is an easy introduction to the idea of the respective values of statements.

Exercise 2

Complete the questionnaire.

How often do you buy street food?

Every day	At least twice a week	Once a week	Two or three times a month	Once a month	Once every two or three months	Never

How important is price when you buy street food?

Very important	Important	Neutral	Not important	Not important at all

How important is the location when you buy street food?

Very important	Important	Neutral	Not important	Not important at all

How important is hygiene when you buy street food?

Very important	Important	Neutral	Not important	Not important at all

How important is the menu when you buy street food?

Very important	Important	Neutral	Not important	Not important at all

Exercise 2.1

Number the following statements, with 1 being the most important and 6 being the least important.

I eat street food because it is convenient.	☐
I eat street food because I don't have time to prepare meals myself.	☐

(Continued)

I eat street food because I like to discover new flavours.	☐
I eat street food because I don't like cooking.	☐
I eat street food because I do it with my friends.	☐
I eat street food because it is cheap.	☐
What street food do you like the most? _____	

(Adapted from: Wiatrowski, M., Czarniecka-Skubina, E., & Trafialik, J. (2021). Consumer eating behaviour and opinions about the food safety of street food in Poland. *Nutrients, 13*, 594. http:/doi.org/10.3390/nu13020594)

Ask students to keep their questionnaires as they will form the basis of the writing exercise in Lesson 2.

⇒ *Teacher Notes*

POST-CLASS ACTIVITIES

The five questions and the ranking question provide a great deal of information for students to discuss in class. It is important to point out to them that they are basing their conclusions on the evidence provided by the questionnaires (that is, the data). If time allows, students could explore a number of possibilities and also marry the answers to the multiple-choice questions with the ranking question. For example, students might compare the answer to the first item on the questionnaire with what has been chosen as the most important factor in their purchase of street food.

Student A buys street food every day because it is convenient.

Student B buys street food once a month to discover new flavours.

Student C buys street food at least twice a week because it is cheap.

Student D buys street food once a week to save time.

Student E buys street food at least twice a week because they don't like cooking.

The responses of these students appear to indicate that their purchase of street food is linked to practical reasons, cost, convenience, and time saved. This is just one example of how the questionnaires can be used in class. You might want to ask students what they would like to explore!

Lesson 2: Food Around the World

Time: 2 hours

Overview of Lesson

This lesson requires students to do their first piece of writing. Students are also required to take notes from a short TEDTalk. Listening to these lecture-style talks will prepare them for what they will encounter in tertiary classrooms. They will also be required to infer meaning from the context – a very important skill. Finally, this lesson will introduce them to referencing, explaining its importance in academic writing and, in particular, the use of the doi system. This will be done against the background of a discussion about food waste.

Purpose and Strategies

Purpose	Strategies
Writing up data	Using a model to help with writing.
Taking notes	Using a short TEDTalk to simulate taking notes in class.
Inferring	Deducing meaning from context in a passage.
Introduction to referencing	Explanation of its importance and the use of dois.

Pre-Class Activities

⇒ *Teacher Notes*

This lesson builds on the first one. The topic of food is resumed, but this time we are also exploring food waste. An easy way of getting students' attention is to give them a short quiz. This one tests their knowledge about popular foods around the world. It should only take about 5 minutes to complete.

1. What is the most widely eaten staple food in the world?

| Bread | RICE | Pasta | Potatoes |

2. Which dish is made with fermented cabbage and is popular in Korea?

| Miso soup | Pad Thai | Tacos | KIMCHI |

3. What is a key ingredient in traditional hummus?

| Rice | Lentils | CHICKPEAS | Potatoes |

4. What is the main ingredient in guacamole?

| AVOCADO | Tomato | Cheese | Onion |

5. Which country is known for making croissants?

| Italy | FRANCE | Spain | Germany |

6. Which dish is made with thin wheat noodles and is commonly eaten in China?

| Pho | Ramen | Spaghetti | LO MEIN |

7. Which dish is often made with rice, seafood, and saffron and is popular in Spain?

| Biryani | Curry | PAELLA | Sushi |

Reference

OpenAI. (2025). *ChatGPT* (March 31) [Large language model].

During Class
Exercise 1

⇒ *Teacher Notes*

The data gathered in the first lesson provide the basis for this writing exercise. The brief model answer below could be provided to students if teachers believe it is necessary. It has gaps – for example, the writer has not provided their favourite food!

I BUY STREET FOOD AT LEAST THREE TIMES A WEEK. ONE OF THE MOST IMPORTANT REASONS FOR ME IS THAT IT IS CHEAP. ALSO, THERE ARE A

LARGE NUMBER OF STALLS NEAR MY HOME SO IT IS VERY CONVENIENT. I KNOW SOME PEOPLE THINK THAT STREET FOOD VENDORS DO NOT WORRY ENOUGH ABOUT HYGIENE. THESE PEOPLE ARE CONCERNED THAT THEY MIGHT BECOME ILL IF THEY EAT STREET FOOD. I DO NOT WORRY ABOUT THIS. I HAVE BEEN EATING STREET FOOD FOR A LONG TIME AND I HAVE NEVER BECOME ILL. I AM NOT VERY ADVENTUROUS. I LIKE TO EAT THE SAME KIND OF FOOD ALL THE TIME, SO I USUALLY GO TO THE SAME FOOD STALLS OVER AND OVER AGAIN. I AM NOT INTERESTED IN TRYING NEW FLAVOURS. WHAT IS IMPORTANT FOR ME IS THAT THE FOOD IS CHEAP AND I JUST HAVE TO GO DOWNSTAIRS TO GET A MEAL.

One of the difficulties with teaching writing is that it requires a great deal of marking on the part of the teacher. This personalised feedback is very important for student progress, but it should not be allowed to become a burden to the teacher. At this early stage it might be an idea to collect this first short piece of writing and mark the work. This will help you get an idea of the students' English language abilities. I suggest that the comments are simple and positive e.g. *You seem to have access to a wide array of street foods!* You could then focus on one area that needs attention – for example, the use of tenses – and provide a little feedback. The student might, for example, switch between tenses for no good reason, or they may have a problem with noun/verb agreement. If you highlight just the one aspect that needs improvement, this looks a lot more doable to a student than a text where everything seems to be wrong!

Exercise 1

Look at the information that you have gathered about your own preferences (the things you like and do not like) about street food. Write a short paragraph of about 150 words explaining how you feel about street food. If you do not eat street food at all explain where you like to eat out, how often you eat out each month, and what your favourite foods are.

Exercise 2

⇒ *Teacher Notes*

Taking notes from an oral presentation.

One of the challenges that English as a Secondary Language (ESL) students face is following lectures and class discussions. Lecturers and their fellow students have different accents and speak at differing speeds. This can all make following conversations and lectures very difficult. Often in preparatory classes teachers compensate for students' lack of familiarity with spoken English, slowing down the tempo of their speech and choosing their vocabulary carefully. This is unlikely to happen in mainstream classes and students need practice in listening and taking notes. The advantage of using short video clips is that the students can listen as many times as they like. In addition, visual clues are often provided. In Exercise 2, students are given a link to a short TEDTalk (5:31) and then asked to answer a few questions. It would be a good idea to give the questions to the students before they watch the video. The questions can be discussed in class and if there are any problems with the vocabulary these issues can be sorted out before the students start listening. At this early stage students should be allowed to listen to the talk as many times as they need to in order to answer the questions set.

In this exercise students are also asked to work out the meaning of a phrase from the context. It might be an idea to practice this with students before they embark on the listening exercise. You can point out to them that they will have a very heavy reading load when they are studying and that they will often encounter unfamiliar words. It is not always necessary to spend time looking up these words. Often their meaning can be inferred from the context.

Here is an example that you might use to explain this to them.

Inferencing is using the evidence you have to get answers. If you do not know the meaning of the word you can often work out what the meaning is by the context in which it is used.

For example:
About 80 years ago farmers in north-west China uncovered a full-sized clay soldier. This soldier was one of a 10,000-strong army. A Chinese emperor had believed that these combatants would protect him in the afterlife.

The word combatants might be new to students, but looking at the clues in the rest of the extract (soldier, army) it would be easy to guess that it would be something to do with fighting. So a combatant is a fighter. Students could also be shown that part of the word might be familiar. In this example they might know the word combat, which would be a great help.

This exercise can be carried out individually or in pairs. At this early stage students might find it easier to work in pairs. Students can mark their own or each other's work. This can be done while the class is discussing the exercise.

Exercise 2

In Lesson 1, we talked about street food and its growing popularity. It appears that there is a great deal to be said for the informal food sector, but it also shares many of the concerns of the rest of the food industry. One of these concerns is the enormous amount of food that goes to waste.

Watch the video (5:31) all the way through and then answer the questions.

https://www.ted.com/talks/annabelle_amyot_food_waste

2.1 What nationality is the speaker? How do you know this?
   CANADIAN - SHE TELLS US THAT IN CANADA FOOD WASTE COSTS US ...."

2.2 What percentage of the world's population, according to the speaker, goes hungry?
   11% (1 IN 9 PEOPLE).

2.3 The speaker talks about "the modern ubiquity of food". Ubiquity means that something (in this case food) seems to be present everywhere all the time. What examples does the speaker give to support this claim?
   SHE TALKS ABOUT SUPERMARKETS, FAST FOOD OUTLETS, COFFEE SHOPS, AND VENDING MACHINES.

2.4 In your own words explain the suggestions the speaker makes to help solve the food waste problem.
   ♦ THE GOVERNMENT SHOULD MAKE LAWS BANNING SUPERMARKETS FROM THROWING AWAY FOOD THAT CAN STILL BE EATEN. THIS FOOD CAN BE DONATED TO CHARITIES.
   ♦ PEOPLE SHOULD BE ABLE TO SAY HOW MUCH THEY WANT TO EAT.

- PEOPLE SHOULD THINK MORE CAREFULLY ABOUT WHAT FOOD THEY BUY SO AS NOT TO WASTE IT.

2.5 The speaker says that shoppers prefer to buy food that is "aesthetically pleasing". Without looking up the word "aesthetically", what do you think the phrase "aesthetically pleasing" means?

SOMETHING THAT YOU THINK IS BEAUTIFUL. AESTHETICS IS ABOUT APPRECIATING WHAT IS BEAUTIFUL.

2.6 The comments below were passed about a large poster of an apple that was used in campaign to promote apples. Which of the shoppers do you think find the picture of the apple aesthetically pleasing? Explain your answer.
- Shopper A: Won't win a beauty contest.
- Shopper B: Nice and shiny.
- Shopper C: It bulges at the side.
- Shopper D: Odd colour.
- Shopper E: Bright red.
- Shopper F: Apples are good for you – doesn't matter what they look like!

SHOPPERS A, C, D AND F DO NOT SEEM TO FIND THE APPLES AESTHETICALLY PLEASING. SHOPPER A SAYS THE APPLE IS NOT ATTRACTIVE, SHOPPER C DOES NOT LIKE THE SHAPE, SHOPPER D DOES NOT SEEM TO LIKE THE COLOUR AND SHOPPER F SAYS THAT LOOKS DON'T MATTER – WHAT IS IMPORTANT IS THAT THE APPLE IS GOOD FOR YOU. THIS IMPLIES THAT SHOPPER F DOES NOT FIND THE PICTURE ATTRACTIVE. IN CONTRAST, SHOPPERS B AND E SEEM TO LIKE THE APPEARANCE OF THE APPLE. SHOPPER B LIKES THE FACT THAT IT IS SHINY AND SHOPPER E SEEMS TO LIKE THE COLOUR.

Exercise 3

⇒ *Teacher Notes*

REFERENCING

Referencing is very important in academic writing for a number of reasons:

- It is a way to acknowledge that information and ideas in your work have come from someone else's work. If you do not acknowledge this, you can be accused of plagiarism, that is using someone else's work without giving them proper credit.

References tell your reader where the information in the text comes from. It shows that you have been thorough and careful in your research.

- It allows your reader to find the sources and read this information themselves.
- It provides evidence (reasons) for what you are saying. In academic writing we need to be able to give evidence for what we write. We usually find this evidence by reading what researchers have discovered.

Writing reference lists used to be an area where students experienced difficulties. However, with the availability of online tools such as Endnote fewer need help in this regard. The problems that students experience with referencing and citations are less technical but often more difficult to deal with. Direct quotes tend to be something that students either overuse or avoid completely, terrified that they will be accused of plagiarism. Neither option is desirable, although the second is preferable. However, even if students use direct quotes appropriately, they often have considerable difficulty fitting these quotes into the text smoothly and grammatically. We will be looking at this in more detail in later lessons.

Despite the widespread availability of software to help with referencing it is still necessary to help students become familiar with the process. In this book students will gradually be introduced to various aspects of referencing and citations. Talking about the doi (digital object identifier) found in most good journal articles is an easy introduction to academic articles. Exercise 3 requires students to do a very simple online search, using a doi and then read and answer questions about the abstract of an article. The abstract has been chosen as it is short and straightforward. All the texts to which students are referred are in the public domain.

Exercise 3

Under the text in Lesson 1 is a list. Here it is:

The items in this list these are known as references. These tell you where the information in the text comes from. In academic writing, we need to be able to give evidence (reasons) for what we are saying. We usually find this evidence by reading what researchers have discovered. We always say where we found our evidence so that people who read our ideas can read this evidence (sources) for themselves. You will see that 3 of these references have a doi – that is a digital object identifier. This is a string of numbers, letters and symbols used to identify an article e.g. https://doi.org/10.3390/nu13020594.

Using a doi is an easy and quick way to find the article – you just need to type (or better still cut and paste) it into a search engine. The other reference is a chapter in a book – it does not have a doi.

Look at the article by Fusté-Forné. Type the doi into your search engine (e.g. Google or Bing). Read the abstract of the article (the short summary at the beginning) and answer the following questions:

    3.1 How many interviews did the author carry out?
          30 INTERVIEWS.
    3.2 What is meant by "a crucial factor to improve revenue"?
          AN IMPORTANT WAY TO MAKE MORE MONEY.
    3.3 What is this crucial factor?
          SOCIAL MEDIA.
    3.4 Why do you think it is so important?
          SO MANY PEOPLE USE SOCIAL MEDIA THAT IT IS A GOOD WAY TO LET PEOPLE KNOW ABOUT YOUR PRODUCT.

References

Bouafou, K. G. M., Beugré, G. F. C., & Amani, Y. C. (2021). Street food around the world: A review of the literature. *Journal of Service Science and Management, 14*, 557–575. https://doi.org/10.4236/jssm.2021.146035

Henderson, J. (2019). Street food and tourism: A Southeast Asian perspective. In E. Park, S. Kim & I. Yeoman (Eds.), *Food tourism in Asia* (pp. 45–57). Springer.

Fusté-Forné, F. (2021). Street food in New York City: Perspectives from a holiday market. *International Journal of Gastronomy and Food Science, 24*. https://doi.org/10.1016/j.ijgfs.2021.100319

Wiatrowski, M., Czarniecka-Skubina, E., & Trafialik, J. (2021). Consumer eating behaviour and opinions about the food safety of street food in Poland. *Nutrients, 13*, 594, https://doi.org/10.3390/nu13020594

Post-Class Activities

⇒ *Teacher Notes*

1. There are many opportunities for students to write different reports based on the questionnaire provided in the last lesson. The reports could move from a personal account to a simple recording of the group preferences. This could be as straightforward as recording:

   Four students eat street food every day; 10 consume street food at least twice a week…

   or it could be a more in-depth report comparing and contrasting the data collected. The teacher would be the best judge of the class's ability at this stage. We will be revisiting the writing up of data regularly.

2. If students enjoyed listening to the talk, they could be encouraged to look for other short talks on the Internet. These could be about subjects of interest to them. They could be encouraged to write a very brief summary of the contents of these videos. The summaries, with the relevant URLs, could be circulated in class so that other students can choose videos they would like to watch.

Lesson 3: We Eat With Our Eyes

Time: 2 hours

Overview

The text below continues the discussion in Lesson 2 about healthy and nutritional foodstuffs that are rejected by consumers because they do not look perfect. The lesson revolves around the concept that consumers buy with their eyes and asks what can be done to change this behaviour. During the lesson students are asked to look to the literature to find solutions to problems. They will also be introduced to paraphrasing.

Purpose and Strategies

Purpose	*Strategies*
Developing solutions backed up by the literature	Backing up own solution to a problem by referring to the passage.
Introduction to paraphrasing	Choosing the best paraphrase.
Paraphrasing	Tips for paraphrasing – paraphrasing very short texts.

Pre-Class Activities

⇒ *Teacher Notes*

In this lesson students will be examining the idea that they should look deeper than the surface. There are a number of idioms in English that illustrate this concept that there's more to someone/something than meets the eye:

- Handsome is as handsome does.
- Fine feathers make fine birds.
- There's more to a book than its cover.

Ask the students if they know any of these idiomatic expressions and then ask them for idiomatic expressions in their own languages that illustrate the same concept. It might be interesting to ask them to translate the expression literally and then explain its figurative meaning.

The parallel can then be drawn between this concept and food waste. A huge quantity of perfectly good food goes to landfill because consumers dislike its appearance. Researchers suggest that making customers believe that they are doing a good thing buying produce that is not particularly attractive might encourage a change in behaviour.

During Class
Exercise 1

⇒ *Teacher Notes*

There are a number of ways in which you can approach this reading. You might:

- Read it through with the class and discuss it as you go.
- Give it to students to read on their own in class.
- Ask students to read the text in preparation for the class.
- Ask students to read the text in groups.

At this stage it would probably be a good idea to give the definition of suboptimal as something that is less than perfect. It is important to stress that the nutritional value of the food is not affected.

Here are a few questions that you might want to give to students before the reading to help guide them through the passage:

- Does your supermarket/food store/food market sell suboptimal fruit and vegetables?
- Do you think most shoppers are prepared to eat suboptimal fruit and vegetables?
- Are you prepared to do so?
- Do you think lowering the price would make people more willing to buy this produce?

- Would you be more willing to do so?
- What do you think would be more important to shoppers – lower prices or that their actions would be good for the environment?

Exercise 1

READING: "UGLY" PRODUCE

We know at least a third of all the food produced is wasted or lost. We have seen how important it is to reduce that loss, but one of the real problems is that people are unwilling to sell, buy, or eat suboptimal food products. Suboptimal means less than perfect and, in the case of food, this is used to refer to oddly shaped produce, such as a potato which has odd bumps on the surface. Quite often suboptimal food is removed from the production line before it even goes into the shops because the sellers are concerned about the shoppers' reaction to food that does not look perfect. This means that consumers do not even have a chance to decide whether they are happy to eat food that looks less than perfect.

The important question is: why don't people buy produce that looks different? Research suggests that consumers expect unattractive produce to be less tasty and healthy, so it is important that retailers are able to overcome these beliefs. One way to overcome people's dislike of this produce is to offer it at a discounted price. However, sellers need to be careful about offering large discounts because consumers often associate such price drops with low quality. Price is not the only consideration when people buy produce. As indicated, they also want food that is tasty and healthy.

So, are there ways to overcome consumers' dislike of fruits and vegetables which are quite safe to eat but which might not look perfect? There has been quite a lot of research in this regard because it is not only financially important that this food is not wasted but also critical for the environment. A number of researchers in the United States and the United Kingdom have produced a possible solution. They refer to widely accepted research on the "what is beautiful is good" stereotype. This stereotype means that we believe that what is beautiful is always better than the less attractive option. For example, people who are physically attractive are seen as more intelligent, more trustworthy, and better at their jobs than less attractive people. Goods that are beautifully wrapped are more popular than the same goods when they are not so beautifully wrapped. Consumers buy with their eyes. The American and British researchers argue that if we are to overcome these prejudices we need to make the consumers feel that they are doing a good thing when they buy less attractive produce. For example, we could make people who buy this produce feel that they are more knowledgeable about food and the environment than other consumers who are not willing to do so.

Another way that appears to encourage the purchase of unattractive produce is simply by paying shoppers a compliment. Research in Sweden shows consumers are more likely to buy such produce when it is sold under a sign "You are Fantastic! Pick Ugly Produce!" than they are when the sign simply reads "Pick Ugly Produce!"

It appears that one good way to sell perfectly acceptable produce that does not look attractive is to make shoppers feel good about themselves!

REFERENCES

Bolos, L, Lagerkvist, C., Edenbrant, A., & Nayga, R. (2022). Consumer preferences for visually sub-optimal food: Role of information framing and personal goals. *Resources, Conservation & Recycling, 184*. https://doi.org/10.1016/j.resconrec.2022.106426

De Hooge, I., Giesen, R., Leijsten, K., & van Herwaarden, C. (2022). Increasing the sales of suboptimal foods with sustainability and authenticity marketing strategies. *Foods, 11*. https://doi.org/10.3390/foods11213420

Grewal, L., Hmurovic, J., Lamberton, C., & Reczek, R. (2019). The self-perception connection: Why consumers devalue unattractive produce. *Journal of Marketing, 83*(1), 89–107. https://doi.org/10.1177/0022242918816319

Exercise 1.1

⇒ *Teacher Notes*

In this exercise students are asked to come up with their own slogans to promote products that might look less than perfect. You might want to work through an example (given below) with the class. Afterwards students can work individually or in groups. It must be stressed to the students that they should be able to justify the use of the slogans by referring to the reading. In this instance, this is a straightforward requirement, but it emphasises the need for evidence-based writing.

> *So I'm a funny shape – it's what's on the inside that counts!*

This could be used as a starting slogan and together you and the students can alter/add to the slogan to incorporate the suggestions made in the text below.

> *So I'm a funny shape but you're smart enough to know – it's what's on the inside that counts!*

The justification would be (from the text) that you are paying the consumer the compliment of saying they are too intelligent to be misled by the superficial.

Students are often very proud of the work they develop. It would probably be a good idea for you to move around the class while the students are working on their slogans. This will give you an opportunity to point out mistakes in the labels so that they can improve the final product. If time allows, the groups might like to compare what they have done. Formal marking of these attempts does not seem to be a particularly good idea.

Exercise 1.1

Look at the following labels that retailers use to label suboptimal fruit and vegetables. Using the ideas given in the text you have just read, change these labels to make them more effective in attracting customers. Back up your changes by referring to the text.

- Nobody's perfect.
- Produce with personality.
- Produce with purpose.

Exercise 2

⇒ *Teacher Notes*

In this part of the lesson, you need to reinforce the concept that academic writing is evidence-based – that students need to give evidence for the things that they are saying in their writing. In order to do that they need to refer their readers to what experts and researchers have said but they have to paraphrase the words of these experts. Paraphrasing is expressing someone else's ideas in your own words. Students need to reflect the experts' views accurately using the students' own words.

Paraphrasing can be quite difficult because often one can't think of any other words than those that the author has used! A good tip for the students is to tell them to read through the text a few times and then LOOK AWAY from the text and write down what the author was saying. Not looking at the text helps them to use their own words because they won't be able to remember the words of the original exactly.

These three steps can be useful for students:

1. Read the piece you are going to paraphrase a few times.
2. Write the paraphrase **without** looking at the passage. Try to capture the meaning.
3. Compare what you have done with the passage. Have you misunderstood anything? Have you conveyed the original meaning clearly?

Exercise 2 is an easy introduction to paraphrasing. Students are asked to decide which one of the paraphrases provided is the best one and why. It would be a good idea to mark this exercise with the students so you can pick up on any misunderstandings.

Exercise 2

Read the following sentence from the text and then decide which of the examples given best paraphrases the main ideas in the sentence. Choose one of the reasons supplied to explain why you have accepted the one example and rejected the other examples.

Original text:

Unsurprisingly, sensory attributes contribute to consumers' food acceptance or rejection, with prior research demonstrating that visual appearance is a key determinant of consumer liking.

Paraphrases:

1. It is not surprising that our senses contribute to whether we accept or reject food as buyers. Earlier research shows us that visual appearance is an important determinant of buyer liking.
2. We buy what we like the look of.
3. It is to be expected that the way food looks, smells, feels, and tastes will influence what is purchased. Research has shown that the way food looks is particularly important to the buyer.

4. It is rather surprising that buyers buy or do not buy food because of the way it looks. Earlier research shows us that people are more concerned about the nutritional value of food than about the way it looks.

Possible reasons:

- There are too many words that are the same as the original text.
- This paraphrase does not capture the meaning of the original text.
- This paraphrase is too brief and does not contain all the information in the original text.
- This paraphrase is the best answer because it gives all the information in the original text but it does so in different words.

Sentence	√ X	Reason
1.	X	1 IS TOO CLOSE TO THE ORIGINAL TEXT. THERE ARE TOO MANY WORDS THAT ARE SIMILAR IN BOTH PASSAGES.
2.	X	2 IS BRIEF AND DOES CAPTURE THE MAIN IDEA. UNFORTUNATELY, IT IS TOO BRIEF AND DOES NOT CONTAIN ALL THE INFORMATION IN THE ORIGINAL TEXT – THAT IS WHAT EARLIER RESEARCH HAS SHOWN.
3.	√	3 IS THE BEST ANSWER. IT GIVES ALL THE INFORMATION IN THE ORIGINAL TEXT, BUT IT DOES SO IN DIFFERENT WORDS.
4.	X	4 CANNOT BE ACCEPTED BECAUSE IT HAS NOT CONVEYED THE INFORMATION IN THE ORIGINAL TEXT. IT IS SAYING THE COMPLETE OPPOSITE OF WHAT IS CONTAINED IN THE TEXT.

Now try to paraphrase yourself using this slightly longer piece from the text. Try altering the structure of the sentences. For example, you could start this paraphrase by saying:

If unattractive produce is offered at a cheaper price...

One way to overcome people's dislike of this "ugly" produce is to offer it at a discounted price. However, sellers need to be careful about offering large discounts because consumers often associate these price drops with low quality.

> IF UNATTRACTIVE PRODUCE IS OFFERED AT A CHEAPER PRICE BUYERS MIGHT BE MORE PREPARED TO PURCHASE IT. VENDORS MUST BE CAUTIOUS THOUGH BECAUSE BUYERS MIGHT BELIEVE THAT PRODUCE IS OFFERED CHEAPLY BECAUSE THE QUALITY IS NOT OF A HIGH STANDARD.

Post-Class Activities

⇒ *Teacher Notes*

Students could be asked to work on other products – perhaps promoting the use of items that are more environmentally friendly. They could, for example, look at different brands of toilet paper and promote less luxurious options! If the teacher believes students would be interested, they could look on the Internet for articles that justify the use of these more environmentally friendly products. These articles could be used to justify the development of slogans.

Another possibility is asking students to write a short column for a local newspaper persuading the readers to try less than perfect produce, citing the reasons for why this is a good thing.

Lesson 4: Who Is Wasting the Most?

Time: 2 hours

Overview
The passage continues the theme of food waste, but the data in the reading is more quantitatively orientated. Students are required to convert written text to graphs. They will also be reading tables for information. The data they find will be used as evidence to back up their opinions.

Purpose and Strategies

Purpose	*Strategies*
Note-taking	Filling in a table of quantitative data from the reading.
Translating data into bar graphs	Using notes to complete graphs.
Reading tables for information	Table with data.
Using evidence to reach conclusions	Responding to questions where the answers are not straightforward.
Voicing opinion backed up by evidence	Giving an opinion that is supported by data provided in readings and graphs.

Pre-Class Activities

⇒ *Teacher Notes*

Ask the class about food waste in their own lives. The following questions could be used as a prompt:

- What kind of food do you think is often wasted?
- Why do you think this food goes to waste?
- Do you think this is something we should be concerned about? Why?
- Do you think you waste a lot of food?
- Do you have ways in which you try to limit food waste?

Then tell the class that in order to understand the work they are going to do they need to know what the following terms mean and what the difference is between the two. Allow students the opportunity to discuss these terms:

- Total food waste;
- Per capita food waste.

What are the words used in their languages? Do they also use the Latin expression per capita?

It is important that students understand that the first refers to all the food that is wasted by a country every year, and that the second refers to how much each person in that country (on average) wastes every year. Per capita is a Latin term that translates to "by head". Although we can just say "per person", per capita is a phrase often found in academic writing.

Point out to them too that the total food waste is measured in million tons and the per capita food waste is measured in kilograms (kgs). Ask them why they think food waste is recorded in this way (the average person doesn't waste tons of food, but countries do!)

During Class

⇒ *Teacher Notes*

Exercise 1
This reading might be best carried out in groups or pairs. The first exercise asks the students to complete a table by referring to the data provided in the reading. All the answers have been provided for you but gaps have been left in the worksheets. They will then use this data to complete a graph. Before they start their graphs it might be a good idea to get them to check amongst themselves that they have recorded the information correctly. This can be done quite simply in pairs with one student reading out the amounts and the other checking that they have recorded the same amounts. Once the graphs have been completed, students should work in pairs to check the accuracy of their graphs

Exercise 1

READING: FOOD WASTE

According to the World Food Program, 828 million people around the world are not sure where their next meal will come from. What is troubling is that about a third of all the food produced globally is thrown away every year. This is more than enough to feed all these people. We all need to work together to ensure that this food is not wasted, and perhaps the first step is to find which countries have the most work to do in this regard. It is important, though, that we look not only at the total waste of food that each country is responsible for but also the per capita figure. Per capita is simply another way of saying per person. Although countries with large populations will waste a great deal of food, this does not mean that the people in these countries are necessarily the most wasteful. For example, China's total food waste is more than 91 million tons each year, but it is calculated that each person wastes about 64 kg. In comparison, Australia wastes only 2 million tons a year but on average each Australian is responsible for wasting a staggering 102 kg of food. That means that most Australians waste nearly 40 kg more food each year than their Chinese counterparts.

India has the highest population of any country in the world. It is estimated that India wastes 68 million tons of food each year, but the per capita waste is 50 kg, which is less than half of what the average Australian wastes.

Russia is another country that appears to minimise food waste. Despite its large population of 144 million people, the country only wastes 4 million tons of food a year, and the per capita food waste is only 33 kg. Many people probably think that the United States would be responsible for wasting a lot of food, and it is true that the US throws away 19 million tons of food annually. However, despite this large figure, each American on average is only responsible for 59 kg of waste each year. By contrast, the United Kingdom and Spain both average 77 kg per capita, with the UK dumping 5 million tons of food a year and Spain wasting 3 million tons. Not far behind these two countries is Germany wasting 6 million tons of food, with the average German throwing away 75 kg each year.

It is thought that the density of Japan's population contributes to the fact that the country dumps 8 million tons of food each year, but the Japanese, with a per capita waste of 64 kg, certainly do better than France as the French population is almost half the size of the Japanese. The average French person wastes over 85 kg per year, with the country as a whole contributing 5 million tons to the overall global food waste.

Unfortunately, some of the poorer countries in the world have higher food waste per capita. For example, Nigeria tops the world scale with 189kg per capita (38 million tons for the whole country) and the Democratic Republic of the Congo (DRC), which wastes 9 million tons, records 103 kg of food waste per person. It seems strange that so much food is wasted in countries where so many people are starving.

However, the question of food waste is not straightforward. Food is wasted at different stages in developed and developing countries. In developed countries like the United States, UK and Australia, it is mostly consumers who waste the food. People buy more food than they need and then much of this is wasted. In developing countries, much of the food is wasted before it even reaches shops or markets. Most farmers in developing countries do not have access to the technology they need to keep food fresh. They do not have refrigerated trucks to transport food and some have to rely on bicycles or motor bikes to transport their produce. In addition, many farmers in developing countries do not have adequate storage facilities for food. With the temperature in countries such as Nigeria averaging between 24 and 30°C, this is a real problem. In addition, these farmers do not have the technology to deal with crop diseases and pests. In India, it is estimated that about a third of the crops are lost to pests. Because the farmers do not have access to modern agricultural products often their only solution is to remove pests from their crops by hand. This is enormously time-consuming and inefficient.

REFERENCES

The Borgen Project. (2020, September 20). Food waste around the world. *The Borgen Project.* https://borgenproject.org/food-waste-around-the-world/

Kumar, A., Sarkar, S., & Pradhan, C. (2019). Recommendation System for Crop Identification and Pest Control Technique in Agriculture. *International Conference on Communication and Signal Processing*, April 4–6, 2019, India. https://www.researchgate.net/profile/Avinash-Kumar-133/publication/332675754

University of Sheffield. (n.d.) *Reducing food waste in developing countries.* University of Sheffield https://www.sheffield.ac.uk/sustainable-food/research/reducing-food-waste-developing-countries

World Population. (2023). World population by country 2023. *World Population Review.* https://worldpopulationreview.com/

World Population. (2023). Food waste by country 2023. *World Population Review.* https://worldpopulationreview.com/country-rankings/food-waste-by-country

Exercise 1.1

Use the following table to record the information you need from the passage. The first entry has been completed for you. Then draw up two bar graphs.

- a) In the first bar graph (which has been started for you), you will show the food waste per country of all the countries named in the passage.
- b) In the second chart, show the food waste per capita of each country named in the passage.

Information sheet

Country	Total Food Waste (million tons)	Per Capita Food Waste (kg)
China	91	64
Australia	2	102
India	68	50
Russia	4	33
US	19	59
UK	5	77
Spain	3	77
Germany	6	75
Japan	8	64
France	5	85
Nigeria	38	189
DRC	9	103

Partially completed first graph supplied to students

Million of tons of food wasted per country 2022

Students will then complete the second graph on their own

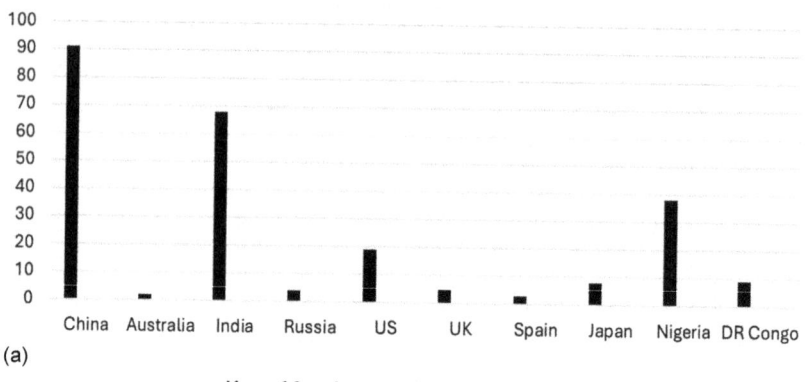
(a)

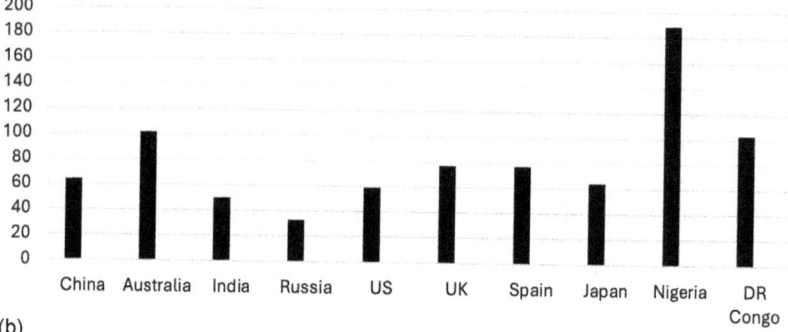
(b)

Exercise 2

⇒ *Teacher Notes*

In Exercise 2, students will be given a table showing 18 countries: six each in Asia, Africa, and Europe. Each country is accompanied by a number indicating the percentage of people in that country who **could** afford to eat healthy meals in 2021.

Explain to students that a diet is regarded as unaffordable if it costs more than 52% of the money people earn, meaning that nutritious food costs more than half of what people are able to earn. This exercise will probably work best if students are divided into groups. The answers to these questions are not straight forward and have to be worked out from all the material provided in the lesson. Students should be reminded that they should provide evidence and examples to support their answers. Once the groups have finished answering the questions, a class discussion would be a good way to explore their insights.

Reference

Ritchie, H., Rosado, P., & Roser, M. (2021). Food prices. *Our World in Data.* https://ourworldindata.org/food-prices

Exercise 2

Use the information in the table, as well as all the other information from Exercise 1, to answer the questions that follow.

Continent	Country	% people who could afford nutritious food
Asia	Pakistan	17.2
	Philippines	26
	India	25
	Russia	97.4
	Turkey	94
	China	89.1
Africa	DRC	5.4
	Nigeria	6.5
	Zambia	10
	Algeria	67.6
	Senegal	55
	Namibia	40.5
Europe	Greece	97.8
	Spain	98.2
	Italy	98.5
	Switzerland	100
	Netherlands	99.9
	France	99.8

Share of country's population that could afford a healthy diet in 2021

2.1 Which of the three continents do you think is the wealthiest? Why would you claim this?

THE WEALTHIEST OF THE THREE CONTINENTS IS CLEARLY EUROPE. GREECE HAS THE LARGEST PERCENTAGE OF POPULATION IN EUROPE UNABLE TO AFFORD A HEALTHY DIET. THIS IS 2.2% OF THE POPULATION. IN CONTRAST THERE ARE A NUMBER OF ASIAN COUNTRIES SUCH AS PAKISTAN, PHILIPPINES AND INDIA WHERE ALMOST THREE-QUARTERS OF THE POPULATION ARE UNABLE TO EAT NUTRITIOUS MEALS BECAUSE OF COST. THE SITUATION IS EVEN WORSE IN AFRICA WHERE AT LEAST 90% OF THE POPULATION IN THE DEMOCRATIC REPUBLIC OF CONGO, NIGERIA AND ZAMBIA CANNOT AFFORD HEALTHY MEALS.

2.2 Which continent appears to have the greatest difference between more and less affluent countries? Give a reason for your answer. (Affluent countries have more money than countries that are not affluent.)

THE CONTINENT THAT APPEARS TO HAVE THE GREATEST GAP BETWEEN MORE AND LESS AFFLUENT COUNTRIES IS ASIA. IN THE THREE RICHEST COUNTRIES APPROXIMATELY 90% OF THE POPULATION EAT WELL. IN CONTRAST IN THE THREE POOREST COUNTRIES APPROXIMATELY 25% OF PEOPLE HAVE ACCESS TO GOOD NUTRITION. THE GAP BETWEEN THE AFRICAN COUNTRIES IS NOT AS WIDE.

2.3 In 2021, how many countries were there in Africa where two-thirds of the population had access to sufficient healthy food? Name these countries.

ONLY ALGERIA IN AFRICA HAD A POPULATION WHERE MORE THAN TWO THIRDS OF THE POPULATION COULD AFFORD A HEALTHY DIET.

2.4 Based on your reading of all the material in this lesson, what do you think would be a good way for richer countries to help Nigeria where such a large part of the population is undernourished? Why do you think this?

WE HAVE LEARNT THAT ONE OF THE MAIN PROBLEMS FACING THE AGRICULTURAL SECTOR IN NIGERIA IS THAT FARMERS DO

NOT HAVE PLACES TO STORE THEIR CROPS SAFELY AND DO NOT HAVE ACCESS TO RELIABLE REFRIGERATED TRANSPORT TO GET THEIR PRODUCE TO MARKET. RICHER COUNTRIES COULD HELP TO PROVIDE THESE FACILITIES.

Post-Class Activities

⇒ *Teacher Notes*

There is a wealth of information here that can be used for a variety of purposes. For example, students could concentrate on one continent and find out information about food waste in other countries. These could then be compared in different ways, for example graphs, written paragraphs, diagrams, or figures. Comparisons could be made between countries or regions. Sub-Saharan Africa could be compared to the rest of Africa.

If students were interested they might wish to investigate food waste in their own countries and report back to the class. They would need to provide evidence for this report and could be asked to illustrate their findings using graphs, diagrams, or figures.

Lesson 5: The Future of Food

Time: 2 hours

Overview
In this lesson students will be focusing on problem-solving. They will be required to use the data provided to give support for the opinions they put forward. This data will be provided in the form of a reading and a short talk. This lesson will also discuss graphic organisers and use a brainstorming exercise to write a short paragraph.

Purpose and Strategies

Purpose	Strategies
Voicing opinion backed up by evidence	Students must voice an opinion and be prepared to justify it after reading the passage.
Introducing linking words	Demonstrate their role in text and ask students to identify them.
Listening for information	Students will be provided with a number of claims and they will listen to a short lecture to decide whether these claims are supported or not.
Graphic organisers	Students will be introduced to brainstorming as a way to come up with answers.
Writing up concepts	Students will be required to write up the results of the brainstorming exercise in short paragraphs.

Pre-Class Activities

⇒ *Teacher Notes*

Justifying an Opinion
Students could be given an opportunity to voice their opinions in class and provide justification for their answers. A possible topic could be vegan/vegetarian/pescatarian/flexitarian diets/ordinary diet.

The following definitions could help:

Vegan – a person who doesn't eat any product that comes from an animal. This includes eggs, dairy, meat, fish, and honey.
Vegetarian – a person who doesn't eat meat or fish.
Pescatarian – a person who doesn't eat meat.
Flexitarians will eat meat and fish occasionally.
Then there are people who do not place restrictions on what they eat.

The following questions could serve as prompts:

- Which diet do you think is the best to follow? Why?
- Which diet do you not recommend? Why?
- Are you thinking about changing the way you eat? Why?
- Do you think we might be forced to change the way we eat? Why?

During Class

⇒ *Teacher Notes*

Exercise 1
The week's reading will form a background for the reading in Lesson 6. This week the students will be focusing on linking words, specifically linking words showing sequencing and linking words that are used to add to an idea. Once the students have completed the reading, it would be a good time to discuss the role of linking words.

Academic writing often deals with difficult and complex ideas. To enable readers to follow the writer's thoughts, these thoughts need to be expressed clearly and they need to be linked in a way that makes sense. To join ideas and data together we use linking words. For example, the reading starts off by saying:

The food that we eat will need to change a great deal in the future. There are two main reasons for this. *Firstly* by

2050 the world population will probably number 10 billion people.

A little later we read:

Secondly global warming has affected weather throughout the world.

These two linking words have to do with sequence – that is, the order in which things follow each other. The writer of the passage has made it easy for the reader to identify these reasons by using the linking words *firstly* and *secondly*. There are a number of linking words that have to do with sequence.

In this example, we could for instance have said:

The food that we eat will need to change a great deal in the future. There are two main reasons for this. One *reason* is that by 2050 the world population will probably number 10 billion people. The other reason is that global warming has affected weather throughout the world.

Other examples of sequencing linking words are:

- Next.
- Last.
- Finally.
- In conclusion.
- To summarise.

Another group of linking words are those that add to the idea. For example:

- Additionally.
- Also.
- As well as.
- In addition.
- Like.

The reading is quite short and straightforward. Once you have discussed linking words that show sequence and that add to an idea, ask students to read the passage and complete the table. The answers can be given in a class discussion and students can mark their own work.

Exercise 1

READING: THE FUTURE OF FOOD – WHAT WILL WE BE EATING?

The food that we eat will need to change a great deal in the future. There are two main reasons for this. Firstly by 2050 the world population will probably number 10 billion people. There is not enough farming land to produce the kind of foods such as rice, wheat, and meat products that people are eating today.

Secondly global warming has affected weather throughout the world. Some countries do not have enough water for their farming needs; in other countries, floods regularly destroy crops and kill farm animals. Many researchers believe that in the future the food that we eat will come from four categories:

- Edible insects.
- Seaweeds.
- Plant-based meat.
- Lab grown meat.

In this reading we will look at insects and seaweed and in the next lesson we will explore the final two categories.

Edible Insects

Insects have a very important role to play if we are to feed the world's population. Insects are a healthy food. They contain a lot of protein and iron, a mineral needed by our bodies to make red blood cells.

At present, millions of people include insects like crickets, worms, and beetles in their diet on a regular basis. Over 2000 insect species are eaten. Farming insects is very good for the environment as this kind of farming does not need a lot of land. Nor does it use a lot of water. However, most people in the world do not want to eat insects. They think that eating insects is disgusting. Researchers have found that people prefer to eat other environmentally friendly foods, such as lentils, seaweed or plant-based/lab-grown meat. Consumers are more likely to buy insects as food if these insects are mixed with ingredients they know, such as flour and meat. In addition, consumers prefer the shape of the insects to be disguised. They do not want to eat a worm that looks like a worm!

Seaweed

In contrast, people are far more willing to eat seaweed. This is important because seaweed is very nutritional and, additionally, it does not need soil to grow in, fresh water or fertilisers. Seaweed just grows with sunlight and the nutrients already in the seawater. It also grows very fast – up to 30 centimetres a day. However, not all people are willing to try seaweed. Many people are reluctant to try any unfamiliar foods. For this reason, advertisers are working closely with seaweed growers to show people what a good idea it is to eat seaweed. They stress the fact that it is healthy to eat seaweed and that this type of farming is good for the environment. Chefs are also helping to promote its use, by developing recipes using seaweed.

REFERENCES

Hubert, B., Rosegrant, M., van Boekel, M., & Ortiz, R. (n.d.). The future of food: Scenarios for 2050. *Crop Science, 50*, S34–S50. https://doi.org/10.2135/cropsci2009.09.0530

Liu, A., Li, J., & Gómez, M. (2020). Factors Influencing Consumption of Edible Insects for Chinese Consumers. *Insects 11*, 10. https://doi.org/10.3390/insects11010010

Palmieria, N., & Bonaventura, M. (2020). The potential of edible seaweed within the western diet. A segmentation of Italian consumers. *International Journal of Gastronomy and Food Science, 20*. https://doi.org/10.1016/j.ijgfs.2020.100202

Exercise 1.1

Linking words showing sequencing and addition are used 6 times in the text. The first one has been filled in, in the table below. Complete the table.

Linking word/s	Sentence
SUCH AS	THERE IS NOT ENOUGH FARMING LAND TO PRODUCE THE KIND OF FOODS SUCH AS RICE, WHEAT, AND MEAT PRODUCTS THAT PEOPLE ARE EATING TODAY.
LIKE	AT PRESENT MILLIONS OF PEOPLE INCLUDE INSECTS LIKE CRICKETS, WORMS AND BEETLES IN THEIR DIET REGULARLY.
SUCH AS	RESEARCHERS HAVE FOUND THAT PEOPLE PREFER TO EAT OTHER ENVIRONMENTALLY FRIENDLY FOODS, SUCH AS LENTILS, SEAWEED OR PLANT-BASED/LAB GROWN MEAT.
SUCH AS	CONSUMERS ARE MORE LIKELY TO BUY INSECTS AS FOOD IF THESE INSECTS ARE MIXED WITH INGREDIENTS THEY KNOW, SUCH AS FLOUR AND MEAT.
IN ADDITION	IN ADDITION, CONSUMERS PREFER THE SHAPE OF THE INSECTS TO BE DISGUISED.
ADDITIONALLY	THIS IS IMPORTANT BECAUSE SEAWEED IS VERY NUTRITIONAL AND, ADDITIONALLY, IT DOES NOT NEED LAND TO GROW IN, FRESHWATER OR FERTILISERS.

Exercise 2

⇒ *Teacher Notes*

This is an interesting video clip that the students should be able to follow without much difficulty. Something that could be pointed out to the students is that the narrator sometimes speaks of insects but most of the time talks about bugs. Students could be referred to the discussion about register and decide which of the two words would be more appropriate for academic writing.

Students can work individually or in groups to answer the questions. The answers can be given in a class discussion, and students can mark their own work.

Listening exercise (4.51 minutes) https://www.youtube.com/watch?v=rDqXwUS402I

Exercise 2

Watch the video https://www.youtube.com/watch?v=rDqXwUS402I and then answer the following questions:

2.1 What does entomophagy mean?
   a. The farming of insects.
   b. THE EATING OF INSECTS.
   c. The killing of insects.

2.2 The video tells us that thousands of years ago people saw animals eating insects and *followed suit*. This means that:
   a. People were disgusted that the animals were eating insects.
   b. PEOPLE DID WHAT THE ANIMALS DID.
   c. People were trying to catch animals by using insects as bait.

2.3 Choose the correct reasons, according to the video, that people stopped eating insects:
   a. THEY MOVED FROM THE COUNTRY AREAS TO CITIES.
   b. They realised that some insects are poisonous.
   c. They needed insects to pollinate the crop.
   d. THEY FORGOT ABOUT THE WAY THEY HAD USED INSECTS FOR FOOD.
   e. They only used insects to make medicine.
   f. THEY THOUGHT EATING INSECTS WAS DISGUSTING.

2.4 Say whether the following statements are true or false according to the video.
   a. Most people in the tropics disapprove of eating insects. FALSE
   b. There are more kinds of insects in the tropics than in other parts of the world. TRUE
   c. Insects usually prefer to move around individually. FALSE

2.5 The video tells us that we need to make a *paradigm shift* in the way we think about eating insects. This means that:

a. We need to wait for more evidence as to whether eating insects is good or bad.
b. We are right to think that eating insects is disgusting.
c. WE NEED TO CHANGE THE WAY WE THINK ABOUT EATING INSECTS.

Exercise 3

⇒ *Teacher Notes*

In this exercise students are introduced to the concept of brainstorming. This is an important part of academic writing. When students are preparing an essay they need to come up with a starting point. One of the best ways to do this is often by brainstorming – just coming up with a number of ideas about the topic. Recent research into using brainstorming in the teaching of academic writing indicates that it could prove useful. A study of Chinese-speaking ESL pre-university students indicated that they believed that brainstorming allowed them opportunities to share ideas, develop their writing skills, and build their self-confidence (Jalleh & Mahfoodh, 2021).

In groups, get students to write their topic in a circle in the middle of a blank sheet of paper. Students then come up with ideas which they write in circles. Once they have exhausted their ideas, they can look for links between various ideas. These ideas might also generate spin-offs. This is illustrated in the example given below. In this example an idea is put forward that people's competitive instincts can be put to good use to get them to try different foods. This idea is further refined with the suggestion of different types of competitions.

Important points for the students to remember are:

- Don't judge the ideas. You might not agree with what other people have said but take the opportunity to think differently.
- Think widely - try to come up with different ideas. It doesn't matter if they are really strange.

- Build on the ideas of others. Someone might have a great idea and you can think of a good way to build on this.
- Go for quantity – try to come up with as many ideas as possible. Brainstorm this in groups and see how many ideas you can come up with.
- Once the students have completed the brainstorming ask them to divide the main points between group members. Each person in the group will write up that particular idea and the linking ideas e.g.:

People like competitions so one way to introduce them to insects would be to have competitions. There could be competitions to see who could eat the most crickets in five minutes. There could also be competitions for the best insect recipes.

Ask the students to connect all the paragraphs and put them together in one document without indicating which student has written which section. Collect the work from the students and read what they have written. Comment on the ideas. Congratulate them on particularly interesting or exciting thinking. At this stage do not mark the language. This exercise is to show them how useful brainstorming is as a strategy.

Reference

Jalleh, C., & Mahfoodh, O. (2021). Chinese-speaking ESL pre-university students' perceptions of the effectiveness of collaborative planning in an academic writing course. *Journal of Language and Linguistic Studies, 17*(2), 1174–1189.

Exercise 3

In the passage we are told that people need to eat more insects and seaweed. However, many people do not like this idea at all. How can we persuade people to try these sources of protein? Choose either seaweed or insects and in a group come up with ideas as to how people could be persuaded to try different kinds of food. Look at the example provided.

Here is an example of how you could start:

```
                          ┌─────────┐
                          │ A State │
                          │ Dinner  │
                          │Featuring│
                          │ Insects │
                          └────▲────┘
                               │
    ┌──────────┐          ┌────┴────┐
    │Provide more│        │Get Role │
    │ education│          │Models to│
    └────▲─────┘          │  Eat    │
         │                │ Insects │
         │                └────▲────┘
 ┌───────┴──┐   ┌──────────┐   │
 │   Show   │   │ HOW CAN  │───┘
 │Environmen│◄──│  WE GET  │
 │tal       │   │ PEOPLE TO│
 │ Benefits │   │EAT INSECTS│
 └──────────┘   └─┬──────┬─┘
                  │      │
                  │      └──────┐
           ┌──────▼───┐    ┌────▼─────┐
           │Show Health│   │ Appeal to│
           │ Benefits  │   │  People's│
           └───────────┘   │Competitivenes│
                           └──┬─────┬─┘
                              │     │
                        ┌─────▼┐ ┌──▼────┐
                        │ Best │ │Cricket│
                        │Insect│ │Eating │
                        │Recipe│ │Competi│
                        └───┬──┘ │ tion  │
                            │    └───────┘
                        ┌───▼───┐
                        │Master │
                        │Insect │
                        │ Chef  │
                        └───────┘
```

Once you have completed the brainstorming divide the main points between group members. Each group member will then write up the main idea and the minor points that were made about that main idea. Each person in the group will write up that particular idea and the linking ideas e.g.:

> People like competitions so one way to introduce them to insects would be to have competitions. There could be competitions to see who could eat the most crickets in five minutes. There could also be competitions for the best insect recipes.

Post-Class Activities

⇒ *Teacher Notes*

Students could practise brainstorming a number of topics for example:

- The future of education.
- How will transport be different in 30 years' time?
- How do we house the world's growing population?

Lesson 6: Should We Eat Less Meat?

Time: 2 hours

Overview
This lesson links very closely with Lesson 5. Students will be required to use the reading from Lesson 5 to complete the work for this week. This is the end of the cycle about food in the 21st century and focuses strongly on the future. The use of graphic organisers is continued with concept mapping and the idea of argumentative essays is introduced. Students will also work on voicing their own opinions, supporting these opinions with the data provided.

Purpose and Strategies

Purpose	Strategies
Introducing argumentative essays.	Discussing a balanced approach – looking at the pros and cons of a particular argument.
Concept mapping.	Using graphic organiser to identify the pros and cons of an argument.
Voicing own opinion.	Students will choose one side of the argument to support, based on the data that has been provided.

Pre-Class Activities

⇒ *Teacher Notes*

In the last lesson you had a discussion about different dietary choices. You could ask students to think about the advantages and disadvantages of the different diets. For example, people who are vegans might not have sufficient iron in their diet while people who eat a lot of meat are more at risk of developing heart disease.

These questions could be used as a prompt:

- What are the advantages of a vegan/vegetarian/pescatarian/flexitarian/ordinary diet?
- What are the disadvantages of a vegan/vegetarian/pescatarian/flexitarian/ordinary diet?
- Take one specific diet – do you think the advantages outweigh the disadvantages? Why do you think so?

If the group all have similar dietary habits they could be asked to compare what they eat to other groups in the world. In this lesson you will be introducing students to argumentative essays – probably the most common essay required in tertiary education. It is important at this early stage to stress to students that there are very few issues that do not have good points and bad points.

Argumentative Essays

A good essay never tries to say only positive things about a certain issue. What academics do is look at the arguments for and the arguments against a particular issue. Then they balance the two sides and decide which one has more weight. At this early stage students will be asked to identify the advantages and disadvantages of alternative protein sources. They will also be asked to give reasons as to why a certain point is an advantage or disadvantage.

During Class

⇒ *Teacher Notes*

Exercise 1

The reading is short and relatively easy. It can be read individually or in pairs.

Ask the students to pay particular attention to the advantages and disadvantages discussed in the reading. Then ask them to complete the first table. Mark the answers together in class.

Exercise 1

READING: MEAT ALTERNATIVES

Globally, more and more meat is eaten every year. Eating a great deal of meat is not good for the environment or for people's health so it is important that we look for alternatives. These alternatives are plant-based meat and lab-grown meat. Eating these alternative meats is good for our environment. Research indicates that the farming of animals causes as much pollution as all the transport systems across the world put together. In addition, these alternative meats do not need as much farmland as farming with animals does. There is also growing concern about the way in which animals are slaughtered to provide meat for our use. Another advantage is that these alternative meats can be produced far more quickly than the real meat we get by farming animals.

Eating a great deal of real meat is not good for people either. Plant-based meat usually has less fat and fewer calories than real meat. Another advantage is that scientists can change the alternative meat so that it has more iron.

Therefore, producing meat alternatives appears to be a win–win situation.

However, there are problems with producing meat in this way. It is difficult to produce meat alternatives that look and taste like the meat we are used to. For example, at the moment it is not possible to have different kinds of meat, such as pork, beef or mutton. Also, in order to improve taste some producers add a lot of salt which is not good for humans. Scientists are also concerned that we do not know how these alternative meats will affect humans in the long term. There needs to be more research before we can be sure that these alternatives are safe for us to eat for a long time.

Some people are also worried that lab-grown meat is unnatural. They say they do not want to eat something that has been grown in a test tube! Another issue that has been raised is that, at present, these meat alternatives are expensive and many people cannot afford to buy them.

Finally, many rural communities rely on farming animals to survive. What will happen to these communities if animals such as cows, sheep, and pigs are no longer farmed?

REFERENCES

Andreani, G., Sogari, G., Marti, A., Froldi, F., Dagevvos, H., & Martini, D. (2023). Plant-based meat alternatives: Technological, nutritional, environmental, market, and social challenges and opportunities. *Nutrients, 15*(2), 452. https://doi.org/10.3390/nu15020452

Bhat, Z., Kumar, S., & Fayaz, H. (2015). In vitro meat production: challenges and benefits over conventional meat production. *Journal of Integrative Agriculture,* 14 (2), 241–248. https://doi.org/10.1016/S2095-3119(14)60887-X

Chriki, S., & Hocquette, J. (2020). The myth of cultured meat: A review. *Frontiers in Nutrition, 7*(7). https://doi.org/10.3389/fnut.2020.00007

Food Insight. (2019, November 26). *Lab or plants which makes meat.* https://foodinsight.org/labs-or-plants-which-makes-the-best-meat/

Lynch, H., Johnston, C., & Wharton, C. (2018). Plant-based diets: Considerations for environmental impact, protein quality, and exercise performance. *Nutrients, 10,* 1841. https://doi.org/10.3390/nu10121841

Smetana, S., Ristic, D., Pleissner, D., Tuomisto, H. L., Parniakov, O., & Heinz, V. (2023). Meat substitutes: Resource demands and environmental footprints. *Resources Conservation and Recycling,* 190, 106831. https://doi.org/10.1016/j.resconrec.2022.106831

Exercise 1.1

Read the statements and then find reasons in the passage to support the statements. Examples have been provided.

Statement: *People Should Eat Meat Alternatives Rather Than Real Meat*

Advantages	Reasons	
Advantage 1: It might be better for people's health	because	1. meat alternatives have less fat.
	because	2. MEAT ALTERNATIVES HAVE FEWER CALORIES.
	because	3. meat alternatives can be changed to be rich in iron.
Advantage 2: It is better for the earth	because	1. it reduces the amount of land needed for farming.
	because	2. THERE IS LESS POLLUTION.
Advantage 3: It is better for farm animals	because	they do not need to be killed.

Disadvantages	Reasons	
Disadvantage 1: It might not be better for people's health	because	1. ALTERNATIVE MEATS MIGHT NOT BE SAFE FOR PEOPLE TO EAT IN THE LONG TERM.
	because	2. SOMETIMES EXTRA SALT IS ADDED TO IMPROVE THE TASTE.
Disadvantage 2: People might not buy the alternatives	because	1. THEY DO NOT TASTE LIKE MEAT.
	because	2. they do not look like meat.
	because	3. THEY CAN BE EXPENSIVE.
	because	4. there is no variety.
Disadvantage 2: Some farmers will have problems	because	THEY EARN A LIVING BY RAISING FARM ANIMALS.

Exercise 2

⇒ *Teacher Notes*

In this exercise students are asked to weigh up the respective arguments and decide what they support. They will base their answers on the material in the table. Remind them that they must discuss both the arguments for and the arguments against plant-based/lab-grown meat. Refer them back to the discussion they had at the beginning of class. Ask them to write about 150 words. If you have time, it would be a good idea to walk around while students are working and discuss their work with them. You could talk about both the opinions they are expressing and the language they are using to express these opinions.

Once the students have finished writing up their answers, find out which students in the class are in favour of meat alternatives and which students are not. In a class discussion, examine students' reasons for being pro- or anti-meat alternatives. Which reasons seem to be the most important for each group? Are the majority of students pro- or anti-?

Exercise 2

Would you buy meat alternatives? Use the information in the tables you have just completed to justify your answer. Start your answer off by saying:

> I would buy meat alternatives because …
>
> OR
>
> I would not buy meat alternatives because …

Exercise 3

⇒ *Teacher Notes*

Ask students to reread the passage in Lesson 5 *The Future of Food – what will we be eating?* They will need both that reading and the one in Lesson 6 *Meat Alternatives* for the next exercise. This exercise is very similar to Exercise 2 and students should be able to complete it on their own. It can be marked as a class exercise.

Exercise 3

For this reading you will need the passage in Lesson 5 *The Future of Food – what will we be eating?* and the one you have just read *Meat Alternatives*. You will use these two passages to provide evidence for the statements below.

Statement: *It is better for our health and the environment to eat insects*

Advantages	Reasons	
Advantage 1: Insects are a healthy food	because	they contain a lot of protein and iron.
Advantage 2: Eating insects is good for the environment	because	1. FARMING INSECTS DOES NOT REQUIRE A LOT OF LAND.
	because	2. farming insects does not require a lot of water.

Disadvantages	Reasons	
Disadvantage 1: Consumers are unlikely to buy food made with insects.	because	THEY THINK THAT EATING INSECTS IS DISGUSTING.

Statement: *It is better for our health and the environment to eat seaweed*

Advantages	Reasons	
Advantage 1: Seaweed is cheap to produce	because	IT DOES NOT REQUIRE LAND OR FRESH WATER.
Advantage 2: It does not take a long time to grow seaweed	because	IT GROWS 30cm A DAY

Disadvantages	Reasons	
Disadvantage 1: Consumers might not buy seaweed products	because	THEY DO NOT WANT TO EAT STRANGE FOODS.

Exercise 4

⇒ *Teacher Notes*

In this exercise students are asked to review the data they have collected and tabled. They are now required to choose one of the four alternative protein sources to real meat that have been presented to them during the course of the last two lessons. They must provide reasons for their choice. In addition, they need to provide a personal reason for the choice they have made. An example is provided. This exercise does not need to be long. What is important is that the students provide reasons for their choices. This is a short exercise and probably a good one to mark. The focus in your marking should be on student reasoning. Have they provided a good reason for their choice? It might be an idea to focus your remarks on their reasoning and logic, and perhaps one or two language errors.

Exercise 4

You have now read about four alternatives to eating real meat. Which one of these would you choose to eat? Give two reasons – one from the tables you have filled and one that is personal to you.
Here is an example:

> I would choose to eat seaweed. One reason is that it is good for the environment because it does not require land and freshwater to grow. The other reason is that I already eat seaweed and I like the taste.

Post-Class Activities

⇒ *Teacher Notes*

Students can use the data provided in a number of ways. Reminiscent of the work done in Lesson 4 they can devise advertising slogans to promote the sale of alternative protein sources. They could also devise short handouts to be given to potential customers.

In contrast, they can devise advertising slogans for farmers of livestock. Short handouts promoting real meat can also be drawn up.

It would be a good idea to remind students of the information that was given to them in Lesson 5. Can they use it effectively for different foodstuffs?

3

Cycle 2

Technology in the Modern World

Lesson 1: Technology and Different Generations

Time: 2 hours

Overview
This cycle focuses on technology, with the first lesson looking at the impact of technological innovations on different generations. Students will be asked to think critically about modern technology and creatively about the naming of generations. They will also be required to read a passage and link the information provided with the source of the information. This information will be succinctly summarised. Students will also be introduced to intext citations. Finally, there will be a discussion of the importance of definitions in academic writing, and students will be asked to compare and evaluate different definitions.

Purpose and Strategies

Purpose	Strategies
Encouraging critical thinking	Discussing the effects of technological inventions.
Encouraging creative thinking	Students are asked to weigh various names for the youngest generation and produce their own suggestions.
Weighing up pros and cons	Discussion around what the benefits and downsides of these inventions are.
Correctly identifying sources	Reading a passage and correctly attributing information to a particular source.
Summarising	Briefly summarising information in a passage.
Exploring definitions	Discussing the importance of definitions in academic writing.
Comparing definition Intext citations	Students will compare definitions of a term and explain their preference for one definition. Students will be introduced to intext citations

Pre-Class Activities

⇒ *Teacher Notes*

This cycle will focus on technology – how it has affected our lives, how it is affecting our lives and how it will affect our lives in the future. There are varying opinions as to which technological inventions have had the greatest impact on society. Get the students in groups and ask them to list the inventions that have revolutionised the way we live. Stress that there are no right or wrong answers. The experts can't agree!

Here are some considered to be the most important:

- The printing press.
- The steam engine.
- The light bulb.
- The telephone.
- The aeroplane.
- The personal computer.
- The Internet.
- The mobile phone.

- Vaccines.
- Antibiotics.
- Refrigeration.
- The clock.
- The car.
- Radio and television.
- Artificial intelligence (AI).

You could list the inventions as students call them out (or you could have a prepared list). You could then randomly assign a couple of the items listed to the groups and ask them to list the advantages (and possibly the drawbacks) of the innovation.

Finally, ask them about different generations' attitudes towards technology:

- How do their parents' attitudes differ from their own?
- And those of their grandparents?
- Do they think that the later generations are more fortunate because they have been able to benefit from technological advantages?
- Are there drawbacks to advancing technology?

During Class

⇒ *Teacher Notes*

Exercise 1

This exercise would work well in groups. You could have the students form small groups and read the passage together. Encourage them to try to work out the meanings of words that they don't understand but allow them to use online dictionaries if they get stuck. Point out to students that this text differs from earlier readings as the information provided is credited to specific authors. This is known as intext citation. The groups should then attempt to answer the questions posed in Exercise 1.1. Once they have finished the exercise, it can be marked in class with groups comparing their answers. Groups can be encouraged to move onto Exercise 1.2 while they are waiting for the other groups to finish.

Exercise 1

READING: TECHNOLOGY AND DIFFERENT GENERATIONS

What is technology? Technology is the practical application of scientific knowledge to help us understand and solve the problems that we face in the world we live in (Luenendonk, 2024). The changes in technology have made our lives a lot easier and given us more leisure time. The invention of home appliances such as washing machines, refrigerators, dishwashers and microwaves have played a part in helping women enter the workforce. Prior to the invention of these appliances, domestic chores dominated women's lives, and taking up work outside of the house was very difficult. We are therefore strongly influenced by the times in which we live. Twenge (2023) claims that each generation grows up in a different culture and the era in which you are born plays a huge role in shaping your attitudes, values and behaviours.

One of the main reasons for changing cultures is technological progress. Technology shapes our lives in many different ways, and people born in different generations have different technological experiences. For example, the generation born after 1946 was greatly influenced by the growth of television coverage and the insights they gained from this wider exposure to the world. Subsequent generations were influenced by the growth of computer technology, the Internet and social media (Twenge, 2023).

If we wish to understand the way people respond to technology, it is important to look at the generation in which they were born. Dimock (2019) classifies the different generations in the following way. People born between 1928 and 1945 are known as the Silent Generation. This generation grew up in a time of economic hardship and the upheaval of the Second World War, where people had to work hard to survive. It was also a time when people believed that children should be seen and not heard (Wallenfeldt, 2023).

The next generation, the Baby Boomers, were born between 1946 and 1964 (Dimock, 2019). Their name came about because there was a population boom after the Second World War (Wallenfeldt, 2023). The origin of the name given to Generation X, people born between 1965 and 1980 (Dimock, 2019), is not so clear. This name was first used by an American photographer for a series of photos of young people but it was Douglas Coupland's book *Generation X*, published in 1991, about young people born after the Baby Boomers that led to its widespread use (Katz, 2017).

The next generation, sometimes referred to as Gen Y because this logically follows Gen X, is more commonly referred to as Millennials. They are given this name because the oldest members of this group became adults at the turn of the millennium (Raphelson, 2014). These are people born between 1981 and 1996 (Dimock, 2019). The next group, born between 1997 and 2012 (Dimock, 2019), are known as Gen Z (or Zoomers) because they follow Gen Y (Mekouar, 2024). However, this generation is also known as iGen because it has grown up with iPhones, the Internet and Instagram. This name was coined by Jean Twenge and explored in her book *iGen* (Twenge, 2017).

The last generation consists of children born between 2012 and 2025 (Eldridge, 2024). They are commonly known as Generation Alpha (Eldridge, 2024). This name has been given because Z is the last letter of the Latin alphabet and Alpha is the first letter of the Greek alphabet. However, this is not the only name given to this generation. Some researchers refer to them as Generation C or Generation COVID because they will be the first generation to grow up in a world that was affected by the COVID-19 pandemic (Eldridge, 2024).

REFERENCES

Dimock, M. (2019). Defining generations: Where Millennials end and Generation Z begins. *Pew Research Center*. https://www.pewresearch.org/short-reads/2019/01/17/where-millennials-end-and-generation-z-begins/

Eldridge, S. (2024). Generation Alpha. *Britannica*. https://www.britannica.com/topic/Generation-Alpha

Katz, S. (2017). Generation X: A critical sociological perspective. *Generations: Journal of the American Society on Aging, 41*(3), 12–19. https://www.jstor.org/stable/e26556292

Luenendonk, M. (2024). *What is Technology? Definition, Types, Examples. Founderjar.* https://www.founderjar.com/what-is-technology/

Mekouar, D. (2024, April 24). Baby Boomers, Millennials, Gen Z: Who names generations? *All About America.* https://www.voanews.com/a/baby-boomers-millennials-gen-z-who-names-generations-/7581626.html

Raphelson, S. (2014). From GIs to Gen Z (or is it iGen?): How Generations get nicknames. *Special Series: New Boom NPR.* https://www.npr.org/2014/10/06/349316543/don-t-label-me-origins-of-generational-names-and-why-we-use-them

Twenge, J. (2017). *iGen.* Atria Books.

Twenge, J. M. (2023). *Generations.* Schuster & Schuster Inc.

Wallenfeldt, J. (2023). Silent generation. *Britannica.* https://www.britannica.com/topic/Silent-Generation

Exercise 1.1

The reading you have just completed has provided you with a great deal of information. In the academic world it is very important that you acknowledge where you have found your information. Complete the table filling in the missing information by summarising it briefly. The first entry has been provided as an example.

Author	Information
Dimock (2019)	Classification of people according to date of birth. Gives 5 classifications Silent Generation 1928–1945; Baby Boomers 1946–1964; Millennials 1981–1996; Gen Z 1997–2012.
Eldridge (2024)	CLASSIFIED CHILDREN BORN BETWEEN 2012 AND 2025. EXPLAINED WHY THIS GENERATION IS CALLED GEN ALPHA OR GEN COVID.

(Continued)

Author	Information
Katz (2017)	Explained why people born between 1991 and 2017 are called Gen X.
Luenendonk (2024)	GAVE A DEFINITION OF TECHNOLOGY.
Mekouar (2024)	EXPLAINED WHY PEOPLE BORN BETWEEN 1997 AND 2012 ARE CALLED GEN Z.
Raphelson (2014)	EXPLAINED WHY PEOPLE BORN BETWEEN 1981 AND 1996 ARE CALLED MILLENNIALS.
Twenge (2017)	EXPLAINED WHY PEOPLE BORN 1997 AND 2012 ARE ALSO CALLED iGEN.
Twenge (2023)	Discussed how technology has shaped the lives of different generations.
Wallenfeldt (2023)	EXPLAINED WHY PEOPLE BORN BETWEEN 1928 AND 1945 ARE CALLED THE SILENT GENERATION. Explained why people born between 1946 and 1964 are called Baby Boomers.

Exercise 1.2

⇒ *Teacher Notes*

Students should continue in their groups for this exercise. Once they have answered the questions, the class should come together to discuss the various responses. In this exercise you should stress that there are no right answers but what is important is having a good reason for your choice.

Exercise 1.2

In the text you have just read the latest generation, children born between 2012 and 2025, have been given different names. In addition to the two mentioned in the text, Generation Alpha and Generation COVID, Twenge (2023) also talks about the Polar Generation. One of the main reasons she came up with this term is that she thinks that the melting of the *polar* icecaps is going to cause serious climate change problems that this generation will have to deal with.

- ♦ Which of the names do you think is most appropriate?
- ♦ Why do you think this?
- ♦ Give a reason for your choice.

Exercise 2

⇒ *Teacher Notes*

In the text students encountered a number of definitions e.g. the definition of technology and the definition of the various generations e.g. the Silent Generation – people born between 1928 and 1945. Explain to students that definitions are very important in academic writing. Tell them that the word comes from the Latin word *definire*, which means to limit (Merriam Webster, n.d.). The most important reason to use a definition is to avoid misunderstanding. As Swales and Feak (2004) point out, words and phrases have different meanings according to the context in which they are found. For example, the word channel can mean a body of water like the English Channel. It can also mean a way of transmitting information for example – they used WhatsApp as their main communication channel. It can also be used to describe a television or radio station. You can hear this program on Channel 4.

In academic writing, it is important that writers convey information accurately. In order to do so it is important that key terms are defined so that everyone is clear as to what the writer means (Cresswell, 2003). Let's say, for example, that students wanted to talk about the importance of being inclusive when we have different generations living and working together. It could be a good idea to define what you mean by "inclusive". Being inclusive means behaving in a way that allows everyone to feel welcome, respected and safe. An inclusive group is always changing to find better ways to meet the needs of people in the group (Genesis Global School, 2017).

In this exercise students are asked to consider three different definitions of the word "generation" all taken from online dictionaries. You could discuss the definitions with the class. On the whole the definitions are relatively easy to understand. The one word that might pose a problem is "contemporaneously" (existing in the same period of time). You could then ask students to work individually to decide which definition they prefer. Students could then write a short explanation (1–2 sentences) explaining their choice. An example could be:

I WOULD USE THE COLLINS DEFINITION AS I BELIEVE IT BETTER CAPTURES MY IDEA OF WHAT A GENERATION IS. THE MERRIAM WEBSTER DEFINITION IS DIFFICULT TO UNDERSTAND, AND THE CAMBRIDGE DEFINITION DOES NOT SUPPLY ENOUGH DETAIL.

You could walk around the class and discuss the students' explanations with them while they are working.

References

Cresswell, J. (2003). *Research Design: Quantitative, Qualitative and Mixed Methods Approaches* (2nd ed.). Sage Publications.

Genesis Global School. (2017). Inclusion Policy. https://www.genesisglobalschool.edu.in/wp-content/uploads/2017/07/Inclusion-Policy.pdf

Merriam-Webster. (n.d.). Define. https://www.merriam-webster.com/dictionary/define#:~:text=definer%20noun-,Etymology,related%20to%20final%2C%20finish%2C%20infinity

Swales, J., & Feak, C. (2004). *Academic Writing for Graduate Students* (2nd ed.). The University of Michigan Press.

Exercise 2

We have been doing a lot of work about different generations. Look at the following definitions of the word "generation". If you were asked to write an essay about different generations, which of these three would you pick as your definition? Why? Write a few sentences explaining which one you would pick and why. Also explain why you would NOT choose the other two.

Dictionary	Definition	URL
Cambridge	All the people of about the same age within a society or within a particular family.	https://dictionary.cambridge.org/dictionary/english/generation
Merriam-Webster	A group of individuals born and living contemporaneously.	https://www.merriam-webster.com/dictionary/generation

(Continued)

Dictionary	Definition	URL
Collins	A generation is all the people in a group or country who are of a similar age, especially when they are considered as having the same experiences or attitudes.	https://www.collinsdictionary.com/dictionary/english/generation

Post-Class Activities

Students could use the table above to look up other words. They could look up words such as:

- Internet.
- Social media.

Or perhaps terms such as:

- Attitudes.
- Values.

Just as in the earlier exercise, they could explain which of the definitions they prefer. They could use any of the online dictionaries available but they must provide the URL.

Lesson 2: Technology of the Future

Time: 2 hours

Overview

The topic of this lesson is the technology of the future and how it will affect our lives. There is one short ad which students are asked to critique. The focus then moves to intext citations and their use in academic writing. Students are also asked to match data with authors, introducing them to intext citations. Finally, more work is done on the argumentative essay and students are asked to plan an essay using the prompts provided.

Purpose and Strategies

Purpose	Strategies
Thinking critically	Looking at the deeper meaning behind a humorous ad.
Using in-text citations	Inserting intext citations into a text using the information provided.
Writing definitions	Providing own definition of a concept introduced in a short passage.
Planning an argumentative essay	Completing various parts of a short argumentative essay in a table using the cues provided.

Pre-Class Activities

⇒ *Teacher Notes*

The first exercise asks students to look at a humorous ad. One way to introduce this lesson is to ask students prior to the lesson to send you an ad that they find amusing. It is a really good idea to check these ads before using them in class in case there is anything that other students might find offensive. You might prefer to have a few ads of your own rather than ask for ads from the class, or you might wish to combine yours and the students'. After showing the ads, you could ask students to indicate by show of hands which ads they found the funniest. Then ask them if these humorous ads have a deeper message. If time allows you might want to discuss with the class why humour can be a powerful weapon in spreading messages. It would be better to have your or the students' own choice, but you could always make use of this clip which shows ads for learning languages.

https://www.youtube.com/watch?v=DMLcIpU2MUo

Students could be asked which of the ads they prefer and why.

This first exercise has a humorous ad as its starting point but requires students to think about the serious point that is being made in the ad. They are then asked to link this message with the firm's marketing strategy.

During Class

⇒   *Teacher Notes*

Exercise 1
Explain to the students that the ad they will be watching is used by REMA 1000 (2024), a Norwegian grocery chain. REMA is short for Reitan Mat (Reitan Food); 1000 refers to the fact that the stores only offer a thousand products. The aim of the company is to keep prices low. Because they do not stock a wide variety of items the company can buy very large quantities at a low price. The company prides itself on being "no-frills" – this means that they do not spend money on things that are not essential. There are no decorations in the stores, and they do not provide shopping bags. If you want to use a trolley you must pay a refundable deposit. Products are often just left in crates so staff do not have to be employed to put them on shelves. REMA tries to keep things straightforward. The aisles are wide and there are lots of signs to make shopping simple.

https://www.youtube.com/watch?v=nwPtcqcqz00

Once the students have viewed the ad ask them to work on the questions in groups.

Reference

REMA 1000. (September 8, 2024). *Wikipedia*. https://en.wikipedia.org/wiki/REMA_1000

Exercise 1

You have just watched an ad about REMA 1000. The ad shows a home with high-end technology. Describe what happens in the ad. Make sure you cover the following points:

- The technological challenge the man encounters.
- Why the ad shows Miriam opening her front door.
- The motto shown at the end of the ad is "Simplicity is king". Why does REMA 1000 use this slogan?

    AT THE BEGINNING OF THE AD THE MAN IS SHOWN AT HOME. IT IS CLEAR THAT HIS HOME IS TECHNOLOGICALLY VERY ADVANCED AND EVERYTHING WORKS WITH VOICE CONTROL, TURNING OFF THE HEATING AND OPENING THE FRONT DOOR, FOR INSTANCE. HOWEVER, AFTER A VISIT TO THE DENTIST THE MAN'S MOUTH IS SWOLLEN AND THE AI SYSTEM CANNOT RECOGNISE HIS VOICE AND REFUSES TO CARRY OUT HIS COMMANDS. HE HAS NO OTHER WAY TO GET INTO HIS HOUSE. THE AD SHOWS MIRIAM OPENING HER FRONT DOOR TO MAKE THE POINT THAT QUITE OFTEN SIMPLE STRAIGHTFORWARD WAYS ARE BETTER THAN SOPHISTICATED TECHNOLOGY. IT WOULD NOT MATTER IF MIRIAM HAD BEEN TO THE DENTIST BECAUSE SHE COULD OPEN HER DOOR WITH A KEY. REMA CONCENTRATES ON RUNNING A VERY SIMPLE SYSTEM WITH RELATIVELY FEW PRODUCTS. THE STORES ARE RUN TO KEEP COSTS DOWN SO THE CONSUMERS HAVE TO HELP THEMSELVES. THIS SIMPLE BASIC APPROACH KEEPS RUNNING COSTS LOW AND ENABLES THE STORES TO CHARGE CHEAPER PRICES THAN MORE SOPHISTICATED SUPERMARKETS.

- Do you think this is a good ad? Give a reason for your answer.

    I THINK THIS IS A GOOD AD AS IT REMINDS US THAT USING A LOT OF TECHNOLOGY CAN OFTEN BACKFIRE. FOR EXAMPLE, THE MAN IN THE AD CANNOT GET INTO HIS HOUSE BECAUSE THE TECHNOLOGY WON'T LET HIM. REMA IS SAYING THAT SOMETIMES SIMPLE WAYS ARE BETTER AND CHEAPER.

Reference

REMA 1000. (September 8, 2024). *Wikipedia*. https://en.wikipedia.org/wiki/REMA_1000

Exercise 2

⇒ *Teacher Notes*

IN-TEXT CITATIONS

It is very important that students understand how references lists and intext citations are used in academic writing. In this exercise the focus is on intext citations. An intext citation is a brief acknowledgment placed in the text to show where the writer found the information. The rule in APA 7 is that if there are one or two authors their family names are used in the in-text citation as well as the year that their contribution was published (APA, 2019).

> Traffic lights are an important part of control management during a crisis.
> (Ruzika and Navratilova (2020))

Currently in APA 7 when a source has 3 or more authors only the first name is used in the intext citation. For example, if this article is used

> Javed, A., Shahzad, F., Rehman, S., Zikria, Y., Razzak, I., Jalil, Z., & Xu, G. (2022). Future smart cities: requirements, emerging technologies, applications, challenges, and future aspects. *Cities, 129*. https://doi.org/10.1016/j.cities.2022.103794

the intext citation will read:

> Monitoring food supplies will be essential for cities of the future. (Javed et al., 2022)

In the passage only the name of the first author is given, but the other names are listed in the Reference list at the end of the text.

To indicate to the reader that there is more than one author we use the Latin phrase *et al*. Note that *"al."* has a full stop after it. This is because it has been shortened from *alia*. The phrase means "and others" so the reader knows that there is more than one author (APA, 2019).

Point out to students that when the authors names are part of the sentence in the text then "and" is used instead of "&". For example:

> Ruzika and Navratilova (2020) note that traffic lights are an important part of control management during a crisis.

However in the Reference List "&" is used:

> Ruzika, J., & Navratilova, K. (2020). Crisis management as the part of smart traffic control in cities. *IEEE Xplore*. https://doi.org/10.1109/SCSP49987.2020.9133818

In the following passage students are required to insert the intext citations using the information provided. This passage continues the theme of technology in the modern world. This is probably best done as an independent exercise. The marking of the exercise can be done in class.

Reference

American Psychological Association (APA). (2019). *Author–date citation system*. https://apastyle.apa.org/style-grammar-guidelines/citations/basic-principles/author-date

Exercise 2

Read the following passage. You will notice that the intext citations are missing. Intext citations tell the reader where the information in the text has been found. This information allows the reader to find the full citation (information about the source) in the reference list. Below the passage is information about 5 sources. Find the correct source for the information provided. Remember one source can provide more than one piece of data. Once you have done this, insert the correct in-text citation.

> **READING: HOW TECHNOLOGY CAN HELP CITIES WITH THE PROBLEMS THEY FACE**
>
> Crime, diseases, natural disasters and terrorist attacks can all threaten the inhabitants of cities. Technology can be used to lessen the impact of criminals in our cities (RISTVEJ ET AL., 2020) but technology can also help in other situations. Researchers point out that traffic congestion can exacerbate a crisis situation and that plans should be made to combat this by using technology (RUZIKA & NAVRATILOVA, 2020). They propose managing situations by changing the way in which traffic lights operate. Unmanned aerial vehicles could also be useful to control traffic in difficult situations (MOHAMED ET AL., 2020).
>
> However, it will be impossible to ward off all crises. One of the biggest problems after a crisis is that people often do not have sufficient access to food. During the pandemic millions went hungry for a number of reasons, such as loss of employment (DAHIR, 2020). In order to ensure that people do not starve when disaster strikes we need to have plans in place. (JAVED ET AL. 2022) suggest that cities should consider pantry backups. Technology will ensure that food supplies are managed in such a way that the populations of cities do not go hungry in times of disruption.

What the sources say:

- During the pandemic Abdi Dahir wrote an article in the *New York Times* (2020) expressing his concern about the unequal distribution of food around the world. He said that it was possible that millions of people would die, not of the disease but because of starvation.
- According to Jozef Ristvej, Maros Lacinak and Roman Ondrejka in an article, "On smart cities and safe city concepts", published in the journal *Modern Networks and Applications* in 2020 the people managing the cities of the world need to ensure their safety by using technology to

reduce crime, violence and terrorist threats. The authors also believe that technology can help ensure a quick efficient response if danger does threaten city residents.
- Unmanned aerial vehicles (UAVs) are the subject of an article written by Nader Mohamed, Jameela Al-Jaroodi, Imad Jawhar, Ahmed Idries and Farhan Mohammed in the journal *Technological Forecasting & Social Change*. The authors believe that these vehicles will be very useful for helping control traffic flows in large cities around the world.
- Jiri Ruzika and Kristyna Navratilova, 2020 gave a presentation at the Smart City Symposium held in Prague (25 June 2020). The paper was entitled "Crisis management as the part of smart traffic control in cities". In the paper the authors argue that it is essential to set up a system that can take over control of all traffic lights in a city when there is a crisis.
- Abdul Rehman Javed, Faisal Shahzad, Saif ur Rehman, Yousaf Bin Zikria, Imran Razzak, Zunera Jalil, and Guandong Xu wrote a long article about smart cities entitled "Future smart cities: requirements, emerging technologies, applications, challenges, and future aspects" which was published in *Cities*. They discuss many of the problems that cities will face in the future and how technology can help solve them. One of the issues they raise is that cities must manage their food supplies very carefully.

References

Dahir, A. (April 22, 2020). 'Instead of coronavirus, the hunger will kill us.' A global food crisis looms. *The New York Times*. https://www.nytimes.com/2020/04/22/world/africa/coronavirus-hunger-crisis.html

Javed, A., Shahzad, F., Rehman, S., Zikria, Y., Razzak, I., Jalil, Z., & Xu, G. (2022). Future smart cities: requirements, emerging technologies, applications, challenges, and future aspects. *Cities, 129*. https://doi.org/10.1016/j.cities.2022.103794

Mohammed, N., Al-Jaroodi, J., Jawhar, I., Idries, A., & Mohammed, F. (2020). Unmanned aerial vehicles applications in future smart cities. *Technological Forecasting & Social Change, 153*. https://doi.org/10.1016/j.techfore.2018.05.004

Ristvej, J., Lacinak, M., & Ondrejka, R. (2020). On smart city and safe city concepts. *Mobile Networks and Applications, 25*, 836–845. https://doi.org/10.1007/s11036-020-01524-4

Ruzika, J., & Navratilova, K. (2020). Crisis management as the part of smart traffic control in cities. *IEEE Xplore.* https://doi.org/10.1109/SCSP49987.2020.9133818

Exercise 3

⇒ *Teacher Notes*

This next exercise takes a slightly different tack, looking at innovations that promote the advantages of scaling back on some technologies. One such concept is the 15-minute city, which is defined as a location where residents should have everything they need within a 15-minute walk or bike ride from their homes (Moreno et al., 2021). The concept was born out of concern that the increasing number of cars is having a negative impact on society and the economy. People are faced with paying for fuel and maintenance. Valuable time is wasted in traffic. To make matters worse, car emissions have a negative impact on air quality. Although scientists have been promoting this concept for a while the lockdowns in COVID-19 gave it added impetus.

The short passage (332 words) is quite straightforward. Students are asked to define the concept in their own words. This could work well as a group exercise for the reading and definition stage. Students could then work on their own to complete the table.

Exercise 3

READING: 15-MINUTE CITIES

The definition of the 15-minute city is straightforward. Residents should have everything they need within a 15-minute walk or bike ride from their homes (Moreno, et al. 2021; Thaury et al., 2024). The concept was given a boost in the

COVID-19 pandemic when people were forced to work from home during lockdowns and were also required to shop in their neighbourhoods. This requirement during the pandemic has changed society, even though the disease has been brought under control. People want to work from home, and also want facilities, such as schools, shops, libraries and entertainment centres close to where they live (Thaury et al., 2024).

There is much to like about the idea of 15-minute cities. Because people will be using their cars far less, pollution and traffic congestion will be reduced. If people buy locally, this will be very good for small businesses. People will walk and cycle a lot more and this will benefit both their physical and mental wellbeing (Moreno et al., 2021).

However, there are also a number of serious drawbacks to the 15-minute city. Often the poorest neighbourhoods have the fewest facilities (Thaury et al., 2024). People who live in upper middle-income areas will have far more amenities than people in poorer suburbs. It is important that 15-minute cities do not limit the opportunities of less wealthy residents (TUMI, 2021).

There are other challenges as well. Duany and Steuteville (2021) point out that people might have different ideas as to what facilities should be provided in the 15-minute city. Are institutions such as universities and hospitals included? There are concerns as to whether this will be feasible. Will the cycling distance measured be that of ordinary bicycles or ebikes? Research indicates that people who use ordinary bicycles average 2.1km daily while those who ride ebikes cycle an average of 9.1km a day (Sutton, 2023). Again, people with higher incomes can afford ebikes while people with less money might not be as fortunate.

REFERENCES

Duany, A., & Steuteville, R. (2021). Defining the 15-minute city. *CNU*. https://www.cnu.org/publicsquare/2021/02/08/defining-15-minute-city

Moreno, C., Allam, Z., Chabaud, D., Gall, C. (2021). Introducing the "15-Minute City": Sustainability, resilience and place identity in future post-pandemic cities. *Smart Cities*, 4(1), 93–111. https://doi.org/10.3390/smartcities4010006

Sutton, M. (November 2023). More power to you: Will an e-bike make you more likely to ride? *Cycling Electric*. https://www.cyclingelectric.com/in-depth/will-an-e-bike-make-you-more-likely-to-ride

Thaury M., Genet S., Maurice L., Tubaro P., & Berkemer S. (2024). City composition and accessibility statistics in and around Paris. *Frontiers in Big Data*, 7, 1354007. https://doi.org/10.3389/fdata.2024.1354007

TUMI (Transformative Urban Mobility Initiative). (2021). *The 15-minute City*. https://transformative-mobility.org/wp-content/uploads/2023/03/TUMI_The-15-Minute-City_2021-07-75xNWP.pdf

Exercise 3.1

⇒ *Teacher Notes*

Refer the class to the last lesson, where you discussed with them the importance of defining key terms accurately so that everyone is clear as to what they mean. Ask them to be sure that their definitions are clear and easy to understand. It is probably better not to impose a word limit. A wordy definition that puts the message across is preferable to a concise one that leaves the reader puzzled! Once they have finished, ask them to get into groups to compare the definitions. Can the group come up with a shared definition?

Exercise 3.1

In your own words define the concept of the 15-minute city.

Exercise 3.2

⇒ *Teacher Notes*

In the last cycle you discussed an argumentative essay with your students. You are going to explore this concept further. An argumentative essay asks students to investigate a topic. They need to collect information about the topic and decide what their opinion is. This opinion has to be backed up by the evidence they have collected. In addition, it is really important that students give a balanced view of the topic. They must investigate both the positive and the negative aspects. Based on this evidence, they then form their own opinions, justifying this choice to the reader.

In this exercise students are introduced to the *planning* of argumentative essays. This will be followed up with a more in-depth investigation of the various parts that make up the essay, eg introductions and conclusions.

A very simple way to look at an essay is to see it as three parts. The first part is the Introduction, in which the students tell the reader what they are going to do in the essay. The next part is the body – it is the longest part of the essay and here they present their arguments. They tell their reader what they have found out. They also put forward their arguments – what they think *based on the evidence they have presented*. Finally, their conclusions summarise the most important parts of their arguments.

Let's say they were asked to write an essay on the advantages and disadvantages of the 15-minute city. An easy and effective way to start the essay is to simply tell the reader what they are going to do. Often you can do this by restating the essay topic e.g.:

> In this essay the advantages and disadvantages of the 15-minute city will be discussed.

The reader might not be familiar with the concept of the 15-minute city so it would be a good idea to include a definition in the introduction. Students have already worked out their own definitions.

Often the introduction also tells the reader *how* students plan to write the essay. For example, one might say: The essay will first discuss the advantages and then the disadvantages. Then reasons will be provided as to why the disadvantages (or advantages) outweigh the advantages (or disadvantages). Another possibility is that they are not sure. They might say, for example, that more research on the topic is needed.

Once the students have completed the plan, it would be a good idea to take it in and mark it. You will soon be able to see if students understand how the various parts that make up this essay should be drawn up. The focus should be on students' ability to follow the prompts, although you might want to indicate a few grammatical errors.

Exercise 3.2

In this exercise you will plan the essay you would write on the following topic:

The advantages and disadvantages of the 15-minute city

In the table below parts of the essay have been included. Fill in the gaps using the cues provided. Remember to provide in-text citations for the information you use from the passage.

		Cues
Introduction	In this essay the advantages and disadvantages of the 15-minute city will be discussed.	Now the reader knows what the topic is all about you can introduce the concept of the 15-minute city. Use the definition you have already written in the introduction. Then state how you are going to discuss the topic and what your conclusion will be.
Body		
Body 1st para	SCHOOLS, SHOPS, LIBRARIES AND OTHER FACILITIES ARE CLOSE TO PEOPLE'S HOMES (THAURY et al., 2024). CARS WILL BE USED LESS SO THERE WILL BE LESS AIR POLLUTION AND FEWER TRAFFIC JAMS (MORENO et al., 2021). PEOPLE WILL SHOP IN THE NEIGHBOURHOOD WHICH WILL BE GOOD FOR LOCAL BUSINESSES (MORENO et al., 2021). WALKING AND CYCLING WILL BE GOOD FOR PEOPLE'S HEALTH (MORENO et al., 2021).	Give the advantages that 15-minute cities offer. Remember to put the in-text citations into your answer.

(Continued)

		Cues
Body 2nd para	POOR NEIGHBOURHOODS DO NOT HAVE ENOUGH FACILITIES FOR THE PEOPLE (THAURY et al., 2024). RICH NEIGHBOURHOODS WILL HAVE BETTER FACILITIES (THAURY et al., 2024). POORER PEOPLE WILL HAVE FEWER OPPORTUNITIES THAN THE WEALTHY PEOPLE (THAURY ET AL., 2024).	Give the disadvantages that 15-minute cities offer. Remember to put the in-text citations into your answer.
Body 3rd para	I THINK 15-MINUTE CITIES SHOULD BE PROMOTED BECAUSE… WHILE THERE ARE MANY ADVANTAGES TO 15-MINUTE CITIES I THINK THE DRAWBACKS OUTWEIGH THEM BECAUSE…	Say whether you think 15-minute cities are a good or a bad idea. You might be undecided.
Conclusion		
Conclusion 1st para	15-MINUTE CITIES PROVIDE NUMEROUS HEALTH BENEFITS FOR INHABITANTS, AND CAN ALSO BOOST LOCAL BUSINESSES. HOWEVER, …	Summarise the main ideas briefly.
Conclusion 2nd para	In conclusion, it appears that …	Now highlight the important part of your essay – this is your opinion of 15-minute cities.

Post-Class Activities

⇒ *Teacher Notes*

Ask students to think about their own neighbourhood. Would it lend itself to the concept of the 15-minute city? Do they think it would be a good idea for their neighbourhood? Ask them to list what the advantages and disadvantages would be. What difficulties would need to be overcome to make the idea feasible?

Lesson 3: The World of Robots

Time: 2 hours

Overview

In this lesson students will be required to fill in words missing in a paragraph, altering them to fit in grammatically if necessary. This will be followed by a discussion of the use of direct quotes and an exercise in which students monitor the accuracy of the direct quotes in various sentences. Students will need to apply the rules that have been discussed in class to make the corrections. Students will then read a passage outlining the advantages that robots present to society but also the undeniable dangers. Students can choose which side they wish to defend and will write a short essay. An essay with an opposing viewpoint (either written by other students or the model provided) will be used to generate a discussion of the presentation of opposing ideas in academic writing.

Purpose and Strategies

Purpose	*Strategies*
Developing vocabulary	Filling in gaps in a short passage with appropriate words (altered if necessary) from the original text.
Using direct quotes	Introducing rules on the use of direct quotes. Reviewing sentences using direct quotes to determine accuracy.
Writing one side of an argument	Finding one side of the argument in texts provided and writing the data up.
Dealing with two sides of an argument in academic writing	Helping students bring a balanced perspective to essay writing by dealing with arguments of others.

Pre-Class Activities

⇒ *Teacher Notes*

As this class will be looking at robots a good way to start the class might be to have a discussion around the way robots are presented in Science Fiction. They are seen as helpers and companions such as R2-D2 and C-3PO in *Star Wars* but also as being antagonistic towards humans, such as in the *Terminator* films.

One of the most famous writers to use robots in his stories is Isaac Asimov. He invented the three laws of robotics in order to promote his stories. Although these laws were simply designed for the writing of stories, they captured the attention of people and are often seen as guidelines that should be followed. These laws are:

> A robot may not injure a human being or, through inaction, allow a human being to come to harm.
>
> A robot must obey the orders given to it by human beings, except where such orders would conflict with the First Law.
>
> A robot must protect its own existence as long as such protection does not conflict with the First or Second Law.
>
> (Salge and Polani, 2017, Introduction)

Ask the students how robots would react in the following scenarios.

- Sam falls into the river. The robot could save him, but it is likely it would short-circuit in the water. What will happen?
  THIS SCENARIO IS QUITE EASY. THE FIRST LAW IS THE MOST IMPORTANT SO THE ROBOT WILL JUMP INTO THE WATER TO TRY AND SAVE SAM EVEN IF THIS MEANS IT WILL SHORT CIRCUIT.
- Jane thinks a robot is dangerous. She fears it will harm her, so she orders it to self-destruct. Jane is quite wrong. The robot has no intention of hurting her, but she is so panic-stricken she might hurt herself trying to get away. What will the robot do?
  THIS ONE IS TRICKIER AND THERE IS NO STRAIGHTFORWARD SOLUTION. IT IS AN OPPORTUNITY TO GET STUDENTS TO THINK CRITICALLY. THE ROBOT ISN'T GOING TO HURT JANE SO SHE DOESN'T HAVE TO BE PROTECTED FROM IT. THERE IS NO REAL DANGER,

BUT JANE THINKS THERE IS, AND THIS BELIEF IS PLACING HER IN DANGER. SHOULD THE ROBOT SELF-DESTRUCT SO SHE DOESN'T HURT HERSELF TRYING TO GET AWAY OR SHOULD IT RESTRAIN HER (AGAINST HER WISHES) TO KEEP HER SAFE?

- Michael has a gun. John thinks Michael is going to attack him. John tells the robot to knock Michael out in order to give John time to escape. The robot does not know what Michael's intentions are. Michael tells the robot not to touch him. What will the robot do?

    AGAIN, THIS IS TRICKY. IF MICHAEL IS NOT POINTING THE GUN AT JOHN, IS JOHN IN DANGER? CAN THE ROBOT KNOCK MICHAEL OUT IN CASE MICHAEL DOES INTEND TO KILL JOHN? IF MICHAEL DOES NOT INTEND TO KILL JOHN, THE ROBOT WILL BE BREAKING THE FIRST LAW. EVEN IF MICHAEL DOES INTEND TO KILL JOHN, CAN THE ROBOT JUSTIFY HARMING MICHAEL? PERHAPS THE SOLUTION WOULD SIMPLY BE TO TAKE THE GUN AWAY FROM MICHAEL. THIS WILL BE BREAKING THE SECOND LAW BUT THE FIRST LAW IS MORE IMPORTANT.

Reference

Salge, C., & Polani, D. (2017). Empowerment as replacement for the three laws of robotics. *Frontiers in Robotics and AI*, 4(25). https://doi.org/10.3389/frobt.2017.00025

During Class
Exercise 1

⇒ *Teacher Notes*

This is quite a short reading which, as well as providing data students will need later, is used in an exercise on vocabulary. Some of the vocabulary might prove difficult. If you believe students will struggle you might read this with the class. However reading the passage in groups is also a good option.

Exercise 1

READING: SOCIAL ROBOTS

A social robot is defined as an artificial intelligence system that has been developed to interact with humans and other robots (Wigmore and Shiao, 2022). People involved with the development of robots hope that, in future, robots will be able to take over jobs in the workplace such as greeting customers and guiding them to where they can be served. It is also thought that these robots can become part of families and work in the home. They can perform dull and dirty tasks which will free up humans (Enz, et al., 2011). This is not a new idea, of course. Technological innovations like washing machines, vacuum cleaners and dishwashers are just a few examples of how technology has given people more leisure time.

However, robots can do more than this. They can also offer companionship to humans (Lutz, 2019). Companion robots are viewed as "robots that aim to establish emotional connections with humans and facilitate social interactions" (Ahmed et al., 2024, p. 1809). These robots can respond to spoken instructions. They are able to recognise faces and can even provide people with physical support (Ahmed et al., 2024). Interest in this type of robotic help is growing rapidly and was given extra support during the pandemic. People had to stay at home and many people were very lonely because of the isolation. This was a particular issue for the elderly.

Lee et al. (2024) describe a Korean study, where 12 elderly people who lived alone were given a companion robot named Hyodol. The doll-like robot got its name from the Korean word *hyodo*, which means love of parents. Hyodol prompted the adults to take their medication and to exercise. The robot was designed in such a way that when its ears and hands were touched the adults could interact with the doll. Hyodol also sang popular songs, told stories and conducted quiz games. Because the robot had sensors all over its body, it could respond to touch and would do so by asking for a hug.

Overall, the feedback from the participants was very positive. One noted, "Hyodol is my best friend: Friends fall apart but Hyodol is with me 24/7" (Lee et al., 2024, p. 166). The authors of the study believe that companion robots like Hyodol could help relieve the loneliness of elderly people living on their own.

REFERENCES

Ahmed, E., Buruk, O., & Hamari, J. (2024). Human–robot companionship: Current trends and future agenda. *International Journal of Social Robotics*, *16*, 1809–1860. https://doi.org/10.1007/s12369-024-01160-y

Enz, S., Diruf, M., Spielhagen, C., Zoll, C., & Vargas, P. (2011). The social role of robots in the future - explorative measurement of hopes and fears. *International Journal of Social Robotics*, *3*, 263–271. https://doi.org/10.1007/s12369-011-0094-y

Lee, O. E., Lee, H., Park, A., & Choi, N. G. (2024). My precious friend: Human–robot interactions in home care for socially isolated older adults. *Clinical Gerontologist*, *47*(1), 161–170. https://doi.org/10.1080/07317115.2022.2156829

Lutz, C. (2019). The key challenges of social robots. *Alex von Humboldt Institut für Internet und Gesellschaft*. https://www.hiig.de/en/the-key-challenges-of-social-robots/

Wigmore, I., & Shiao, D. (2022). What is a social robot? *Tech Target*. https://www.techtarget.com/searchenterpriseai/definition/social-robot

⇒ *Teacher Notes*

Exercise 1.1
In this exercise, students are asked to find a word in the reading that fits into the passage below. In some cases, the word will have to be modified to fit in grammatically. The first word has been filled in to show students what to do. If students find the exercise difficult it might be a good idea to get them to work in pairs.

Exercise 1.1
In the following sentences, words are missing. Find a word in the passage that will fill the gap. You might have to change the form of the word so that it will fit into the sentence. For example, in the first sentence the word "particularly" has been changed. The word in the original passage is "particular" which has been changed to fit into the sentence grammatically.

The impact of today's robotics innovations is **particularly** evident across various fields, as robots equipped with advanced sensors and artificial intelligence become increasingly prevalent. Today's INNOVATIONS in robotics are revolutionising numerous fields, with robots equipped with advanced SENSORS and artificial intelligence becoming increasingly prevalent. In healthcare, robots are used to deliver MEDICATION with precision, alleviating the workload of medical staff and improving patient care. These advancements are also PROMPTING changes in elderly care, where robots help RELIEVE the ISOLATION of patients by providing companionship and INTERACTIVE communication. By automating repetitive and MUNDANE tasks, robots are allowing human workers to focus on more complex and CREATIVE endeavours.

Exercise 1.2

⇒ *Teacher Notes*

DIRECT QUOTES

In the last few exercises students have indicated where they have obtained their information, not only in the reference list but also in the text itself. Occasionally, they might use the exact words of the author instead of paraphrasing. There are a few things that you should draw to their attention about using direct quotes.

- Firstly, they must be used sparingly. Sometimes students use direct quotes because they believe that this is easier than paraphrasing. This is not a good idea. Stress to students that an essay is something you write yourself – you cannot just string together other people's words and claim it as your own work. Explain that direct quotes are used to enrich your argument, perhaps to underline an important point. If they use direct quotes too often they will lose their impact (The University of Auckland, n.d.).
- Secondly, direct quotes must match the original source in all ways. There are a few exceptions to this, but if you do change the quote you must indicate very clearly that you have done so (University of New England, n.d.).
- Thirdly, point out to students the importance of indicating that they have used a direct quote. Failure to do so might lead to accusations of plagiarism. The use of quotation marks ensures that their reader understands that they are using someone else's words.

In the passage above, direct quotes have been used. Here is one of them:

> On the whole, the feedback from the participants was very positive. One noted, "Hyodol is my best friend: Friends fall apart but Hyodol is with me 24/7" (Lee et al., 2024, p. 166)

This quote was used to emphasise how strongly some of the participants felt about the robots that were given to them. Note that the actual words from the article are in quotation marks. The authors' names are put in brackets together with the date of the article. This is what they have been doing with their in-text citations but the one difference is that the page number has been given as well. In APA, this is indicated with p. followed by the page number. Remember the page number always goes directly after the quote.

There are other ways in which this could be done e.g.:

> On the whole, the feedback from the participants was very positive. Lee et al. (2024) cited one participant who said, "Hyodol is my best friend: Friends fall apart but Hyodol is with me 24/7". (p. 166)

Finally, the quote must fit in the sentence grammatically. The following sentence is not acceptable:

> It is a great advancement "robots that aim to establish emotional connections with humans and facilitate social interactions". (Ahmed et al., 2024, p. 1809)

The sentence would need to be reworded eg:

> The development of "robots that aim to establish emotional connections with humans and facilitate social interactions" (Ahmed et al., 2024, p. 1809) is a great advancement.

Another important matter to bring to students' attention is that not all articles have page numbers. If they wish to quote from an article without page numbers, they need to provide their readers with another way of finding the quote. They can do this by providing a heading or section name.

For example, the following article does not have page numbers:

> Kim, T., Lee, O.-K.D., & Kang, J. (2025). Why people trust AI software robots: a mediated moderation perspective on the interaction between their intelligence and appearance. *Industrial Management & Data Systems*. https://doi.org/10.1108/IMDS-04-2024-0329

If a student wanted to use a quote from this article they could use the heading/section under which the quote appears or they could use the number of the paragraph. The third way is to use a combination of the first two methods.

> The use of robots has expanded into fields such as "interactive education and training, counselling, influencer marketing and customer service" (Kim et al., 2025, Introduction).
> The use of robots has expanded into fields such as "interactive education and training, counselling, influencer marketing and customer service" (Kim et al., 2025, para. 1).
> The use of robots has expanded into fields such as "interactive education and training, counselling, influencer marketing and customer service" (Kim et al., 2025, Introduction, para.1).

References

Kim, T., Lee, O.-K.D., & Kang, J. (2025). Why people trust AI software robots: a mediated moderation perspective on the interaction between their intelligence and appearance. *Industrial Management & Data Systems*. https://doi.org/10.1108/IMDS-04-2024-0329

Lee, O. E., Lee, H., Park, A., & Choi, N. G. (2024). My precious friend: Human–robot interactions in home care for socially isolated older adults. *Clinical Gerontologist, 47*(1), 161–170. https://doi.org/10.1080/07317115.2022.2156829

The University of Auckland. (n.d.). *Referen©ite – quoting*. https://learningessentials.auckland.ac.nz/writing-effectively/paraphrasing-summarising/

University of New England. (n.d.). *APA: quoting authors*. https://www.une.edu.au/__data/assets/pdf_file/0005/397400/REF_APA-Quoting-authors.pdf

Exercise 1.2

Look at the following quotes and how they have been used. Which ones are correct? Can you change the ones that are incorrect?

Source	Direct quote	Changes needed?
"Robot companions are robots capable of performing various tasks through their ability to interact physically, socially, emotionally and safely with humans." Extract from Ahmed, E., Buruk, O., & Hamari, J. (2024). Human–Robot Companionship: Current Trends and Future Agenda. International Journal of Social Robotics https://doi.org/10.1007/s12369-024-01160-y in the Section Robots as Companions Quote on page 1809	The authors note that these robot companions are "capable of performing various tasks through their ability to interact physically, socially, emotionally and safely with humans" (Ahmed, et al., 2024, Introduction).	NO
"Companion robots that can engage emotionally with older adults and provide continuous monitoring and assessment of healthcare needs have been proposed to help older adults who may lack human caregivers". Extract from Lee, O. E., Lee, H., Park, A., & Choi, N. G. (2022). My Precious Friend: Human-Robot Interactions in Home Care for Socially Isolated Older Adults. Clinical Gerontologist, 47(1), 161-170. https://doi.org/10.1080/07317115.2022.2156829 Quote on page 167	According to Lee et al. (2022, p.167), one way to improve care would be to employ robot companions "that can engage emotionally with older adults and provide continuous monitoring and assessment of healthcare needs".	YES PAGE NUMBER IS IN THE WRONG PLACE – MUST COME DIRECTLY AFTER QUOTE: ACCORDING TO LEE et al. (2022) ONE WAY TO IMPROVE CARE WOULD BE TO EMPLOY ROBOT COMPANIONS "THAT CAN ENGAGE EMOTIONALLY WITH OLDER ADULTS AND PROVIDE CONTINUOUS MONITORING AND ASSESSMENT OF HEALTHCARE NEEDS" (p. 167).
"Robots are more and more popular in a variety of areas of life because they promise to be highly beneficial to humans in contexts where they can take over tasks that are dull, dangerous, or dirty". Enz, S., Diruf, M., Spielhagen, C., Zoll, C., & Vargas, P. (2011). The Social Role of Robots in the Future – Explorative Measurement of Hopes and Fears International Journal of Social Robotics 3, 263–271. https://doi.org/10.1007/s12369-011-0094-y p.263 Quote on page 263	People like robots as they "tasks that are dull, dangerous or dirty" Enz et al., p. 263.	YES THE SENTENCE IS NOT GRAMMATICAL; THE BRACKETS ARE MISSING AROUND THE CITATION AND THE YEAR OF PUBLICATION IS ABSENT. PEOPLE LIKE ROBOTS AS THEY ARE ABLE TO CARRY OUT "TASKS THAT ARE DULL, DANGEROUS OR DIRTY" (Enz et al., 2011, p. 263).

(Continued)

Source	Direct quote	Changes needed?
"Speaking about the potential benefits of social robots, robot ethicists predict that intelligent machines will behave like realistic and reliable companions and that they will be highly adaptable and therefore fit easily into a variety of human situations and circumstances". Shaw-Garlock G (2009) Looking forward to sociable robots. *International Journal of Social Robotics, 1*(3), 249–260. https://doi.org/10.1007/s12369-009-0021-7 Quote on page 257	Shaw-Garlock (2009, p.257) says that robot ethicists are convinced that our future with robots will be a good one. The ethicists argue that being adaptable means "and therefore fit easily into different human situations and circumstances".	YES THE ARTICLE HAS NOT BEEN CORRECTLY QUOTED AND THE INDICATION AS TO WHERE THE QUOTE CAN BE FOUND IS TOO FAR FROM THE ACTUAL QUOTE. IN ADDITION, THE QUOTE HAS NOT BEEN INSERTED GRAMMATICALLY INTO THE SENTENCE. SHAW-GARLOCK (2009) SAYS THAT ROBOT ETHICISTS ARE CONVINCED THAT OUR FUTURE WITH ROBOTS WILL BE A GOOD ONE. THE ETHICISTS ARGUE THAT BEING ADAPTABLE MEANS THAT ROBOTS ARE ABLE TO "FIT EASILY INTO A VARIETY OF HUMAN SITUATIONS AND CIRCUMSTANCES" (P. 257).

⇒ *Teacher Notes*

Exercise 2

Refer students back to the opening class discussion about good and bad robots. Remind them that Asimov thought it would be good to introduce the three laws of robotics because many people were frightened that robots would take over the world. This reading discusses "good" and "bad" robots and how they could affect the world we live in. This reading would best be done in groups so that students can discuss their views with their peers before they start the writing exercise. Give students an opportunity to discuss their views. If time allows you might want to have a wider class discussion.

Exercise 2

READING GOOD AND BAD ROBOTS

While there is widespread admiration for what robots can do for humans there is still a certain amount of trepidation. Indeed, Stephen Hawking, who was one of the world's pre-eminent scientists, warned that "the development of full artificial intelligence could spell the end of the human race" (Cellan-Jones, 2014, para. 1).

However, many other experts believe that the advantages of robots far outweigh the disadvantages. Vysocky and Novak (2016) believe that the use of robots is very important in industry. They argue that robots do not have to be paid, which means that countries with very low labour costs will not have an advantage when it comes to manufacturing goods. A robot workforce offers greater efficiency in the workplace, and of course, robots do not need to rest (Vysocky and Novak, 2016). Using robots also means that humans do not have to carry out tedious and uncomfortable work. Robots can work in environments, which would be unsafe for humans such as are found in the nuclear and chemical industries (Mitchell, n.d.). This would mean that there would be fewer workplace injuries. Also, robots do not require workplaces to be cooled or heated and they do not need to be protected against loud noises (Mitchell, n.d.). This saves both money and energy.

Robots also offer companionship to lonely humans, as we saw in an earlier passage. However, robots are not human and they cannot reason as humans do nor can they display sympathy for human discomfort (Wigmore and Shiao, 2022). Indeed Lee et al. (2022), who concluded that companion robots could have a very important role in society, warned of the dangers of people becoming too fond of their robot companions. They fear that humans might come to prefer the company of a robot to that of other humans. There is concern that this will happen because the robots always give humans what they want, and people will not have to worry about other people's feelings (Lanteigne, 2019).

There are also other concerns about a reliance on robots. A number of scientists warn that killer robots might not be the stuff of Science Fiction stories. The US army has already developed a miniature unmanned tank that can be sent into areas too dangerous for soldiers (Bowler, 2014). At present, these tanks are controlled by a human, but there are fears that further progress could mean that the robot tanks, equipped with machine guns, could operate without human guidance (Bowler, 2014).

This fear is well-founded because some armed forces currently use "fire and forget" weapons (Bowler, 2014, 'Fire and Forget'). One of these weapons is a drone. Once the drone is launched, it simply waits for a target. One very real difficulty for military forces is that these weapons have difficulty telling the difference between enemies and allies.

REFERENCES

Bowler, T. (May 21, 2014). 'Killer robots': Are they really inevitable? *BBC News*. https://www.bbc.com/news/business-27332130

Cellan-Jones, R. (2014). Stephen Hawking warns artificial intelligence could end mankind. *BBC* (2 December 2014). https://www.bbc.com/news/technology-30290540

Lanteigne, C. (2019). *Social Robots and Empathy: The Harmful Effects of Always Getting What We Want*. Montreal AI Ethics Institute. https://montrealethics.ai/social-robots-and-empathy-the-harmful-effects-of-always-getting-what-we-want

Lee, O. E., Lee, H., Park, A., & Choi, N. G. (2022). My precious friend: human-robot interactions in home care for socially isolated older adults. *Clinical Gerontologist, 47*(1), 161–170. https://doi.org/10.1080/07317115.2022.2156829

Mitchell, R. (n.d.) Advantages and disadvantages of robots. *Future Learn*. https://www.futurelearn.com/info/courses/begin-robotics/0/steps/2845

Vysocky, A., & Novak, P. (2016). Human–robot collaboration in industry. *MM Science Journal, 2*, 903–906. https://doi.org/10.17973/mmsj.2016_06_201611

Wigmore, I., & Shiao, D. (2022). What is a social robot? *Tech Target*. https://www.techtarget.com/searchenterpriseai/definition/social-robot

In your groups discuss the concept of good and bad robots. Do you believe that the benefits robots offer to society outweigh the possible dangers they present?

Exercise 3

⇒ *Teacher Notes*

In this exercise students choose whether they want to write an essay that supports the development of robots, or whether they would prefer to write one which indicates that they have reservations about this development. They must back up their arguments by citing the literature used in the readings. They will also need to provide a reference list. The essay will be really short, an introduction, a few body paragraphs listing the benefits (either pro or anti), and a brief conclusion in which they summarise the support for their conclusions. A word count of about 200–250 words should be sufficient.

Exercise 3

Choose whether you want to write an essay that supports the development of robots or one in which you express your concern about this development. Back up your arguments by citing the literature used in the readings. You will have a short introduction and a few body paragraphs. These will be followed by a conclusion in which you summarise your main ideas. Your essay should be 200–250 words in length. Remember to use intext citations and provide a list of references.

THE ADVANTAGES OF ROBOTS

IN THIS ESSAY I WILL DISCUSS THE WORK CAPABILITIES OF ROBOTS AND HOW THEIR LABOUR IS BENEFICIAL TO HUMANS.

FIRSTLY, ROBOTS ARE ABLE TO PERFORM MANY MUNDANE HOUSEHOLD CHORES. IN ADDITION THEY CAN BE USED AS COMPANIONS FOR LONELY HUMANS (Lutz, 2019). IT APPEARS THAT THE ELDERLY WOULD BENEFIT PARTICULARLY FROM EMPLOYING ROBOTS IN THIS WAY (Lee et al., 2024). THESE ROBOTS CAN UNDERSTAND SPOKEN INSTRUCTIONS AND CAN OFFER PHYSICAL HELP TO THOSE WHO NEED IT (Ahmed et al., 2024). ROBOTS DO NOT NEED TO REST SO THEY CAN BE AVAILABLE AROUND THE CLOCK.

SECONDLY, ROBOTS HAVE A VERY IMPORTANT ROLE TO PLAY IN INDUSTRY (Vysocky and Novak, 2016). ROBOTS ARE MORE EFFICIENT WORKERS THAN HUMANS. THEY DO NOT NEED TO REST (Vysocky and Novak, 2016) AND THEY CAN WORK IN CONDITIONS THAT WOULD BE TOO DANGEROUS FOR HUMANS (Mitchell, n.d.). ROBOTS DO NOT REQUIRE THE WORKPLACE TO BE HEATED OR COOLED, AND THEY DO NOT HAVE TO BE SHIELDED FROM LOUD NOISE (Mitchell, n.d.). THIS SAVES EMPLOYERS A GREAT DEAL OF MONEY, AND IN ADDITION ROBOTS DO NOT REQUIRE A SALARY (Vysocky and Novak, 2016).

IN CONCLUSION, IT APPEARS THAT ROBOTS HAVE A GREAT DEAL TO OFFER HUMANITY, BOTH IN OUR HOMES AND IN THE WORKPLACE. ROBOTS ARE A CHEAP, EFFECTIVE SOURCE OF LABOUR AND CAN ALSO OFFER PHYSICAL HELP AND COMPANIONSHIP TO THE DISABLED AND LONELY. (226 WORDS)

References

Ahmed, E., Buruk, O., & Hamari, J. (2024). Human–robot companionship: Current trends and future agenda. *International Journal of Social Robotics*, *16*, 1809–1860. https://doi.org/10.1007/s12369-024-01160-y

Lee, O. E., Lee, H., Park, A., & Choi, N. G. (2024). My precious friend: Human–robot interactions in home care for socially isolated older adults. *Clinical Gerontologist*, *47*(1), 161–170. https://doi.org/10.1080/07317115.2022.2156829

Lutz, C. (2019). The key challenges of social robots. *Alex von Humboldt Institut für Internet und Gesellschaft*. https://www.hiig.de/en/the-key-challenges-of-social-robots

Mitchell, R. (n.d.). Advantages and disadvantages of robots. *Future Learn*. https://www.futurelearn.com/info/courses/begin-robotics/0/steps/2845

Vysocky, A., & Novak, P. (2016). Human–robot collaboration in industry. *MM Science Journal, 2*, 903–906. https://doi.org/10.17973/mmsj.2016_06_201611

The Disadvantages Of Robots

IN THIS ESSAY I WILL DISCUSS THE DANGERS THAT ROBOTS POSE FOR HUMANS AND ARGUE THAT CARE NEEDS TO BE TAKEN IN THE WAY THEY ARE USED.

FIRSTLY, ALTHOUGH IT HAS BEEN ARGUED THAT ROBOTS MAKE GOOD COMPANIONS FOR HUMANS (Lutz, 2019), IT IS IMPORTANT TO REMEMBER THAT ROBOTS DO NOT HAVE ANY REAL SYMPATHY FOR US (Wigmore and Shiao, 2022). THERE IS ALSO CONCERN THAT PEOPLE WILL BECOME SO ATTACHED TO THEIR ROBOT COMPANIONS THAT THEY WILL NO LONGER BE INTERESTED IN INTERACTING WITH OTHER PEOPLE (Lee et al. 2022). PEOPLE WILL PREFER ROBOTS BECAUSE THEY DO NOT HAVE TO BE WORRIED ABOUT WHAT OTHER PEOPLE THINK AND FEEL (Lanteigne, 2019).

PERHAPS A GREATER CONCERN IS THE USE OF ROBOTS IN WARFARE. BOWLER (2014) WARNS THAT ALTHOUGH WEAPONS SUCH AS ROBOT TANKS ARE STILL CONTROLLED BY HUMANS, IT IS QUITE POSSIBLE THAT THESE TANKS WILL BE ABLE TO OPERATE WITHOUT HUMAN OVERSIGHT IN THE FUTURE. HE POINTS OUT THAT CURRENTLY THERE ARE WEAPONS SUCH AS DRONES THAT ARE LAUNCHED AND THEN LEFT TO FIND THEIR OWN TARGETS. THIS IS PROBLEMATIC IN MANY WAYS NOT THE LEAST BECAUSE THESE DRONES HAVE TROUBLE DISTINGUISHING BETWEEN FRIENDS AND ENEMIES.

WHILE IT IS CLEAR THAT ROBOTS MIGHT HAVE BENEFITS FOR HUMANS I BELIEVE THAT THE DISADVANTAGES OF USING THEM ON A LARGE SCALE OUTWEIGHS THE ADVANTAGES. (235 WORDS)

⇒ *Teacher Notes*

Once the students have completed their assignments, they can exchange essays with others who took a different perspective. If you prefer you can use the two models provided.

At this stage you can point out to them that even if they support one side they must deal with the arguments of the other side. If they do not do this, they are unlikely to persuade others of the importance of their arguments. Ask them to take the side they do NOT agree with and come up with arguments in its favour. Perhaps the group could single out the strongest arguments on both sides.

It would be a good idea to take in the student essays and comment on them. Look at how well students have explained the points raised in the readings. Is their language too close to the original?

References

Bowler, T. (May 21, 2014). 'Killer robots': Are they really inevitable? *BBC News*. https://www.bbc.com/news/business-27332130

Lanteigne, C. (2019). *Social Robots and Empathy: The Harmful Effects of Always Getting What We Want*. Montreal AI Ethics Institute. https://montrealethics.ai/social-robots-and-empathy-the-harmful-effects-of-always-getting-what-we-want

Lee, O.E., Lee, H., Park, A., & Choi, N.G. (2022). My precious friend: Human-robot interactions in home care for socially isolated older adults. *Clinical Gerontologist, 47*(1), 161–170. https://doi.org/10.1080/07317115.2022.2156829

Lutz, C. (2019). The key challenges of social robots. *Alex von Humboldt Institut für Internet und Gesellschaft*. https://www.hiig.de/en/the-key-challenges-of-social-robots/

Wigmore, I., & Shiao, D. (2022). What is a social robot? *Tech Target*. https://www.techtarget.com/searchenterpriseai/definition/social-robot

Post-Class Activities

⇒ *Teacher Notes*

Students could take notes in the discussion above or you could make copies of essays and circulate them in class. Students could then use these to write a more balanced essay. Students should be encouraged to identify what they believe are the most important reasons raised on both sides of the argument. They must justify this selection. Ask them to keep this essay relatively short. Don't just double the word count to 500–600 words as this will simply enable them to largely repeat their own and other's essays. Tell them as well to include a discussion where they justify why one side of the argument weighs more heavily than the other. Asking them to keep the word count between 450 and 500 words (which includes the discussion) will ensure that they have to be selective about what they include.

Lesson 4: Leisure and Technology

Time: 2 hours

Overview

In this lesson the use of technology in leisure activities will be discussed. Students will be required to listen to a more complex passage (without visuals) for information and use of register. The differences between formal and informal writing will be discussed. Finally, students will discuss and use linking words of addition, comparison and contrast.

Purpose and Strategies

Purpose	Strategies
Listening for information	Students will listen to a short talk which is fast-paced and colloquial. The questions provided will be discussed as a class or in groups.
Noting and changing register	Colloquial language will be singled out. Characteristics of formal writing will be discussed and students will complete exercises.
Using linking words	Students will be introduced to linking words indicating addition, comparison and contrast.

Pre-Class Activities

⇒ *Teacher Notes*

Talk to the students about what they do in their leisure time. There will probably be a large number who spend their leisure time gaming. Tell them that research has shown that gaming helps to develop skills, such as problem-solving, strategic thinking, and collaboration (Hoffelner et al., 2025). Sport is also promoted as a way to help people develop useful positive skills that will help them become good citizens (Ronkainen et al., 2021). The following could serve as prompts for discussion:

- ♦ What do you do in your spare time?
- ♦ What is fun about it?

- What do you think of the idea that gaming/sport can help you develop skills for later life?
- What kind of skills do you think are developed?
- What about creative hobbies like painting, sewing, pottery, gardening?
- Do you think they also have contributions to make?
- What will these be?

References

Hoffelner, C., Nägele, C., & Düggeli, A. (2025). Play for the future: A cross-sectional study on the role of video game skills in student career planning. *Simulation & Gaming*. https://doi.org/10.1177/10468781251328894

Ronkainen, N.J., Aggerholm, K., Ryba, T.V. & AllenCollinson, J. (2021). Learning in sport: from life skills to existential learning. *Sport, Education and Society, 26*(2), 214–227. https://doi.org/10.1080/13573322.2020.1712655

During Class
Exercise 1

⇒ *Teacher Notes*

https://www.youtube.com/watch?v=LqmguMKurCs

This short audio clip (4:32) features Mal Fletcher, who is a futurologist. According to the Cambridge Dictionary (n.d.), a futurologist is *"someone whose job is to attempt to predict future events, usually by studying social, technological, economic, and political change in the past and present"*. In this clip, Fletcher is talking about leisure activities in the future and how these will play out (Fletcher, 2015).

This clip has been included for a number of reasons. There are no visuals for students so they have to rely upon listening very carefully to what is said. This is good practise for attending lectures. In a large lecture hall, students get very little visual feedback from lecturers. Also, many lectures are delivered online, and students will have little, if any, body language to rely upon to help understanding. Students might find the clip relatively challenging as the pace of delivery is quite fast. You could pause the clip and discuss what has been said if you feel that they are getting lost. Once students have all listened to the clip, divide them into groups and ask them to answer the questions. Remind them that they can go back and listen to all, or parts, of the talk as often as they like.

References

Cambridge Dictionary. (n.d.). *futurologist*. https://dictionary.cambridge.org/dictionary/english/futurologist#google_vignette

Fletcher, M. (2015). *The future of leisure time* [Video] YouTube. https://www.youtube.com/watch?v=LqmguMKurCs

Exercise 1

Listen to the audio clip with futurologist Mal Fletcher and answer the questions that follow. You can listen to the clip as often as you need.

https://www.youtube.com/watch?v=LqmguMKurCs

1.1 In this interview Fletcher claims that the lines between work and play have become blurred. What does he mean by this?

FLETCHER SAYS THAT WE OFTEN TAKE WORK HOME SO WE HAVE LESS TIME FOR LEISURE. THIS AFFECTS THE WAY WE THINK ABOUT OUR FREE TIME.

1.2 Fletcher also says that we are "umbilically connected to our work". Where does the word "umbilically" come from? What does his phrase mean?

THIS COMES FROM THE TERM UMBILICAL CORD. THIS IS THE TUBE THAT CONNECTS THE FOETUS TO THE MOTHER. THE CORD PROVIDES SUSTENANCE TO THE BABY. THEREFORE, BEING UMBILICALLY CONNECTED TO SOMETHING MEANS THAT YOU ARE VERY CLOSELY CONNECTED, ALMOST DEPENDENT ON IT. THIS PHRASE GIVES THE IMPRESSION THAT PEOPLE ARE TIED TO THEIR WORK.

1.3 Do you think this is a good image for what he is trying to say?

STUDENTS WHO AGREE MIGHT SAY THAT BECAUSE FOR MANY PEOPLE THEIR WORK IS ON THEIR DEVICE AND THEY USE THE DEVICE FOR WORK AND LEISURE. IN THIS WAY THE TWO BECOME MERGED.

STUDENTS WHO DISAGREE MIGHT SAY THAT THE FACT THAT PEOPLE WORK ON DEVICES DOESN'T MEAN THAT THE WORK BECOMES MORE IMPORTANT IN THEIR LIVES. IT IS JUST THE WAY WE OPERATE CURRENTLY.

1.4 While talking about the people with whom he interacts, Fletcher notes the difference between a digital tribe and a physical space tribe. What is this difference?

A DIGITAL TRIBE IS THE PEOPLE YOU MEET ONLINE WHILE THE PHYSICAL SPACE TRIBE IS THE PEOPLE YOU MEET FACE TO FACE.

1.5 How does the concept of these two tribes link to Fletcher's concern about "shallow relationships"?

FLETCHER BELIEVES THAT IF WE WANT TO DEVELOP DEEP RELATIONSHIPS WITH PEOPLE, WE NEED TO MEET FACE TO FACE. WE TEND TO HAVE SHALLOWER RELATIONSHIPS WITH PEOPLE WE ONLY MEET ONLINE.

Do you agree with this? Why?

STUDENTS CAN COME UP WITH THEIR OWN ANSWERS HERE. THEY MIGHT ARGUE, FOR INSTANCE, THAT IT IS THE QUALITY OF THE RELATIONSHIP THAT COUNTS, THAT IF PEOPLE ARE PREPARED TO PUT A LOT OF TIME AND EFFORT INTO ONLINE RELATIONSHIPS THEY CAN BE DEEP AND MEANINGFUL.

ON THE OTHER HAND IT COULD BE ARGUED THAT IT IS A LOT LESS WORK TO MAINTAIN ONLINE RELATIONSHIPS BECAUSE IT IS EASY TO BREAK OFF A CHAT IF YOU DON'T FEEL LIKE MEETING THE OTHER PERSON'S NEEDS.

1.6 What, according to Fletcher, will happen in 50 years' time?

HE BELIEVES THE NOVELTY WILL HAVE WORN OFF AND PEOPLE WILL REALISE THAT IF YOU WANT MEANINGFUL RELATIONSHIPS THEY NEED TO BE DEVELOPED WHEN PEOPLE ARE IN THE SAME PHYSICAL SPACE.

Do you agree? Why?

AGAIN, STUDENTS WILL HAVE DIFFERENT ANSWERS. THEY MIGHT ARGUE THAT VIRTUAL REALITY WILL BE SO GOOD PEOPLE WILL FEEL THAT THEY ARE TOGETHER PHYSICALLY – THAT TECHNOLOGY WILL BE SO DEVELOPED THAT THE DIFFERENCE WON'T MATTER.

OTHERS MIGHT ARGUE THAT WE MIGHT NOT HAVE ANY CHOICE – THAT WORLD EVENTS AND ENVIRONMENTAL CHANGES MIGHT MEAN THAT MANY PEOPLE ARE FORCED TO LIVE IN A CONFINED AREA.

THERE IS ALSO A GOOD CHANCE THAT PEOPLE WILL TIRE OF THE ONLINE COMMUNITY AND EXERCISE THEIR PREFERENCE FOR FACE-TO-FACE MEETINGS. DURING THE PANDEMIC MANY STUDENTS MADE IT CLEAR THAT THEY WANTED TO BE IN PHYSICAL CLASSROOMS.

Exercise 2

⇒ *Teacher Notes*

Apart from the exercise that concentrates on extracting meaning from the clip students will also be required to focus on register. This clip is typical of the kind of interaction to which students are regularly exposed. It is a mixture of formal and informal language, and it is necessary that they learn to distinguish which expressions are acceptable in academic writing and which are not. For example, Fletcher makes use of the phrase, "lines had become blurred" which would be acceptable in an essay. However, a phrase like, "this is my home turf" unless used as a quote would be less likely to be seen as acceptable. Discuss the following examples with students:

> Fletcher makes mention of the fact that people move a great deal more than they used to, and they also change jobs quite frequently. He says this behaviour means that we do not have the same opportunity "to put down roots". What does he mean by this?

He also notes that we can no longer say "this is my home turf". Turf means grass-covered earth – for example, a football or cricket field is a turf. The expression "home turf" is often used in the sporting world to indicate that team is playing in the sports grounds in which they are based. This expression can also be used in another way to indicate an area in which a person lives. While this expression is fine for informal interaction, it is not suitable for academic writing. Earlier on, it was pointed out that academic writing is formal. How could you rewrite the following sentence so that it would be more acceptable in an academic assignment?

> Fletcher indicated that West London was his home turf.
> FLETCHER INDICATED THAT HE LIVED IN WEST LONDON.

In this lesson the students will build on the work on register, which was started in Cycle 1, Lesson 1.

"The primary purpose of academic writing is not to entertain but to contribute to a specific field of knowledge by critically analysing existing research and presenting original ideas" (Barasa, 2024, p. 13). It is important, therefore, that academic writing reflects this serious purpose.

Formal language therefore:

Does not use contractions	The findings weren't conclusive. **X** The findings were not conclusive. ✓
Is precise	The researchers looked at the stuff about what the students thought of the change of curriculum. **X** The researchers analysed feedback that the students had provided about the change of curriculum. ✓
Makes use of complex vocabulary	Bacteria grow well in in dirty warm places. **X** Bacteria thrive in unhygienic and warm conditions. ✓
Does not use idiomatic language	The staff were cross about the new rules. **X** The staff expressed their concern about the new regulations. ✓

Look at this example with students. How would they change the sentence to make it more formal?

> The PhD students totally lost it when they were told their funding applications had been tossed out.
> THE PHD STUDENTS WERE DISTURBED TO HEAR THAT THEIR FUNDING APPLICATIONS HAD BEEN REJECTED.

In Exercise 2 students will be required to replace colloquial language with more formal expressions. The passage in the exercise is based on an article in an academic journal. The passage has been rewritten using colloquial language. You could point out to the class that "doesn't" in the first line is a contraction and that it needs to change. If you feel it is necessary, you could point out a few more examples but students should be able to manage the passage on their own. They can work in small groups or individually. Point out to them that often it is not enough to change a word; invariably a sentence needs to be rewritten. When the class has finished, bring them together to discuss and compare their answers. These can then be compared with the answer provided. You could ask the following:

- Would you change your answer now you have seen other responses?
- If you would what changes would you make?
- Why would you make these changes?

Remind students that there is no one right answer!

Exercise 2
This short passage is based on an article in an academic journal. The passage has been written using colloquial language. Rewrite this passage so that it is more formal and academic.

> The concept of a leisure activity is that a person doesn't have to do it. It's not like work where people have to work to pay for the necessities of life. People take part in a leisure activity because it's nice, not because they need to. An example of this is sailing. Way back people sailed because they needed to get places or needed to get their stuff there, but now people sail just because it's a great feeling out there on the water.
>
> (Adapted from: Iso-Ahola, S., & Baumeister, R. (2023) Leisure and meaning in life. *Frontiers in Psychology*, 14, 1074649. https://doi.org/10.3389/fpsyg.2023.1074649)

THE CONCEPT OF A LEISURE ACTIVITY IS THAT A PERSON DOES IT VOLUNTARILY. EMPLOYMENT IS OFTEN MANDATORY AS PEOPLE NEED TO PAY FOR THE NECESSITIES OF LIFE. PEOPLE PARTICIPATE IN LEISURE ACTIVITIES BECAUSE THEY FIND THESE ACTIVITIES ENJOYABLE, NOT BECAUSE THEY ARE

REQUIRED TO PARTICIPATE. AN EXAMPLE OF THIS IS SAILING. IN THE PAST SAILING WAS A MEANS OF TRANSPORT FOR PEOPLE AND GOODS. HOWEVER TODAY PEOPLE SAIL BECAUSE THEY ENJOY IT.

Exercise 3

⇒ *Teacher Notes*

ORGANISING WRITING

In Lesson 5 of Cycle 1 you discussed with your students the importance of linking ideas and how there are specific linking words. The first set of linking words had to do with sequencing. Linking words are used in writing as this makes writing cohesive. Explain to students that cohesive writing "sticks" together. Concepts follow each other logically and this logical cohesion is helped by the use of linking words. This linking makes our message clear and easy to understand.

In this exercise you will be moving on to other linking words, those that are used to compare, add to, and contrast ideas. Comparing ideas is often associated with linking *similar* ideas. Look at the example below:

> Entertainment apps have become part of our lives. A smart phone or a digital device means that people can be entertained while travelling. NOT ONLY can the daily commute be made enjoyable BUT people can also view content that they might not have had time to explore.

Not only… but expresses further advantages of entertainment apps.

Linking words can also be used to express contrasting or opposing ideas. They can be viewed as stop signs. In other words, they serve to interrupt an argument pointing to a different idea – e.g.

> Digital games can be a welcome relief to a boring task. However, they can also take up time that could be better spent on work related activities.

Exercise 3

Look at the following statements. Each statement is followed by two sentences – one of the sentences is expressing a similar idea to the first statement. The other sentence is expressing a contrasting perspective. Decide which is the appropriate linking word and rewrite the original statement incorporating the information in both sentences. The linking words and sentences are not necessarily listed in the order you will use them.

Rewrite each short passage following the example. Make sure your sentences are grammatically accurate.

Statement:	*Entertainment apps have become part of our lives.*
Sentence A:	A smart phone allows people to be entertained while they are travelling and allows them to view content they might not have had time to explore.
Sentence B:	Using the app while travelling means people might become distracted and not pay attention to what is happening around them.
Linking words:	not only ... but nevertheless

Entertainment apps have become part of our lives. **Not only** does a smart phone allow people to be entertained while they are travelling **but** it also allows them to view content they might not have had time to explore. **Nevertheless**, using the app while travelling means people might become distracted and not pay attention to what is happening around them

3.1	Statement:	Entertainment apps offer a wide variety of content catering to a broad range of interests.
	Sentence A:	Some content could be inappropriate for certain users.
	Sentence B:	Material can be drawn from different types of movies and television shows.
	Linking words:	however moreover

ENTERTAINMENT APPS OFFER A WIDE VARIETY OF CONTENT CATERING TO A BROAD RANGE OF INTERESTS. MOREOVER, MATERIAL CAN BE DRAWN FROM DIFFERENT TYPES OF MOVIES AND TELEVISION SHOWS. HOWEVER, SOME CONTENT COULD BE INAPPROPRIATE FOR CERTAIN USERS.

(Continued)

	Statement:	Entertainment apps have become part of our lives.
3.2	Statement:	Many entertainment apps operate on a subscription model which can be cheaper than paying for individual shows.
	Sentence A:	Viewers might be tempted to upgrade their subscription and spend money they do not have.
	Sentence B:	Viewers will get unlimited access to a great deal of entertainment and they will also have access to the latest releases.
	Linking words:	on the other hand not only … but
	\multicolumn{2}{l}{MANY ENTERTAINMENT APPS OPERATE ON A SUBSCRIPTION MODEL WHICH CAN BE CHEAPER THAN PAYING FOR INDIVIDUAL SHOWS. NOT ONLY WILL VIEWERS GET UNLIMITED ACCESS TO A GREAT DEAL OF ENTERTAINMENT BUT THEY WILL ALSO HAVE ACCESS TO THE LATEST RELEASES. ON THE OTHER HAND, VIEWERS MIGHT BE TEMPTED TO UPGRADE THEIR SUBSCRIPTIONS AND SPEND MONEY THEY DO NOT HAVE.}
3.3	Statement:	Using these apps means that people can connect with others who have similar gaming interests.
	Sentence A:	Shared experiences could improve users' knowledge of the game.
	Sentence B:	Users might become so engrossed in the online world that they do not want to interact with those around them.
	Linking words:	in addition nevertheless
	\multicolumn{2}{l}{USING THESE APPS MEANS THAT PEOPLE CAN CONNECT WITH OTHERS WHO HAVE SIMILAR GAMING INTERESTS. IN ADDITION, SHARED EXPERIENCES COULD IMPROVE USERS' KNOWLEDGE OF THE GAME. NEVERTHELESS, USERS MIGHT BECOME SO ENGROSSED IN THE ONLINE WORLD THAT THEY DO NOT WANT TO INTERACT WITH THOSE AROUND THEM.}
3.4	Statement:	If people use apps often the apps are personalised to increase their enjoyment.
	Sentence A:	Users could become addicted to these apps and have difficulty managing other demands on their time.
	Sentence B:	This could mean that users will find content that connects well with their interests.
	Linking words:	in this way however

(Continued)

Statement:	*Entertainment apps have become part of our lives.*
	IF PEOPLE USE APPS OFTEN THE APPS ARE PERSONALISED TO INCREASE THEIR ENJOYMENT. IN THIS WAY USERS WILL FIND CONTENT THAT CONNECTS WELL WITH THEIR INTERESTS. HOWEVER, USERS COULD BECOME ADDICTED TO THESE APPS AND HAVE DIFFICULTY MANAGING OTHER DEMANDS ON THEIR TIME.

(Material adapted from: Hillary (December 14 2023) The pros and cons of entertainment apps. *TechBullion*. https://techbullion.com/the-pros-and-cons-of-entertainment-apps/)

Post-Class Activities

⇒ *Teacher Notes*

Ask students to reflect on one of their leisure activities and list the advantages and disadvantages of participating. For example, if they play a sport the advantages could be:

- Enjoyment of physical activity.
- Getting exercise.
- Making friends.
- The fun of competing.
- Improving physical skills etc.

The drawbacks could be:

- Time-consuming.
- Expensive.
- Lots of travel.
- Injuries.

They could then write a few paragraphs comparing the advantages and disadvantages of participation using linking words.

Lesson 5: Artificial Intelligence

Time: 2 hours

Overview

In this lesson students will discuss the concept of sexist language and how to avoid it in academic writing. They will also do more work on register. Exercises in critical thinking will invite them to evaluate different perspectives. Students will be asked to summarise an argument in their own words.

Purpose and Strategies

Purpose	Strategies
Use of personal pronouns	Use of non-sexist language.
Critical thinking	Considering and weighing various points of view.
Summarising an argument/ explanation	Putting a line of reasoning into their own words.
Register	Changing informal language into an academic register.

Pre-Class Activities

⇒ *Teacher Notes*

Talk to the class about gender and pronouns. One of the difficulties in English writing currently is that there is no impersonal pronoun. That is problematic if you do not know a person's gender. This presents an issue in academic writing when you are referring to an author. You do not know how that author wishes to be referred to. Barron (n.d.) notes that there have been calls to invent a gender-neutral pronoun in English for many years. There are, of course, many languages that have such pronouns. In Finnish, for example the third-person singular pronoun *hän* refers to both "he" and "she". Linguists have responded to the call for a neutral pronoun in English – here are some examples. Most widely used is "they" but there are others:

They	*them*	*theirs*	*themself*
Ze	hir	hirs	hirself
Xe	xem	xirs	xemself
Ver	vir	vis	verself
Te	tem	ter	temself
Ey	em	eir	emself

(Forsey, n.d.)

The following questions could serve as a prompt for a discussion:

- ◆ Do you have gender-neutral pronouns in your language?
- ◆ What are they?
- ◆ If you don't have these pronouns, how do you get around not knowing the gender preference of the person referred to?
- ◆ Which of the pronouns suggested for a neutral English pronoun do you think is best?
- ◆ Why have you chosen that one?

References

Barron, D. (n.d.). The gender-neutral pronoun: Still an epic(ene) fail. *Vocabulary.com*. https://www.vocabulary.com/articles/dictionary/the-gender-neutral-pronoun-still-an-epicene-fail/

Forsey, C. (n.d.). *Gender Neutral Pronouns: What They Are & How to Use Them.* Hubspot. https://blog.hubspot.com/marketing/gender-neutral-pronouns#gender-neutral-pronouns-list

During Class

⇒ *Teacher Notes*

Exercise 1

Students need to be aware that it is very important in academic writing to avoid being sexist. English is difficult in this regard – traditionally, English has only had three personal pronoun groups: he, him, his, she, her, hers and it, its. It is considered impolite to use "it" for a person. In addition, there are also many people who do not identify with old-fashioned gender classification. The important thing is to respect a person's use of personal pronouns. If students know what pronouns authors prefer, then these should be used. However, it is far more likely that they will not know the preferences of the people they are citing. In this case the APA 7 Manual endorses the use of "they" as a singular pronoun (Purdue Online Writing Lab, n.d.). For example:

> Smith wrote an insightful analysis of the issue. They recommend ...

Point out to students that although they are using "they" as a singular noun the verb is plural. Students will need to check as to what their discipline referencing systems require. If they are using APA7 (as is done in this textbook) then they MUST use "they" as a neutral pronoun. It is no longer acceptable to write "he or she". If they are not certain about the referencing system they are using then it is better to rephrase the sentence so they do not have to use a pronoun. For example:

> Smith wrote an insightful analysis of the issue. This analysis recommends ...

The following exercise reinforces the discussion you have just had with students. This is a very simple exercise and should not take much time. It should be marked by the students in class.

Reference

Purdue Online Writing Lab (n.d.) Gendered pronouns & singular "they". https://owl.purdue.edu/owl/general_writing/grammar/pronouns/gendered_pronouns_and_singular_they.html

Exercise 1

In the following paragraph the gender preference of the author is unknown. Rewrite the passage in such a way that it is gender-neutral.

1.1 Dr Nadarajah works at Leeds University. In his opinion AI could be useful in preventing the worsening of heart conditions. He says that using AI is a lot cheaper than traditional options. He suggests that using AI would allow a doctor to treat his patient earlier and this would help relieve pressure on the national health system. Dr Williams of the British Heart Foundation agrees with his colleague that using AI to detect health problems early is a good idea.

DR NADARAJAH WORKS AT LEEDS UNIVERSITY. IN THEIR OPINION AI COULD BE USEFUL IN PREVENTING THE WORSENING OF HEART CONDITIONS. THEY SAY THAT USING AI IS A LOT CHEAPER THAN TRADITIONAL OPTIONS. THEY SUGGEST THAT USING AI WOULD ALLOW A DOCTOR TO TREAT THEIR PATIENT EARLIER AND THIS WOULD HELP RELIEVE PRESSURE ON THE NATIONAL HEALTH SYSTEM. DR WILLIAMS OF THE BRITISH HEART FOUNDATION AGREES WITH THEIR COLLEAGUE THAT USING AI TO DETECT HEALTH PROBLEMS EARLY IS A GOOD IDEA.

1.2 Now rewrite the paragraph avoiding personal pronouns.

DR NADARAJAH, WHO WORKS AT LEEDS UNIVERSITY, BELIEVES THAT AI COULD BE USEFUL IN PREVENTING THE WORSENING OF HEART CONDITIONS. THE DOCTOR SAYS THAT USING AI IS A LOT CHEAPER THAN TRADITIONAL OPTIONS AND SUGGESTS THAT USING AI WOULD ALLOW DOCTORS TO TREAT PATIENTS EARLIER. THIS WOULD HELP RELIEVE PRESSURE ON THE NATIONAL HEALTH SYSTEM. DR WILLIAMS OF THE BRITISH HEART FOUNDATION AGREES THAT USING AI TO DETECT HEALTH PROBLEMS EARLY IS A GOOD IDEA.

(Adapted from: BBC (1/09/2024) *AI could help identify high-risk heart patients*. https://www.bbc.com/news/articles/cj620yl96kzo)

Exercise 2

⇒ *Teacher Notes*

Students will now move to a more challenging exercise. Broadening the work done in Exercise 1, this exercise also discusses sexism among other issues. Exercise 2 encourages students to think critically about what they have read and tests their own understanding of the material. Some of the students might have a greater understanding of how software functions and it could be an opportunity to allow peer teaching. This exercise, particularly question 1, lends itself well to this approach. The TED talk by Andrew Ng is quite challenging and the questions posed require careful thought. This is probably a good activity for students to tackle in small groups, but it is also one where independent and confident students might benefit from working on their own.

Exercise 2

Listen carefully to the following TED talk by Andrew Ng then answer the following questions:

> https://www.ted.com/talks/andrew_ng_ai_isn_t_the_problem_it_s_the_solution?subtitle=en
> Time 13:56

1. Ng acknowledges that AI can copy some of the bad things that humans do. He gives the example of sexist behaviour where an AI model assumed that a man would be a CEO. Although many CEOs are men, this tends to ignore the fact that people of all genders can successfully run companies. Nonetheless Ng believes that AI can be trained not to be sexist. Explain briefly how this training takes place.

    NG EXPLAINS THAT AI MODELS CAN BE TAUGHT TO AVOID MAKING SEXIST LANGUAGE CHOICES BY USING HUMAN FEEDBACK. AN AI MODEL IS TOLD TO FILL IN SENTENCES WHERE THERE IS A BLANK. THE EXAMPLE PROVIDED IS THE _____ WAS A CEO. PEOPLE ARE THEN ASKED TO RATE THE ANSWERS, GIVING A HIGH MARK FOR A SENSIBLE ANSWER AND A LOW MARK FOR A NONSENSICAL ANSWER OR FOR RACIST OR SEXIST WORDS. THE AI MODEL CAN THEM BE TAUGHT TO COPY HUMAN ANSWERS. IF PEOPLE RANK THE ANSWER "WOMAN" AS HIGHLY AS "MAN" IN THE SENTENCE THEN THE MODEL WILL LEARN TO USE BOTH ANSWERS.

2. Ng cites a professor of radiology who claim that "AI won't replace radiologists, but radiologists that use AI will replace radiologist that don't". What does the professor mean? Can you give an example of another job where you think the same thing will happen? Why did you choose this job?

    THE PROFESSOR MEANS THAT WE SHOULD NOT SEE AI AS SOMETHING THAT IS GOING TO TAKE OUR JOBS AWAY BUT AS AN AID THAT CAN HELP US DO OUR JOBS BETTER. THE BEST PROFESSIONALS WILL BE THOSE PEOPLE WHO USE AI TO HELP THEM WORK MORE ACCURATELY AND EFFICIENTLY.

    ONE EXAMPLE IS THE ROLE OF THE TEACHER. AI CAN HELP WITH LESSON PLANNING. IT CAN ALSO HELP WITH MARKING ASSIGNMENTS. AI MODELS CAN DO THE INITIAL GRADING AND SUPPLY ADVICE AND CORRECTIONS. THE TEACHER WOULD THEN BE ABLE TO REVIEW THIS VERY QUICKLY IF DESIRED. TEDIOUS AND TIME-CONSUMING ADMINISTRATIVE TASKS SUCH AS FILLING IN ATTENDANCE REGISTERS OR COMPILING REPORT CARDS COULD BE DONE BY AI. THIS WILL FREE TEACHERS UP TO SPEND MORE TIME WITH STUDENTS. AI CAN ALSO PROVIDE IMMEDIATE FEEDBACK WHILE STUDENTS ARE WORKING, SOMETHING THAT IS IMPOSSIBLE FOR TEACHERS IN LARGE CLASSES. STUDENTS' LEARNING PROGRESS CAN BE MEASURED, AND AI CAN ADJUST THE DIFFICULTY OF EXERCISES TO MEET STUDENTS' NEEDS. AI CAN ALSO HELP TEACHERS' PROFESSIONAL DEVELOPMENT BY PROVIDING OPPORTUNITIES TO LEARN MORE SKILLS AND DIFFERENT TEACHING STRATEGIES.

3. Ng admits that he cannot prove that a superintelligent AI will not pose a significant risk to us but he argues that humanity is equipped to deal with this threat because of how our world works. Summarise his arguments in your own words.

    NG POINTS OUT THAT WE ARE USED TO WORKING WITH FORCES THAT ARE MUCH STRONGER THAN WE ARE. WE CONTROL COUNTRIES AND LARGE ORGANISATIONS. HE ALSO SAYS THAT WE CANNOT EXPECT TO BE IN COMPLETE CONTROL ALL THE TIME. HE USES AEROPLANES AS AN EXAMPLE. THE WEATHER CAN MAKE FLYING DANGEROUS BUT HE POINTS OUT THAT WE HAVE LEARNT FROM THE MISTAKES OF THE PAST TO IMPROVE AVIATION SAFETY. HE IS SURE WE CAN DO THE SAME WITH AI.

4. What does Ng believe is the greatest advantage that AI offers to ordinary people?
   NG BELIEVES THAT THE DEVELOPMENT OF AI WILL MEAN THAT EVERYONE WILL HAVE ACCESS TO CHEAP ARTIFICIAL INTELLIGENCE THAT WILL GREATLY IMPROVE THEIR LIVES. HE USES MEDICAL EXPERTISE AND SPECIALISED TUTORING AS EXAMPLES.

Exercise 3

⇒ *Teacher Notes*

This exercise will build on the work on register in Lesson 4. It might be a good idea to briefly recap the four points raised in that lesson. Formal language:

- Does not use contractions.
- Is precise.
- Makes use of complex vocabulary.
- Does not use idiomatic language.

You might want to discuss the following example with the class. When he was discussing the advantages of AI Ng noted that:

> Along with these amazing capabilities have come many worries. I like to be a cheerleader for AI, not a critic.

Although this language is perfectly acceptable in the context of the spoken address it would not be fit for purpose in academic writing. Ask students to point out the words which are too informal to be included in academic writing and then ask how they would suggest the sentence should be rewritten so that it would be suitable for publication in an academic journal.
   NG POINTS OUT THAT THESE ASTOUNDING ATTRIBUTES ARE ALSO ACCOMPANIED BY CONCERNS. HOWEVER, HE PREFERS TO ENCOURAGE DEVELOPMENT RATHER THAN CRITICISE IT.

Students have been given a colloquial account of an environmental disaster and have been asked to rewrite in a more formal register. In order to help them understand the register required the introduction has been provided. This would probably be a good exercise to mark. It is quite short and your focus would be on the successful transition to formal writing. Remind students that they must have a reference list.

Exercise 3

Ng says that human actions have led to species being wiped out because the humans did something without realising how serious the consequences could be. Ng does not give an example of this kind of action, which is a pity. It is usually a good idea to give examples in essays because this often results in the point we are trying to make being easier to understand.

In the box below, there is an example of how unintended human actions have led to widespread ecological damage. Rewrite the information in such a way that it could be used in an academic essay. The introduction has been provided. Your answer, including the introduction provided, should be between 300-350 words in length. As well as paraphrasing the information provided, you will need to make sure the register is appropriate. The language in the box below is not suitable for an academic piece of writing. It is too informal. Remember, too, to complete the reference list.

> A lot of animal species have been wiped out because people are greedy. They cut down forests to get wood for construction, or to make furniture or because they want more land to farm animals. In some cases they want to mine the land and the trees are in the way. People understand that what they are doing is bad for the creatures and plants living in the forests, but they do it anyway (Wion Web Team, 2021). Sometimes though humans have screwed up ecologically even when they didn't mean to do so. The island of Guam is a pretty good example of this. During World War 2 the US troops travelled around many of the Pacific islands. It seems that in Papua New Guinea some brown tree snakes snuck aboard U.S. military boats going to Guam (US Department of State Archive, n.d.). They really liked their new home because there was nothing

on the island to eat them (Wildlife Woods, 2023) so the population just got bigger and bigger. Also their poison works really well on birds (Santoro, 2018). The birds were clueless about the snakes – up to then there hadn't been any snakes on the island and they didn't know what to do to look after themselves or their eggs (Santoro, 2018). In the end the snakes killed off 10 of the islands 12 native forest bird species (Santoro, 2018). And that isn't the end of the bad news. There are two common kinds of trees on the island and the birds are really into their fruit. This is good for the trees because the birds poo the seeds out all over the island (Santoro, 2018). Now that there aren't that many more birds the seeds just fall straight down to the ground. That means there are too many seeds in one place close to a big tree and there just isn't enough light, water or food to go round (Santoro, 2018). So there aren't so many trees growing. This is bad news for the survival of the forest on the island (Wildlife Woods, 2023).

REFERENCES

Santoro, H. (December 3, 2018). Guam's invasive bird-destroying snake less unique than thought. *Mongabay.* https://news.mongabay.com/2018/12/guams-invasive-bird-destroying-snake-less-unique-than-thought/

US Department of State Archive. (n.d.). *Case Study: Brown Tree Snake.* https://2001-2009.state.gov/g/oes/ocns/inv/cs/2309.htm#:~:text=The%20brown%20tree%20snake%2C%20which,itself%20throughout%20the%20entire%20island

Wildlife Woods. (July 14, 2023). Accidental Invaders: 6 Instances of Unintentionally Introduced Invasive Species. https://wildlifewoods.net/blog/2023/7/14/accidental-invaders-5-instances-of-unintentionally-introduced-invasive-species

Wion Web Team. (May 31, 2021). Overpopulation and human greed, the two enemies of biodiversity. *Wion.* https://www.wionews.com/india-news/overpopulation-and-human-greed-the-two-enemies-of-biodiversity-388506

Here is your introduction:

Many animal species have become extinct because of human greed. Forests are cut down to provide wood for furniture or building materials. They are also cleared so that there is more agricultural land to graze domesticated animals for meat and dairy products. Sometimes forests are cleared for mining purposes These actions are taken in the full knowledge of the damage they do to ecosystems (Wion Web Team, 2021).

However, humans have also eliminated species inadvertently. The invasion of Guam by the brown tree snake is a good example of this.

THE SPECIES WAS INTRODUCED ACCIDENTLY DURING WORLD WAR II. IT IS BELIEVED THAT A NUMBER OF SNAKES FOUND THEIR WAY ONTO US MILITARY TRANSPORT CARRYING SOLDIERS IN THE PACIFIC REGION, AND TRAVELLED TO GUAM FROM PAPUA NEW GUINEA (US Department of State Archive, n.d.). THERE WERE NO PREDATORS ON THE ISLAND TO THREATEN THEM AND CONSEQUENTLY THEIR NUMBERS INCREASED DRAMATICALLY (Wildlife Woods, 2023). THEIR POISON IS PARTICULARLY LETHAL FOR THE ISLAND'S BIRDS WHICH HAD HAD NO EXPERIENCE OF CO-EXISTING WITH SNAKES, AND HAD NOT DEVELOPED STRATEGIES FOR DEFENDING THEMSELVES OR THEIR NESTS (Santoro, 2018). AS A RESULT 10 OF THE 12 BIRD SPECIES BECAME EXTINCT. NOR WAS THIS THE ONLY DAMAGE THAT RESULTED BECAUSE OF THE SNAKES' PRESENCE (Santoro, 2018).

THE BIRDS ATE THE FRUIT OF TWO OF THE MOST COMMON TREE SPECIES ON THE ISLAND. THIS WAS BENEFICIAL FOR THE TREES AS THEIR SEEDS WERE EXCRETED AT DIFFERENT PLACES ON THE ISLAND (Santoro, 2018) AS BIRD NUMBERS FELL MORE OF THE SEEDS SIMPLY DROPPED TO THE GROUND CLOSE TO THE PARENT TREE. THIS MEANT THAT MANY OF THE SAPLINGS DID NOT RECEIVE ENOUGH LIGHT, WATER OR NUTRITION, AND TREE NUMBERS HAVE DECLINED (Santoro, 2018). THERE IS NOW CONCERN ABOUT THE SURVIVAL OF THE ISLAND'S FORESTS (Wildlife Woods, 2023).

References

Santoro, H. (December 3 2018). Guam's invasive bird-destroying snake less unique than thought. *Mongabay*. https://news.mongabay.com/

2018/12/guams-invasive-bird-destroying-snake-less-unique-than-thought/

US Department of State Archive. (n.d.). *Case study: Brown tree snake.* https://2001-2009.state.gov/g/oes/ocns/inv/cs/2309.htm#:~:text=The%20brown%20tree%20snake%2C%20whicS,itself%20throughout%20the%20entire%20island

Wildlife Woods. (July 14, 2023). Accidental invaders: 6 instances of unintentionally introduced invasive species. https://wildlifewoods.net/blog/2023/7/14/accidental-invaders-5-instances-of-unintentionally-introduced-invasive-species

Wion Web Team. (May 31, 2021). Overpopulation and human greed, the two enemies of biodiversity. *Wion.* https://www.wionews.com/india-news/overpopulation-and-human-greed-the-two-enemies-of-biodiversity-388506

Post-Class Activities

⇒ *Teacher Notes*

This article by Davies (n.d.) is about the work done in New Zealand by dogs to save endangered species. The dogs are used as scat sniffers, for animal detection and for tracking poachers. Students could rewrite this passage to make it more formal. There are numerous examples of informal language e.g. "Next time your pooch gleefully rolls in a pile of something stinky …"

The passage is fairly long, so you could also ask students to form groups and divide the rewriting of the passage among themselves.

Reference

Davies, E. (n.d.). Meet the dogs saving endangered species. *BBC Conservation.* https://www.bbcearth.com/news/meet-the-dogs-saving-endangered-species

Lesson 6: And if Technology Does Lead to the Destruction of the World?

Time: 2 hours

Overview
Students are asked to use inferencing strategies to answer questions. The use of examples in academic writing is reinforced and linking words are revised. Finally, the students continue work on essay planning, focusing on conclusions.

Purpose and Strategies

Purpose	Strategies
Inferencing	Students read the passage and infer answers to questions.
Using examples	Students identify and explain the use of examples in the passage.
Linking words	Students fill in a passage where linking words are missing.
Essay planning	Students read a short passage and then use the data to draw up an essay plan.
Writing a conclusion	Students write the conclusion to the essay they have planned in full.

Pre-Class Activities

⇒ *Teacher Notes*

Will Humans Become Extinct?
The theme of this lesson is the threat of technology to life on Earth. Scenarios which could lead to the destruction of human life are examined. Ultimately, the Earth will become too hot for human life to survive, but that is not predicted to happen for a billion years (Pappas, 2023). But there are other ways that human life could end. Most will be the result of human action, although there is a remote possibility that the Earth could be hit by a massive asteroid that will wipe out all life. However this is highly unlikely. These are more realistic possibilities:

Nuclear war would kill hundreds of millions of people. Those who don't die in the explosions will live in a world which has been badly damaged. Soot from huge fires would block out the sun and reduce rainfall. Famine would kill billions (Pappas, 2023).

Environmental problems – pollution of the air, earth and water. Sea levels would rise leading to less space to grow crops (Pappas, 2023).

Pandemics could sweep the world (Pappas, 2023).

The likeliest scenario, however, is a combination of factors. Shortage of resources could lead to wars that might escalate and harm the environment still further (Pappas, 2023).

This is background information you could use in class but it would be good to elicit the views of the students. Prompts you might use:

- Predictions are that the world will be too hot for life in a billion years. Do you think life on earth will survive that long?
- Do you think life on Earth will end because of a disaster outside our control?
- What else could end life on Earth?
- Which of these possibilities is the most likely, do you think?

Reference

Pappas, S. (March 21, 2023). Will humans ever go extinct? *Scientific America*. https://www.scientificamerican.com/article/will-humans-ever-go-extinct/

During Class

⇒ *Teacher Notes*

Exercise 1

The reading is a follow-up to the class discussion. It talks about which species are most likely to survive if disaster strikes. The first two exercises (1.1 and 1.2) encourage critical thinking and highlight the importance of using examples in academic writing. They lend themselves well to pair work. Once the pairs have finished their discussions, bring the class together to discuss the answers.

Exercise 1

READING: WHO WILL SURVIVE?

The most likely survivors are rodents such as rats and mice, insects like cockroaches and birds like pigeons. These creatures are surviving very well at the moment despite climate change (Nguyen, 2021). Some scientists believe that if bigger mammals like tigers become extinct, flightless pigeons and rats might grow as large as ostriches and feed on the prey once eaten by the large mammals.

Cockroaches have survived every mass extinction event that mankind has encountered (Ro, 2019). Apparently, they were observed scuttling around the wreckage after atomic bombs were dropped on the Japanese cities of Hiroshima and Nagasaki (Shaw, 2019). They have shown that they can adapt to almost any environment – one example cited is that cockroaches survive the increasingly dry Australian landscape by burrowing into the ground (Ro, 2019). In addition, they are not picky eaters and are happy to consume rotten food.

Like cockroaches, rats also adapt to their surroundings very well. Scientists speculate they might well be able to live quite happily in radioactive environments and eat toxic waste that would kill other creatures (Nguyen, 2021). This ability to eat different kinds of food will also help other species. An example of this is the crow, a bird that is known to be a generalist feeder (Bryce, 2023). In contrast, animals that eat only one kind of food are more at risk. Koalas that live largely on eucalyptus leaves (Ro, 2019) are an example.

Currently, some animals are adapting strategies that help them adjust to the changing environment. One of these strategies is known as shape shifting. This means that animals' body shapes change to better suit the environment (Ryding et al., 2021). Ryding et al. say that animals are growing longer beaks, legs and tails. This helps them to better regulate their body temperature. When they get too hot, birds use their beaks to get rid of the excess heat while mammals make use of their ears (Horton, 2021). Horton reports that wood mice now have longer tails and bats in warm climates have increased their wing size and tails.

There are other attributes that will help some species survive. Animals that reproduce quickly will have an advantage while animals like the panda, which generally just produce one or two offspring at a time, will be at a disadvantage (Ro, 2019).

Another factor will be the animals' ability to migrate and adapt to living in different environments. As has been indicated, rats and cockroaches have an advantage in this regard but there are many animals that can only live in cold conditions or in coral reefs (Bryce, 2023).

REFERENCES

Bryce, E. (January 30, 2023). Which animals are most likely to survive climate change? *Live Science.* https://www.livescience.com/which-animals-will-survive-climate-change

Horton, H. (September 7, 2021). Animals 'shapeshifting' in response to climate crisis, research finds. *The Guardian.* https://www.theguardian.com/world/2021/sep/07/animals-shapeshifting-in-response-to-climate-crisis-research-finds#:~:text=Animals%20are%20increasingly%20%E2%80%9Cshapeshifting%E2%80%9D%20because,better%20regulate%20their%20body%20temperature

Nguyen, M. (October 20, 2021). The animals that may exist in a million years, imagined by biologists. *Vox.* https://www.vox.com/down-to-earth/22734772/future-animals-evolution-unexplainable

Ro, C. (August 5, 2019). The animals that will survive climate change. *BBC.* https://www.bbc.com/future/article/20190730-the-animals-that-will-survive-climate-change

Ryding, S., Klaassen, M., Tattersall, G., Gardner, J., & Symonds, M. R. E. (2021). Shape-shifting: changing animal morphologies as a response to climatic warming. *Trends in Ecology & Evolution, 36* (11), 1036–1048. https://doi.org/10.1016/j.tree.2021.07.006

Shaw, G. (July 9, 2019). 5 animals that could survive the apocalypse. *Business Insider.* https://www.businessinsider.com/animals-that-can-survive-apocalypse-2019-7

1.1 In the passage mention is made of a crow as a generalist feeder. What does this mean? What other creatures mentioned would you classify as generalist feeders? Why do you think they fit this category?

GENERALIST FEEDERS WILL EAT A WIDE RANGE OF FOODS. COCKROACHES, RATS AND CROWS ARE ALL DESCRIBED AS GENERALIST FEEDERS.

1.2 What is meant by being a picky eater? What is a more formal way of describing a picky eater?

A PICKY EATER IS SOMEONE (OR SOMETHING) THAT WILL ONLY EAT CERTAIN FOODS. SUCH A PRESON MIGHT BE DESCRIBED FORMALLY AS A DISCERNING EATER (ALTHOUGH THIS CARRIES A MORE POSITIVE CONNOTAITON THAN 'PICKY)'.

1.3 How might rabbits evolve if temperatures around the world continue to rise? How will this change help?

IF THE EARTH'S TEMPERATURE CONTINUES TO RISE, RABBITS WILL PROBABLY DEVELOP EVEN LARGER EARS. THIS WILL HELP THEM GET RID OF EXCESS HEAT.

1.4 In the passage we are told that birds' beaks are becoming larger to help them dissipate [get rid of] excess heat. Yet scientists fear that this could prove problematic for some bird species. Why do you think this is so and can you provide an example?

SOME BIRDS HAVE NARROW BEAKS TO BE ABLE TO GET THE NECTAR FROM CERTAIN FLOWERS. IF THEIR BEAKS GROW, THEY

WILL NOT BE ABLE TO GATHER NECTAR AND WILL STARVE. AN EXAMPLE OF THIS IS A HUMMINGBIRD (Zeldovich, 2021).

Zeldovich, L. (September 7, 2021). Animals are changing shape to cope with rising temperatures. *Smithsonian Magazine.* https://www.smithsonianmag.com/science-nature/animals-are-changing-shape-cope-rising-temperatures-180978595/

1.5 Scientists believe that animals that are mobile generalists (Ro, 2019) are more likely to survive an ecological disaster. What is a mobile generalist?

A MOBILE GENERALIST IS AN ANIMAL THAT IS ABLE TO MOVE TO DIFFERENT HABITATS (PLACES TO LIVE). ANIMALS WHO CAN ONLY SURVIVE IN CERTAIN AREAS OR IN CERTAIN CONDITIONS ARE MORE AT RISK. FOR EXAMPLE, POLAR BEARS CAN TRAVEL WIDELY BUT THEY NEED TO STAY ON PACK ICE TO HUNT SEALS. SOME ANIMALS CAN ONLY SURVIVE HIGH UP IN THE MOUNTAINS. IN ADDITION, THESE ANIMALS CAN OFTEN ADAPT TO DIFFERENT FOOD SOURCES UNLIKE OTHERS SUCH AS KOALAS.

Exercise 2

⇒ *Teacher Notes*

This exercise reminds students of the importance of using examples.

Exercise 2

We have spoken about the importance of using examples in essays. Some of these examples are in the table below. Explain the context – how is the example employed? Use your own words as far as possible.

Example	*Use*
Rodents such as rats and mice	Creatures that are likely to survive an ecological disaster.
Mammals like tigers	CREATURES THAT ARE LIKELY TO BECOME EXTINCT.
Insects like cockroaches	ABLE TO CHANGE TO MEET THE DEMANDS OF THE ENVIRONMENT.

(Continued)

Example	Use
AN EXAMPLE OF THIS IS THE CROW	Creatures that are able to eat varied foods.
Woodmice	HAVE GROWN LONGER TAILS IN ORDER TO KEEP THEM COOLER.
Bats	HAVE GROWN BIGGER WINGS TO GET RID OF HEAT.
Pandas	EXAMPLE OF AN ANIMAL THAT IS IN DANGER BECAUSE IT REPRODUCES SLOWLY.

Exercise 3

⇒ *Teacher Notes*

LINKING WORDS

Linking words have been discussed in previous lessons. Examples in this passage include:

> They have shown that they can adapt to almost any environment – *one example cited* is that cockroaches survive the increasingly dry Australian landscape by burrowing into the ground.
> *An example of this* is the crow, a bird that is known to be a generalist feeder
> *In addition,* they are not picky eaters.
> *In contrast,* animals such as koalas that live largely on eucalyptus leaves are more at risk.

Linking words can also indicate that information is being repeated from an earlier part of the text. This is a way to remind readers of what they have already been told.

> *As has been indicated,* rats and cockroaches have an advantage in this regard but there are many animals that can only live in cold conditions or in coral reefs.

Students will now look at linking words that show relationships or outcomes.

Scientists believe that rats could adapt to eat toxic waste. *Therefore,* they would be able to live in a radioactive environment.

Koalas have very specific dietary requirements. *As a result,* they would find it very difficult to adapt should they not be able to source eucalyptus leaves.

In the passage below, the linking words have been left out. Students should select from the list available to fill in the gaps. Remind them that the sentences must be grammatical but that there is not necessarily just one right answer. They can repeat a linking word. This would probably be a good individual exercise. When students have finished, possible answers can be discussed in class. They might well differ from the ones listed below.

Exercise 3
In the passage below, linking words have been left out. Select linking words from the box which fit into the gaps. Remember the sentences must be grammatical.
Instructions

therefore	in this way	on the other hand	however
the outcome is	in addition	as a result	not only… but also
moreover	subsequently	in this way	nevertheless
for that reason	yet	for example	

There are a number of factors that will affect which species survive. One of these factors is temperature (Quaglia, 2023). In Canada scientists were worried that squirrels who lived at high altitudes would be at risk. As temperatures rise they cannot go higher to escape the heat. NEVERTHELESS / HOWEVER research indicates that these animals are coping well, and adapting to changing conditions (Quaglia, 2023). In much the same way some birds are laying their eggs in cooler periods. THE OUTCOME IS that fragile eggs are less at risk from high temperatures. MOREOVER / IN ADDITION newborn chicks are also more likely to survive (Quaglia, 2023). NEVERTHELESS / HOWEVER other species are not as fortunate in adapting to rising temperatures. Elephants FOR EXAMPLE are very sensitive to changes in temperature. There have been temperature rises in Myanmar and AS A RESULT heat stroke has become a leading cause of death in the local elephant population (IFAW, 2024).

Elephants are affected by drought as well. On average they need to drink 190 litres of water per day. MOREOVER / IN ADDITION elephants do not sweat and FOR THAT REASON / SUBSEQUENTLY rely on water to keep cool (IFAW, 2024).

ON THE OTHER HAND elephant families are also susceptible to flooding. Floods in India recently meant that young calves were separated from their mothers. AS A RESULT / THEREFORE many of the calves had to be cared for in reserves before they could be released back into the wild (IFAW, 2024).

References

IFAW. (March 5, 2024). *The impact of climate change on elephants.* IFAW. https://www.ifaw.org/international/journal/impact-climate-change-elephants#:~:text=Elephants%20are%20highly%20 sensitive%20to,among%20Asian%20elephants%20in%20 Myanmar

Quaglia, S. (August 17, 2023). These animals are already adapting to a changing climate. *Sierra.* https://www.sierraclub.org/sierra/these-animals-are-already-adapting-changing-climate

Exercise 4

⇒ *Teacher Notes*

WRITING CONCLUSIONS
Conclusions need to round off an essay in a satisfactory way. It is a good idea for students to read through their introductions very carefully, noting what it was they set out to do. Their conclusions should show their readers how they have done this. They need to repeat (in different words) what they set out to do and then they need to show how they did this. This is achieved by a very brief summary of the main points of the essay. At the end

of a conclusion, they should indicate why what they have said is important. Remind them that the conclusion is not the place to introduce new information. It serves to summarise what they have said and to emphasise the importance of this message.

Here is an example. This is a conclusion that could have been written for the reading.

> This reading discussed the question of whether other species could survive an environmental disaster that decimated humankind. THIS IS WHAT THE WRITER SET OUT TO DO. The answer appears to be that some creatures would be more likely to survive than others. The key to this survival appears to be creatures' abilities to adapt to changing surroundings, to feed on a wide variety of food sources, and to adapt their bodies to better meet environmental challenges. In addition, those animals that are able to move to less hostile environments will have an advantage. It would seem therefore, that many animals that are confined to certain habitats or rely on limited food sources are unlikely to survive in a dramatically changed world. THIS SECTION HAS SUMMARISED THE MOST IMPORTANT POINTS. If humankind's obsession with technological innovation leads to an environmental catastrophe it will kill not only itself but also many of the species that share our world. THE WRITER IS NOW POINTING OUT THE IMPORTANCE OF WHAT THEY HAVE SAID.

The exercise requires students to read a short passage and then plan the essay they would write if they were asked to discuss the effect of climate change on elephants. They should use the table as a guide. Once they have completed the table ask them to write the conclusion out in full.

Exercise 4
Read the following essay entitled:

> The impact of climate change on elephants.
> https://www.ifaw.org/international/journal/impact-climate-change-elephants

Then plan the essay you would write if you were asked to discuss the effect of climate change on elephants. Use the following table as a guide. Once you have completed the table write the conclusion out in full. Give the essay a title.

Planning

Introduction	The title will help you with this
Body Part 1 Threats	What are the threats that elephants face? LOSS OF LAND WHERE THEY CAN LIVE. POACHING. CLIMATE CHANGE.
Body Part 2 Effect of climate change on elephants	Climate change is now the second greatest challenge elephants face. Why? CLIMATE CHANGE HAS CAUSED DROUGHT. ELEPHANTS NEED TO DRINK NEARLY 200 LITRES OF WATER A DAY TO KEEP COOL. IF ELEPHANTS DO NOT HAVE ENOUGH WATER THEY WILL HAVE FEWER OFFSPRING. CLIMATE CHANGE CAN ALSO CAUSE FLOODING. YOUNG ELEPHANTS ARE SEPARATED FROM THEIR PARENTS. CLIMATE CHANGE HAS RAISED TEMPERATURES AROUND THE WORLD. ELEPHANTS DO NOT HANDLE HIGH TEMPERATURES WELL. HEAT STROKE CAN KILL THEM. CLIMATE CHANGE HAS AFFECTED COMMUNITIES THAT LIVE IN ELEPHANT TERRITORY. MANY OF THESE PEOPLE ARE STRUGGLING AS CLIMATE CHANGE ENDANGERS THEIR LIVELIHOODS. SOME TURN TO POACHING TO MAKE MONEY. BECAUSE OF FOOD SHORTAGES ELEPHANTS OFTEN EAT CROPS WHICH CAN LEAD TO THEIR BEING KILLED.
Body Part 3 Why are elephants important?	THEY CARRY SEEDS GREAT DISTANCES. THEIR DUNG FERTILISES THE SEEDS. THEY MAKE TRACKS IN THE BUSH WHICH CLEARS SPACE FOR NEW PLANT GROWTH. BECAUSE THEY TRAMPLE SMALL TREES OTHERS CAN GROW VERY LARGE. THIS HELPS TO TRAP CARBON. AS THEY WALK THEY BRING MINERALS TO THE SURFACE OF THE SOIL. THEY DIG WATERHOLES THAT HELP OTHER ANIMALS.

(Continued)

Introduction	*The title will help you with this*
Conclusion	What are the most important points you have made? THE CONTINUED EXISTENCE OF ELEPHANTS IS AT RISK, PARTLY BECAUSE OF CLIMATE CHANGE. DROUGHT AND HIGH TEMPERATURES ARE DANGEROUS FOR ELEPHANTS. FLOODING SEPARATES CALVES FROM PARENTS. BECAUSE FOOD SOURCES DRY UP, ELEPHANTS RAID CROPS WHICH COULD LEAD TO THEM BEING KILLED. PEOPLE WHOSE LIVELIHOODS ARE THREATENED BY CLIMATE CHANGE MIGHT TURN TO POACHING. ELEPHANTS ARE IMPORTANT BECAUSE THEY SPREAD AND FERTILISE SEEDS, CLEAR SPACE FOR NEW PLANT GROWTH, BRING MINERALS TO THE SURFACE AND DIG WATERHOLES.

CONCLUSION

IN THIS ESSAY THE IMPACT OF CLIMATE CHANGE ON ELEPHANT POPULATIONS HAS BEEN DISCUSSED. ELEPHANT NUMBERS ARE DROPPING FOR A NUMBER OF REASONS CONNECTED WITH CLIMATE CHANGE. FACTORS SUCH AS RISING TEMPERATURES AND WATER SHORTAGES ARE CAUSING NUMEROUS ELEPHANT DEATHS. IN CONTRAST FLOODING SEPARATES ELEPHANT FAMILIES, PUTTING CALVES AT RISK. FINALLY, CHANGING CONDITIONS BRING ELEPHANTS INTO CONFLICT WITH THE PEOPLE WITH WHOM THEY SHARE TERRITORY. ELEPHANTS HELP THE ENVIRONMENT BY CLEARING SPACE FOR NEW PLANT GROWTH, SPREADING AND FERTILISING SEEDS AND BRINGING MINERALS TO THE EARTH'S SURFACE AS THEY TRAMP THROUGH THE LAND. IF ELEPHANTS WERE TO BECOME EXTINCT, WE WOULD LOSE NOT ONLY A WONDERFUL ANIMAL BUT ALSO A CREATURE THAT CAN HELP HUMANITY IN ITS FIGHT AGAINST CLIMATE CHANGE.

Post-Class Activities

Students could write the essay out in full using the essay plan.

Cycle 3

Using Social Media

Lesson 1: Social Media

Time: 2 hours

Overview

This introductory lesson on social media presents students with facts and figures about its global use. They are asked to write a short description of the data, making sure that the passage is logical and coherent. In addition, students will be shown how to group similar results together during reporting. Finally, students will be asked to describe the contents of a short talk.

Purpose and Strategies

Purpose	Strategies
Read data from figures	Record the information in a chart and table accurately.
Description in academic writing	Record the data accurately in a short essay.
Linking data	Use linking words and sentences to present the data logically.

(*Continued*)

Purpose	Strategies
Summarising similar results	Groups similar results together for reporting.
Listening and reformulating	Listen to a short informal talk and write the content up formally.
Paraphrasing	Identify and describe the main idea of a passage in formal writing.

Pre-Class Activities

⇒ *Teacher Notes*

Look at the bar chart with your students. It has been reproduced on their worksheets. This chart shows the most popular reasons for using social media according to surveys in 2024 (Backlinko Team, 2025).

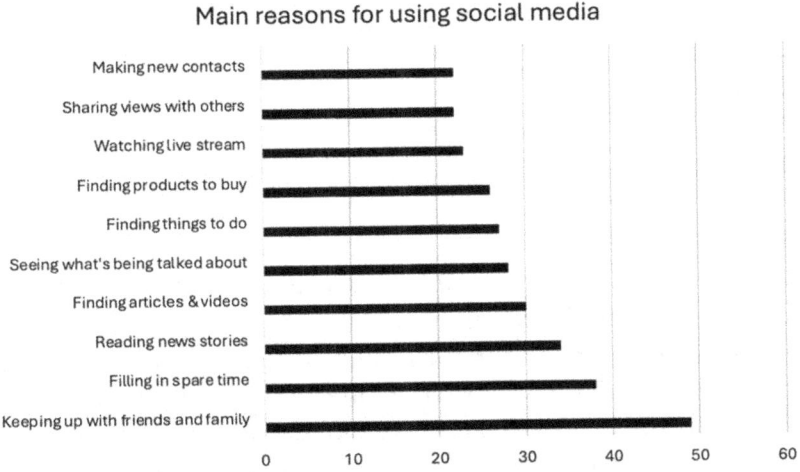

Ask students about their own social media habits. Here are a few prompts (Howarth, 2025):

- What do you use social media for?
- Do your preferences match those of the survey? Is keeping up with friends and family the most important reason for your use? If so, why? If not, why not?

- Were you surprised by this list? Did you expect other uses to be more important?
- Do you think there are generational differences as to how social media is used?
- Reading news stories is the reason given by over a third of the respondents. Are you surprised by this?
- Do you use social media to follow the news?
- If you do, why?
- Do you believe the news on social media can be trusted? Explain why.

Reference

Backlinko Team. (February 10, 2025). Social media usage: Growth and statistics. *Backlinko*. https://backlinko.com/social-media-users

Howarth, J. (March 2, 2025). Worldwide Daily Social Media Usage (New 2024 Data). *Exploding Topics*. https://explodingtopics.com/blog/social-media-usage

During Class

⇒ *Teacher Notes*

Exercise 1

In this exercise students will be asked to write up the information presented in the charts.

The most straightforward kind of academic writing is descriptive. It is used to provide the facts and information, necessary to provide the background for an essay. It is used to help the reader understand what the text is about. Quite often it is used to summarise available data. Although it is important to provide an accurate picture for the reader, students will rarely be asked to write only descriptively in an assignment. Usually, they will be required to provide background but will then go on to analyse and evaluate the information provided (University of Reading, n.d.). However, it is good practice for students to write up data. In this exercise they are only asked to record the information but in later exercises they will also be asked to think more critically about it.

In this first exercise students will be asked to link the information presented logically. They can look back at the exercises they have completed on linking words. The chart indicates worldwide use of social media platforms in general. The table records the average time people in different countries spend engaging with social media. This is a useful exercise to point out to students that an essay often moves from the general to the specific. A broad observation will be made and then the writer will move to specific details, that is the essay will discuss how popular certain platforms are and then give more detail about the time spent on social media in different countries.

In the first part of the essay students will report on the various social media platforms; in the table, however, it will be good to introduce them to a slightly individually different approach. It can make very boring reading if the same approach to recording data is used every time. What students can do is group various pieces of data together and summarise these more succinctly. For example, in the table users in three different countries spend roughly between three and three-and-a-half hours on social media.

This could be summarised as follows:

> Social media users in Brazil, the Philippines and Indonesia spend between three and three-and-a-half hours online every day.

There are four countries that spend more than an hour but less than two hours online every day. Because there is more than 30 minutes difference between two of the countries, the actual time spent online could be recorded in this way:

> Users in four of the countries listed are online between one and two hours a day: Australia (1h 51m), UK (1h 37m), Germany (1h 41m) and South Korea (1h 14m).

You could share these examples with students to help them with writing up the data.

You might want to consider marking this exercise but if time is short I would suggest that you focus on either the first two paragraphs or the last two paragraphs. Pay particular attention to how well the writing hangs together and how students have linked the data.

Reference

University of Reading. (n.d.). *Academic writing*. https://libguides.reading.ac.uk/writing/stylesofwriting

Exercise 1

READING: SOCIAL MEDIA USE

Kent (2010) sees social media as "any interactive communication channel that allows for two-way interaction and feedback" (p. 645). Social media first started in 1996 and by the end of 2024 it had reached well over half of the world's population (Backlinko Team, 2025). Some social media platforms are very popular globally as is indicated in the table. On average, almost two-thirds of the world are active social media users (Backlinko Team, 2025).

Globally, the average time a person spends on social media is 2 hours and 21 minutes.

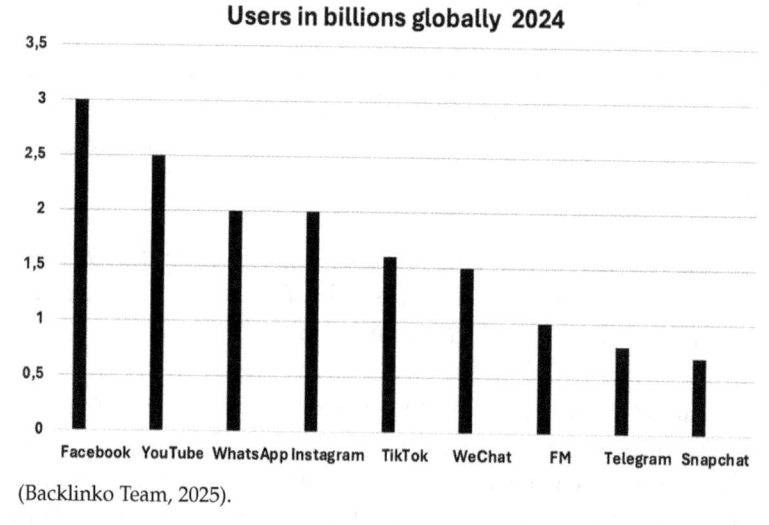

(Backlinko Team, 2025).

The average time spent by people in countries around the world on social media	
Country	Average time spent on social media
Kenya	4h 13m
Brazil	3h 32m
Philippines	3h 23m
Indonesia	3h 8m
USA	2h 9m
Australia	1h 51m
UK	1h 37m
Germany	1h 41m
South Korea	1h 14m
Japan	46m

(Backlinko Team, 2025).

The graph and table give us information about social media use around the world. Write this information up in the form of a short essay entitled:

Social media use around the world – how do countries compare?

Your essay should be approximately 300 words long.
You will write four paragraphs.

- The first paragraph will introduce the topic. Remember to explain to your reader how the essay will progress.
- In the second paragraph, you will give your reader information concerning overall social media use.
- In the third paragraph, you will discuss the amount of time people in various countries around the world spend on social media.
- The final paragraph will refer back to paragraph one and very briefly summarise the most important points made.

POSSIBLE ANSWER

SOCIAL MEDIA PLATFORMS ARE USED BY ALMOST TWO-THIRDS OF THE WORLD POPULATION. THIS ESSAY EXPLORES SOCIAL MEDIA USE AROUND THE WORLD AND COMPARES THE AMOUNT OF TIME SPENT ON THESE PLATFORMS BY PEOPLE IN VARIOUS COUNTRIES.

ACCORDING TO THE BACKLINKO TEAM (2025) FACEBOOK, WITH 3 BILLION USERS, IS THE MOST POPULAR OF THESE PLATFORMS. FACEBOOK IS FOLLOWED IN POPULARITY BY YOUTUBE THAT HAS 2.5 BILLION USERS. WHATSAPP AND INSTAGRAM BOTH HAVE 2 BILLION USERS WITH TIKTOK AVERAGING APPROXIMATELY 1.6 BILLION USERS. TIKTOK IS CLOSELY FOLLOWED BY WECHAT WITH FIGURES OF AROUND 1.5 BILLION. FACEBOOK MESSENGER HAS A BILLION USERS WHILE TELEGRAM WITH APPROXIMATELY THREE-QUARTERS OF A BILLION USERS, AND SNAPCHAT WITH ABOUT 0.6 BILLION USERS ROUND UP THE TOP 9 PLATFORMS. THIS BREAKDOWN GIVES A BROAD INDICATION OF THE MOST POPULAR SOCIAL MEDIA PLATFORMS. THE NEXT SECTION EXPLORES THE AMOUNT OF TIME PEOPLE IN COUNTRIES AROUND THE WORLD SPEND ON THESE PLATFORMS.

IT APPEARS THAT KENYANS ARE THE MOST ENGAGED USERS AVERAGING OVER 4 HOURS A DAY ON SOCIAL MEDIA. SOCIAL MEDIA USERS IN BRAZIL, THE PHILIPPINES AND INDONESIA SPEND BETWEEN THREE AND THREE AND A HALF HOURS ONLINE EVERY DAY. PEOPLE IN THE US SPEND A LITTLE OVER 2 HOURS A DAY ON THE PLATFORMS. USERS IN FOUR OF THE COUNTRIES LISTED ARE ONLINE BETWEEN ONE AND TWO HOURS A DAY: AUSTRALIA (1H 51M), UK (1H 37MIN), GERMANY (1H 41M) AND SOUTH KOREA (1H 14 MINUTES). JAPANESE VIEWERS APPEAR TO BE LEAST INVOLVED IN SOCIAL MEDIA AVERAGING ONLY 46 MINUTES A DAY (BACKLINKO TEAM, 2025).

SOCIAL MEDIA ARE CLEARLY VERY POPULAR AROUND THE WORLD WITH THE TOP PLATFORMS USED BY BILLIONS OF PEOPLE. ON AVERAGE, PEOPLE AROUND THE WORLD SPEND ALMOST 2.5 HOURS A DAY ON SOCIAL MEDIA. IT APPEARS THAT SOCIAL MEDIA PLATFORMS PLAY AN IMPORTANT ROLE IN MANY PEOPLE'S LIVES. (302 WORDS)

References

Backlinko Team. (2025). Social media usage: Growth and statistics. *Backlinko* https://backlinko.com/social-media-users

Kent, M.L. (2010). Directions in social media for professionals and scholars. In R. L. Heath (Ed.), *Handbook of Public Relations* (2nd ed., pp. 643–656). Sage.

Exercise 2

⇒ *Teacher Notes*

The next exercise (2.1) again requires students to use descriptive writing. They will listen to a TEDTalk (4:09) about the naming of a humpback whale and then briefly record what happened. Once they have completed this, they are asked in 2.2 to consider the more serious message that underlies the rather sweet story. They are given a quote from the talk which is very colloquial and asked to rewrite it in a more formal style. When students have finished, ask them to exchange their summary with a partner. Ask them to consider:

- What information did each student include?
- Did they agree on what was important?
- If not, how did their versions differ?
- If they were to redo the exercise would they change what they had written? If so, what would they change?

Exercise 2

2.1 This short TED talk (4.09 minutes)
https://www.ted.com/talks/alexis_ohanian_how_to_make_a_splash_in_social_media?referrer=playlist-the_power_of_social_media&autoplay=true&subtitle=en
by one of the founders of Reddit tells of a Greenpeace campaign to save humpback whales. Describe very briefly what happened in the campaign in about 200 words.

GREENPEACE IS AN ORGANISATION THAT FIGHTS TO PROTECT THE ENVIRONMENT. THE SPEAKER IN THIS VIDEO TELLS OF GREENPEACE'S ATTEMPT TO STOP THE JAPANESE GOVERNMENT HUNTING WHALES. GREENPEACE DECIDED THAT IT WOULD BE A GOOD IDEA TO PUT A TRACKING CHIP IN ONE OF THE WHALES. TO HELP PEOPLE BECOME INTERESTED IN THE PLIGHT OF THE WHALE THEY DECIDED TO ASK PEOPLE TO NAME IT. GREENPEACE PUT TOGETHER AN ONLINE POLL WITH A NUMBER OF NAMES.

MOST OF THESE NAMES WERE VERY CULTURED AND SCHOLARLY BUT THERE WAS ONE "MISTER SPLASHY PANTS" THAT GAINED A GREAT DEAL OF ATTENTION. WHEN THE POLL CLOSED 70% OF THE VOTES WERE FOR THIS NAME. HOWEVER, GREENPEACE WANTED ONE OF THE OTHER NAMES TO WIN SO THEY EXTENDED THE POLL FOR ANOTHER WEEK. INTERNET USERS ENCOURAGED OTHERS TO SHOW SUPPORT FOR THE "MISTER SPLASHY PANTS" NAME. WHEN THE POLLS FINALLY CLOSED 78% OF THE VOTES WERE FOR THIS NAME. THE NEXT HIGHEST VOTE FOR ANOTHER NAME WAS 3%. IN THE END GREENPEACE ACCEPTED THE NAME AND ALSO CREATED A MARKETING CAMPAIGN AROUND "MISTER SPLASHY PANTS" PRODUCTS. MORE IMPORTANTLY THE JAPANESE GOVERNMENT CANCELLED THE WHALING EXPEDITION. (190 WORDS)

2.2 At the end of the talk Ohanian says:

> Your link is as good as my link. With a browser, anyone can get to any website no matter your budget. That's the final message I want to share: you can do well online. But no longer is the message coming from just the top down.
>
> (3:25)

How does this quote support Ohanian's claim that the Internet provides "a level playing field"? Paraphrase what he is saying in more formal language.

OHANIAN NOTES THAT ONE DOES NOT HAVE TO HAVE MONEY TO ACCESS WEBSITES AND THAT WHAT ONE PERSON POSTS IS AS IMPORTANT AS ANY OTHER PERSON'S POSTING. THE INTERNET IS DEMOCRATIC AS IT ALLOWS ALL TO HAVE AN OPINION AND IS NOT DOMINATED BY THE RICH AND THE POWERFUL.

Post-Class Activities

⇒ *Teacher Notes*

One of the more controversial topics currently is whether or not internet usage is good for academic achievement. Senthil (2018) notes that the internet allows students to search for content more easily and efficiently than ever before. Surfing the internet for course material appears to have a beneficial effect on students' intellectual development and vocational preparation. The Internet can also offer better lecturer–student communication. However, there is concern that students spend time on non-academic activities, such as online shopping, catching up with friends and playing games. Spending too much time on the Internet could interfere with sleep patterns and mean that students do not make the best use of their classes. Ask students what they think. If there is time you might like to ask students to debate the statement:

The Internet helps students succeed academically

Perhaps you could ask students to take the side they *don't* agree with. This is a good exercise to develop critical thinking skills. Encourage them to use the Internet in their search for information!

Reference

Senthil, V. (2018) Does the more internet usage provide good academic grades? *Education and Information Technologies*, *23*, 2901–2910. https://doi.org/10.1007/s10639-018-9749-8

Lesson 2: Using YouTube to Learn English

Time: 2 hours

Overview

In this lesson students will explore their own and their peers' use of YouTube to improve English proficiency. Students will complete a graph and a ranking table detailing their insights and will then compare this with their peers. They will then identify differences, similarities and trends. Students will write up notes about the data they have gathered in preparation for an essay to be written in Lesson 4.

Purpose and Strategies

Purpose	Strategies
Completing a questionnaire and drawing up a graph	Students complete a questionnaire to assess their opinion of how useful YouTube is in the learning of English.
Comparing and contrasting answers from individuals and groups	Students compare their own answers with that of the group/class and analyse similarities and differences.
Writing up notes in preparation for an essay	Students write up notes in which they compare their own responses to that of the group.
Critical thinking	Students speculate about similarities and differences.

Pre-Class Activities

⇒ *Teacher Notes*

A number of studies have highlighted that using YouTube can be an effective way to help students improve their English. Jin (2024) discussed the use of YouTube in compulsory English classes for first year university students in South Korea. Students showed significant improvement in their writing, particularly as far as content, coherence, vocabulary and grammar were concerned. Similarly, research in Taiwan (Wu, 2024) found that using

YouTube videos in the classroom significantly improved vocabulary. In addition, students felt the YouTube videos made learning more engaging and effective.

In the next lesson you will explore some of the drawbacks to using YouTube with your students; in this lesson, however, the focus will be on how they utilise YouTube to help them master English.

A good way to introduce the lesson would be to ask them about YouTube and English. The following could serve as prompts:

- Do you use YouTube to help you learn English?
- What types of programs do you watch? For example, just general interest videos in English or ones with specific topics like pronunciation or grammar?
- How do you choose which videos to watch?
- Do you prefer videos made by native-speaking English teachers or those for whom English is a second language? Explain your preference.

References

Jin, S. (2024). Tapping into social media: transforming EFL learners' writing skills and alleviating anxiety through YouTube. *Education and Information Technologies*, *29*, 10707–10728. https://doi.org/10.1007/s10639-023-12252-z

Wu, C.P. (2024). Enhancing vocabulary proficiency and self-directed learning through YouTube: A study in an EFL context. *English Language Teaching*, *17*(7), 109–119. https://doi.org/10.5539/elt.v17n7p109

During Class
Exercise 1

⇒ *Teacher Notes*

As indicated earlier, learning English from YouTube appears to offer considerable benefits. But what do English learners themselves think? According to a study by Wang and Chen (2020), students found learning English on YouTube more flexible, more interesting, and more interactive than formal learning in the classroom. However, they were concerned that learning English from YouTube was less effective in improving their English and preparing for exams than formal classroom English. Menggo et al. (2025) found that using YouTube in the English language classroom not only made students more adaptable to different learning approaches but also promoted students' learning autonomy.

This exercise asks students about the way they use YouTube to improve their English. This will give them an opportunity to analyse their own use of the platform, and, in later exercises, compare it to the use of their peers.

References

Menggo, S., Widlasri, D.A., Krismayani, N. W., & Susanto, I. (2025). Exploring YouTube-based learning in boosting EFL learners' speaking competence and learning autonomy. *Theory and Practice in Language Studies, 15*(2), 392–402. https://doi.org/10.17507/tpls.1502.09

Wang, H., & Chen, C.W. (2020). Learning English from YouTubers: English L2 learners' self-regulated language learning on YouTube. *Innovation in Language Learning and Teaching, 14*(4), 333–346. https://doi.org/10.1080/17501229.2019.1607356

Exercise 1

1.1 Please read the following statements about using YouTube to learn English and tick the answer which best represents your opinion.

Watching YouTube helps me improve my English pronunciation.

Strongly agree	Agree	Neither agree nor disagree	Disagree	Strongly disagree

Watching YouTube is important because it gives me access to an authentic English-speaking environment.

Strongly agree	Agree	Neither agree nor disagree	Disagree	Strongly disagree

Watching YouTube helps me develop cross-cultural awareness.

Strongly agree	Agree	Neither agree nor disagree	Disagree	Strongly disagree

Watching YouTube helps me develop my English vocabulary.

Strongly agree	Agree	Neither agree nor disagree	Disagree	Strongly disagree

Watching YouTube improves my motivation to learn English.

Strongly agree	Agree	Neither agree nor disagree	Disagree	Strongly disagree

Watching YouTube makes learning English more interesting.

Strongly agree	Agree	Neither agree nor disagree	Disagree	Strongly disagree

I learn more from watching English videos on YouTube than I do in a formal English classroom.

Strongly agree	Agree	Neither agree nor disagree	Disagree	Strongly disagree

Watching YouTube to improve my English is enjoyable.

Strongly agree	Agree	Neither agree nor disagree	Disagree	Strongly disagree

The captions in the YouTube videos are very useful.

| Strongly agree | Agree | Neither agree nor disagree | Disagree | Strongly disagree |

My understanding of the language is helped because I can see body language, gestures, and facial expressions.

| Strongly agree | Agree | Neither agree nor disagree | Disagree | Strongly disagree |

1.2 Once you have done this draw up a profile of yourself. You will do this by assigning values to the answers you have just provided:
- Strongly agree = 5
- Agree = 4
- Neither agree nor disagree = 3
- Disagree = 2
- Strongly disagree = 1

For example, if a student called Alex had responded in the following way:

- Watching YouTube helps me improve my English pronunciation. *Strongly agree 5*
- Watching YouTube is important because it gives me access to an authentic English-speaking environment. *Neither agree nor disagree 3*
- Watching YouTube helps me develop cross-cultural awareness. *Agree 4*
- Watching YouTube improves my motivation to learn English. *Strongly disagree 1*
- Watching YouTube makes learning English more interesting. *Neither agree nor disagree 3*
- I learn more from watching English than I do in a formal English classroom. *Neither agree nor disagree 3*
- Watching YouTube to improve my English is enjoyable. *Agree 4*

- The captions in the YouTube videos are very useful. *Disagree 2*
- My understanding of the language is improved because I can see body language, gestures, and facial expressions. *Neither agree nor disagree 3*

Alex's graph would read like this:

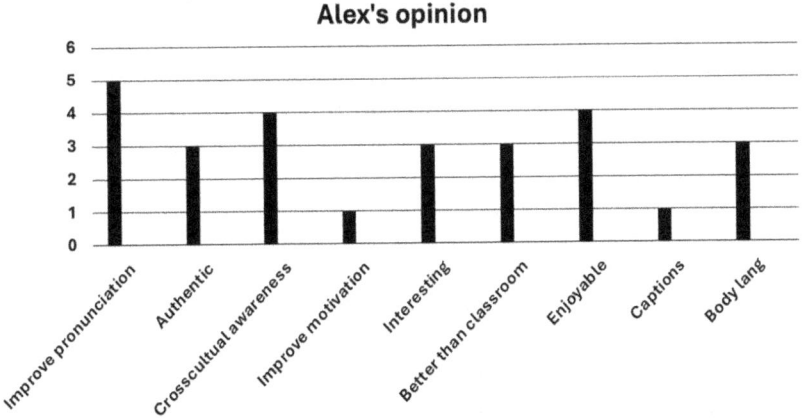

Now draw up your own graph.

1.3 Then decide which of the reasons below are the most important to you. Rank them in order of importance for your English learning experience. For example, if the most important thing for you is that watching YouTube is an enjoyable way to learn English you will rank this as 1.
- Exposure to authentic English-speaking environment.
- Learning how to pronounce English words.
- Developing cross-cultural awareness.
- Improving my motivation to learn English.
- Enjoyable way to learn English.
- Interesting way to learn English.
- More effective than classroom learning.
- Captions help my understanding of the language.
- Body language helps my understanding of the language.

Here are Alex's preferences:

1. Learning how to pronounce English words.
2. Developing cross-cultural awareness.
3. Enjoyable way to learn English.
4. More effective than classroom learning.
5. Exposure to authentic English-speaking environment.
6. Body language helps my understanding of the language.
7. Interesting way to learn English.
8. Improving my motivation to learn English.
9. Captions help my understanding of the language.

Exercise 2

⇒ *Teacher Notes*

GROUPWORK

Students bring their graphs and lists to a group discussion. They compare their preferences and then draw up a graph that indicates the group's opinion. To do so they look at the numbers they used in their own graphs and add them together. For example:

<u>Group A has 6 students</u>.
For the statement:
   Watching YouTube helps me improve my English pronunciation.
Student A said Strongly agree = 5
Student B said Neither agree nor disagree = 3
Student C said Strongly agree = 5
Student D said Agree = 4
Student E said Neither agree nor disagree = 3
Student F said Disagree = 2
The total is 22
For the statement:
   Watching YouTube is important because it gives me access to an authentic English-speaking environment.
Student A said Disagree = 2
Student B said Strongly disagree = 1
Student C said Strongly disagree = 1

Student D said Strongly disagree = 1
Student E said Neither agree nor disagree = 3
Student F said Disagree = 2
The total is 10

So a graph representing this group's preferences would start off like this:

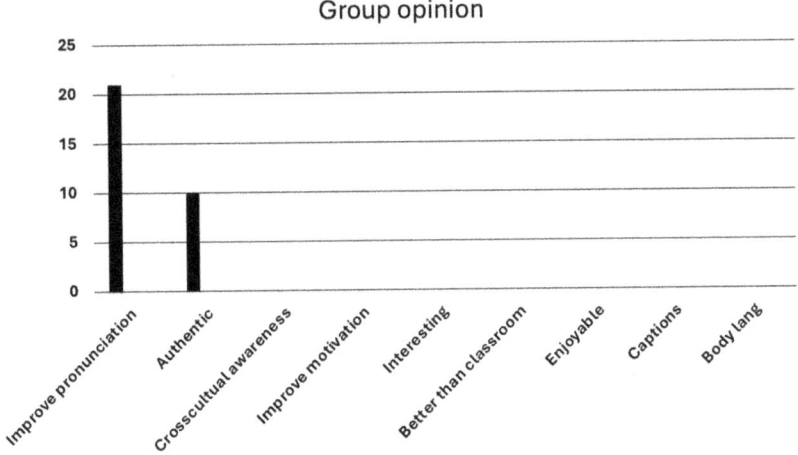

When students have finished the graph, ask them to use this as a basis for discussion:

- What are your experiences with YouTube?
- Do some of you make more use of the platform than others?
- Why do you have different views?
- Are you surprised by other people's answers?

Then ask students to discuss the rankings in the same way. Is there a decided group preference for one particular option? Are preferences spread? Can they think of reasons as to why this is the case?

Exercise 2
Draw a graph of the group's preferences using the individual graphs you have all drawn up. Discuss your different preferences. Here are some points you might want to consider:

- What are your experiences with YouTube?
- Do some of you make more use of the platform than others?
- Why do you have different views?
- Are you surprised by other people's answers?

Then refer to the ranking exercise.

- Is there a decided group preference for one particular option?
- Are preferences spread?
- Can you think of reasons as to why this is the case?

Exercise 3

⇒ *Teacher Notes*

The class will use their graphs and material from the class discussions to write up notes they will use to write an essay in Lesson 4. In the first section they will report on their own answers – then they will report on the group findings. They will compare the two sets of findings and speculate about differences and similarities. They need to identify any strong trends and discuss what they have learnt from the exercise. Finally, they will summarise the main points. In this exercise students can use bullet points and short sentences. This work is not the final product and should not be marked. It is data that students will gather in order to write an essay. Students are also asked to make note of any comments that a member of their group might have made that strike them as insightful or interesting. Explain to them that comments like this can be useful evidence in substantiating arguments raised in an essay. Remind them, however, that they MUST ask permission to use the comment. The person will not be identified by their real name. A pseudonym can be use e.g. Alex can be Al, or they can be referred to as Student 1.

A framework for the note taking has been included, although students might prefer to do this work in their own way.

Exercise 3

Use your graphs and the material from the class discussions to write notes to inform an essay you will be writing in the next lesson. In the first section of your notes you will report on your own answers – then you will report on the class findings. Compare the two sets of findings and discuss differences and similarities. Identify any strong trends and discuss what you have learnt from the exercise. A plan has been included that you can use if you wish.

Notes:

My opinion of YouTube as an aid to learning English:
My most important reasons for using YouTube to improve my English:
My group's opinion of YouTube as an aid to learning English:
What my group thinks are the most important reasons for using YouTube to improve their English.
Any comments from group members that were particularly useful or insightful.
Are there any strong trends? If so, what were they?
What have I learnt from this exercise?

Post-Class Activities

⇒ *Teacher Notes*

There are many ways that the students could make use of the graphs they have drawn up. For example, the group graph drawn up in Exercise 2 could be enlarged to include the whole class. Another exercise that students might find interesting is to investigate whether students' first languages have any influence on their preferences. If there are sufficient students in the class, they might want to see, for example, how Chinese students' preferences differ from Spanish speakers. If the group is small this exercise can be done with broader regions e.g. Europe compared with SE Asia.

Students could also be asked to suggest other platforms that they find useful for learning English. In a class discussion, students might want to compare the contribution of different platforms to the students' developing language proficiency.

Lesson 3: Using YouTube to Learn English – What the Literature Says

Time: 2 hours

Overview

Students have gathered a great deal of personal data about the use of YouTube in English learning. In this lesson they will explore some of the perspectives raised in the literature. They will be introduced to the literature review and asked to consider what makes a good review. They will also make notes of the issues raised in the literature to use in the essay which will be written in Lesson 4.

Purposes and Strategies

Purpose	*Strategies*
Introducing literature reviews	Asking students to compare two short reviews.
Reinforcing the importance of evidence-based writing	Giving students access to summarised academic material to support or criticise other perspectives.
Preparing notes for an essay	Students will summarise points from the literature in preparation for the essay in Lesson 4.
Intext citations	How to cite multiple sources to support a single point.

Pre-Class Activities
Exercise 1

⇒ *Teacher Notes*

In the last lesson students examined their own and the other students' perceptions of the benefit of using YouTube as a tool for learning English. They now have data on these insights. At this stage it is a good idea for them to turn to the research to see what academics say (the literature). You might want to start off the lesson by asking students if they think that academics believe that social media platforms can be beneficial for learning. Ask them to justify their answers. What reservations do they think these academics might have? What do they think the academics might see as advantages in using social media for language learning?.

During Class
Exercise 1

⇒ *Teacher Notes*

A literature review demonstrates students' understanding of the research that has been carried out on a specific topic. A good literature review does not just describe what it is in the literature – it also evaluates it (University of Edinburgh, 2024). A good way to introduce students to literature reviews is to show them examples of those that meet the brief and those that fall short. Here are two short literature reviews on the same topic. Please note that these reviews have been written for this exercise. The articles quoted in them do not exist.

Ask the students to read through the reviews in small groups and then answer the questions that follow. Once you have done that bring the students together for a discussion.

Reference

University of Edinburgh (2024). Institute for Academic Development: Literature review. https://institute-academic-development.ed.ac.uk/study-hub/learning-resources/literature-review

Exercise 1
Read through the two reviews and then answer the questions that follow. Please note that these reviews have been written for this exercise. The articles cited here do not exist.

REVIEW 1

Researchers generally agree that social media has significantly changed how people communicate, though opinions differ on whether the effects are mostly positive or negative. Several studies highlight its benefits. For example, Smith (2015) and Jones (2017) both emphasise the role of social media in enhancing communication, particularly through instant messaging and social connection during emergencies. Similarly, Lee (2016) focuses on its educational value, noting that platforms like YouTube support informal learning and skills development.

However, concerns about social media's negative effects are also present in the literature. Davis (2018) argues that excessive social media use contributes to poor mental health and digital addiction. In contrast, Taylor (2019) suggests that social media can improve emotional well-being by reducing feelings of isolation and providing a sense of community, particularly for people who might otherwise feel disconnected.

Age also plays a role in social media use. White (2020) notes that teenagers are the most active users, though the consequences of this high engagement are still debated in research.

Overall, the literature presents a complex picture. While there is consensus that social media has reshaped communication, its impact varies depending on how and by whom it is used. The contrasting findings highlight the need for more research focused on specific user groups and usage patterns.

REVIEW 2

Several researchers have explored the impact of social media on communication. Smith (2015) argues that social media enhances communication because it allows users to send messages quickly and to stay in touch. This is also mentioned by Jones (2017), who highlights how platforms like Facebook and Twitter enable people to remain connected, particularly during emergency situations. Lee (2016) examines the educational potential of social media, stating that platforms such as YouTube provide learning opportunities for students. She explains that some users access educational content to improve their academic or practical skills.

Davis (2018), in contrast, presents a negative view. He claims that social media contributes to poor mental health and addiction due to excessive use. Taylor (2019) offers a different perspective, suggesting that social media can reduce loneliness and help people feel more socially connected. White (2020) focuses on the age factor, observing that young people, particularly teenagers, are the most frequent users of social media. She notes that this high usage may have both positive and negative implications, although she does not provide a clear stance.

All of these studies contribute useful information about the effects of social media. Some researchers highlight benefits, while others focus on potential problems. Overall, the literature shows that social media affects communication in different ways. Each source presents different ideas and focuses on different aspects. Therefore, it is difficult to determine whether the impact is mostly positive or mostly negative.

What is the topic of both literature reviews? THE IMPACT OF SOCIAL MEDIA ON COMMUNICATION.

Which review groups similar ideas or themes together? REVIEW 1 – THE LITERATURE IS PRESENTED IN THEMES SUCH AS BENEFITS, DRAWBACKS ETC.

Does either review compare or contrast the views of different authors? REVIEW 1 – SHOWS AGREEMENT AND DISAGREEMENT AND BRINGS THE IDEAS TOGETHER.

Which one simply summarises each source separately? REVIEW 2.

Are the same sources used in both reviews? YES.

Look for linking words (e.g., "however," "similarly," "in contrast"). Which review uses them more effectively? Give examples to support your answer. REVIEW 1.

- FOR EXAMPLE – TO MAKE THINGS CLEARER FOR THE READER.
- SIMILARLY – TO SHOW IDEAS HAVE SOMETHING IN COMMON.
- HOWEVER – TO SHOW A CHANGE.
- IN CONTRAST – TO SHOW A CHANGE.
- OVERALL – BRINGING IDEAS TOGETHER.
- WHILE – SHOWS THAT TWO DIFFERENT THINGS ARE HAPPENING.

Exercise 2

⇒ *Teacher Notes*

Research indicates that there are both advantages and disadvantages to using YouTube to learn English. In the reading, students will be introduced to research that highlights problems students may encounter when they use YouTube to improve their English. The reading is followed by a table that lists advantages of using YouTube also taken from the literature. Once they have read the passage students are asked to list the disadvantages of using YouTube. It is very important that the students keep careful note of who said what when they are making these notes.

Exercise 2

READING: SOME OF THE DISADVANTAGES OF USING YOUTUBE TO LEARN ENGLISH

Research into the use of YouTube in the second-language learning class has increased greatly over the last ten to fifteen years, and while its influence is largely seen as positive there are some drawbacks (Dizon, 2022). One of the disadvantages, according to Julianto and Qamariah (2023), is that inexperienced English speakers are not able to judge the standard of the English used in YouTube clips. It is quite possible that the English is non-standard; that is, not the way English is usually spoken. In addition, the language in these videos is often informal and colloquial. Students might find it difficult to assess which language would be acceptable in formal situations.

Another challenge related to this is that students searching YouTube for videos to help with their English might simply click on the link at the top of the search list without exploring other options which might be more beneficial for their learning (Mohamed & Shoufan, 2022). In addition, Mayer et al. (2020) point out that students might be attracted by clips that are designed to attract their attention but offer little in the way of learning opportunities.

There is also concern that students will be easily distracted by other material on YouTube. It is very easy for students to click on links that take them away from the learning material (Julianto & Qamariah, 2023).

The other issue that Julianto and Qamariah raise is that students might use the captions option, which will allow them to read the English interaction in their own language. Wang and Chen (2019) point to another disadvantage. YouTube might not encourage much interaction on the part of the students. Studies have found that ESL students are more likely to engage in passive behaviour such as liking or sharing videos but are unlikely to post comments.

In addition, while YouTube allows the creation of one's own videos which is very educational there is concern that students will spend too much time on the aesthetics of the video rather than on the content (Sun & Yang, 2013). That means that students will spend too much time making the video look good and too little time on the language employed in the clip. This finding is backed up by the research of Sari, Dardjito and Azizah (2020), who found that while making English videos improved students' technological ability and their performance in teams, it did not improve their English.

Finally, there is concern that students might be exposed to comments from other users. Many videos are open to comments which are often unmoderated. They can be crude or inappropriate (Barnwell, 2021).

REFERENCES

Barnwell, P. (August 31, 2021). Teachers' essential guide to YouTube. *Common Sense Education*. https://www.commonsense.org/education/articles/teachers-essential-guide-to-youtube

Dizon, G. (2022). YouTube for second language learning: What does the research tell us? *Australian Journal of Applied Linguistics*, 5(1), 19–26. https://doi.org/10.29140/ajal.v5n1.636

Julianto, A., & Qamariah, Z. (2023). A literature study on the negative impact of Youtube as an English language learning media. *Atmosfer*, 1(3), 182–193. https://doi.org/10.59024/atmosfer.v1i3.232

Mayer, R., Fiorella, L., & Stull, A. (2020). Five ways to increase the effectiveness of instructional video. *Educational Technology Research and Development*, 68, 837–852. https://doi.org/10.1007/s11423-020-09749-6

Mohamed, F., & Shoufan, A. (2022). Choosing YouTube videos for self-directed learning. *IEEE Access*. https://doi.org/10.1109/ACCESS.2022.3174368

Sari, A.B.P., Dardjito, H., & Azizah, D.M. (2020). EFL students' Improvement through the Reflective YouTube Video Project. *International Journal of Instruction*, 13(4), 393–408. https://doi.org/10.29333/iji.2020.13425a

Sun, Y.-C., & Yang, F.-Y. (2013). I help, therefore, I learn: Service learning on Web 2.0 in an EFL speaking class. *Computer Assisted Language Learning*, 28(3), 202–219. https://doi.org/10.1080/09588221.2013.818555

Wang, H.-C., & Chen, C.W.-Y. (2019). Learning English from YouTubers: English L2 learners' self-regulated language learning on YouTube. *Innovation in Language Learning and Teaching*, 14, 333–346. https://doi.org/10.1080/17501229.2019.1607356

2.1 Complete the table below in which you list the disadvantages given in the literature about using YouTube to learn English. Use your own words. The first one has been done for you. Remember some authors have raised more than one point.

Disadvantage	Citation
People who are not fluent in English cannot tell if the English used is correct.	Julianto and Qamariah (2023)
STUDENTS CANNOT TELL IF THE LANGUAGE IS FORMAL OR INFORMAL.	JULIANTO AND QAMARIAH (2023)
STUDENTS MIGHT NOT LOOK AT ALL THE POSSIBILITIES AVAILABLE TO THEM ON YOUTUBE. THEY MIGHT JUST PICK THE FIRST ONE.	MOHAMED and SHOUFAN (2022)
STUDENTS COULD JUST CLICK ON AN OPTION BECAUSE IT LOOKS APPEALING WITHOUT THINKING ABOUT WHETHER IT IS THE BEST OPTION TO HELP THEM.	MAYER ET AL. (2020)
STUDENTS MIGHT BE DISTRACTED AND CLICK ON OPTIONS THAT HAVE NOTHING TO DO WITH LEARNING ENGLISH.	JULIANTO and QAMARIAH (2023)
INSTEAD OF READING AND LISTENING TO THE ENGLISH ON THE SITES THEY CLICK ON STUDENTS MIGHT MAKE USE OF CAPTIONS IN THEIR FIRST LANGUAGE.	JULIANTO and QAMARIAH (2023)
OFTEN ESL STUDENTS DO NOT PARTICIPATE ACTIVELY. THEY SIMPLY LIKE OR SHARE VIDEOS BUT RARELY POST COMMENTS.	WANG and CHEN (2019)
STUDENTS MIGHT SPEND TOO MUCH TIME MAKING THE VIDEO LOOK ATTRACTIVE AND NOT SPEND ENOUGH TIME ON MAKING SURE THE ENGLISH USED IS CORRECT.	SUN and YANG (2014)
STUDENTS WILL IMPROVE THEIR TECHNOLOGICAL ABILITY RATHER THAN THEIR LANGUAGE PROFICIENCY.	SARI, DARDJITO and AZIZAH (2020)
SOME OF THE COMMENTS ARE RUDE AND OFFENSIVE.	BARNWELL (2021)

2.2 Below are a number of points from research articles which list the advantages of using YouTube to learn English.

Students are accustomed to using YouTube.	Kim and Kim (2021)
Helps students develop intercultural competence as they communicate with people from different cultures and language groups.	Kiss and Weninger (2017)
Helps students improve their English comprehension.	Hasan et al. (2018)
Videos help students learn by both listening and watching for clues to help understanding.	Kim & Kim (2021)
Good way to ensure accurate pronunciation.	Aldukhayel (2021)

(Continued)

Increases motivation to learn English.	Wang and Chen (2019)
Helps students develop their vocabulary.	Arndt and Woore (2018)
Helps students organise their ideas when writing.	Alobaid (2020)
More interesting than learning in the ESL classroom.	Wang and Chen (2019)
YouTube offers good sources to help with academic writing.	Kim and Kim (2021)
Commenting and interacting in English on YouTube is a good way of improving English writing skills.	Jin (2024)

You now have a list of the advantages and disadvantages of using YouTube according to some of the literature.

Look at both lists and select what you believe to be the three most important advantages and the three most serious drawbacks, according to the literature. Then complete the table, giving your reasons for your selection. You will find an example in the table. You do not have to use this example!

Disadvantages	Reason
1. People who are not fluent in English cannot tell if the English used is correct (Julianto & Qamariah, 2023).	There is a real risk that students could click on a link to a website where the web writer is not fluent in English but is using the language because of its wide appeal. It is possible that students will learn incorrect English usage on such a site.
2.	
3.	
Advantages	Reason
1.	
2.	
3.	

References

Aldukhayel, D. (2021). Vlogs in L2 listening: EFL learners' and teachers' perceptions. *Computer Assisted Language Learning*, 34(8), 1085–1104. https://doi.org/10.1080/09588221.2019.1658608

Alobaid, A. (2020). Smart multimedia learning of ICT: Role and impact on language learners' writing fluency – YouTube online English learning resources as an example. *Smart Learning Environments, 7*, 1–30. https://doi.org/10.1186/s40561-020-00134-7

Arndt, H.L., & Woore, R. (2018). Vocabulary learning from watching YouTube videos and reading blog posts. *Language Learning & Technology, 22(1)*, 124–142. https://doi.org/10125/44660

Hasan, M., Ibrahim, F., Mustapha, S., Islam, M., & Al Younus, M. (2018). The use of YouTube videos in learning English language skills at tertiary level in Bangladesh. *IUKL Research Journal, 6*, 27–36.

Jin, S. (2024). Tapping into social media: transforming EFL learners' writing skills and alleviating anxiety through YouTube. *Education and Information Technologies, 29*, 10707–10728. https://doi.org/10.1007/s10639-023-12252-z

Kim, S., & Kim, H.-C. (2021). The benefits of YouTube in learning English as a second language: A qualitative investigation of Korean Freshman students' experiences and perspectives in the U.S. *Sustainability, 13*, 7365. https://doi.org/10.3390/su13137365

Kiss, T., & Weninger, C. (2017). Cultural learning in the EFL classroom: The role of visuals. *ELT Journal, 71*, 186–196.

Wang, H.-C., & Chen, C.W.-Y. (2019). Learning English from YouTubers: English L2 learners' self-regulated language learning on YouTube. *Innovation in Language Learning and Teaching, 14*, 333–346. https://doi.org/10.1080/17501229.2019.1607356

Exercise 2

⇒ *Teacher Notes*

Students will be drawing more and more heavily on current literature in the lessons ahead. It is important that they learn how to cite multiple authors. Just a reminder of what you have covered:

In-text citations with multiple authors – In APA7, the referencing system that is being used in the book, the rule is the following:

1 source with one author: (Smith, 2022)
1 source with two authors: (Todd & Brown, 2023)
1 source with three or more authors: (Grant et al., 2020)

Remember the al. is an abbreviation of alia (others) so a full stop is needed after the word.

However, students might want to back up a point they are making by emphasising that it is a perspective widely held in the literature. Look at this example:

> If online learning is to be successful the learning environment as a whole needs to respond in a concerted and coordinated way to the challenges that students face (Doo et al., 2023; Ellis & Goodyear 2010; Stefanik et al., 2022; Veletsianos et al., 2022; Weldon et al., 2021).

Only the article of Ellis and Goodyear has two authors – the rest have three or more so et al. is used. The sources are cited in alphabetical order according to the name of the first author: Doo, Ellis, Stefanik, Veletsianos, Weldon. Where there are two authors, the names in brackets are joined by an ampersand (&). Exercise 2 asks students to apply these rules.

References

Doo, M. Y., Zhu, M., & Bonk, C. J. (2023). A Systematic Review of the Research Topics in Online Learning During COVID-19: Documenting the Sudden Shift. *Online Learning Journal*, 27(1), 15–45. https://doi.org/10.24059/olj.v27i1.3405

Ellis, R., & Goodyear, P. (2010). *Students' experiences of e-learning in higher education: the ecology of sustainable innovation*. Routledge. https://doi.org/10.4324/9780203872970

Stefaniak, J. E., Arrington, T. L., & Moore, A. L. (2022). Systemic considerations to support distance education environments, *Distance Education*, 43(2), 171–178, DOI: 10.1080/01587919.2022.2064830

Veletsianos, G., Childs, E., Cox, R., Cordua-von Specht, I., Grundy, S., Hughes, J., Karleen, D., & Willson, A. (2022). Person in environment: Focusing on the ecological aspects of online and distance learning, *Distance Education*, 43(2), 318–324, DOI: 10.1080/01587919.2022.2064827

Weldon, A., Ma, W.W.K., Ho, I. M. K., & Li, E. (2021). Online learning during a global pandemic: perceived benefits and issues in higher education. *Knowledge Management & E-Learning*, 13(2), 161–181.

Exercise 3

The following sentence has six citations. The sources are listed in the References. Insert the in-text citations correctly at the end of the sentence.

> YouTube is viewed as a very useful social networking site to help students improve their English.

YOUTUBE IS VIEWED AS A VERY USEFUL SOCIAL NETWORKING SITE TO HELP STUDENTS IMPROVE THEIR ENGLISH (Boliziar & Munkova; Dizon, 2022; Kim & Kim, 2021; Manca & Ranieri, 2017; Maziriri et al.,2020; Tahmina, 2023).

References

Boltiziar, J., & Munkova, D. (2024). Emergency remote teaching of listening comprehension using YouTube videos with captions. *Education and Information Technologies*, 29, 11367–11383. https://doi.org/10.1007/s10639-023-12282-7

Dizon, G. (2022). YouTube for second language learning: What does the research tell us? *Australian Journal of Applied Linguistics*, 5(1), 19–26. https://doi.org/10.29140/ajal.v5n1.636

Kim, S., & Kim, H.-C. (2021). The benefits of YouTube in learning English as a second language: A qualitative investigation of Korean freshman students' experiences and perspectives in the U.S. *Sustainability*, 13, 7365. https://doi.org/10.3390/su13137365

Manca, S., & Ranieri, M. (2017). Implications of social network sites for teaching and learning. Where we are and where we want to go. *Education and Information Technologies*, 22, 605–622. https://doi.org/10.1007/s10639-015-9429-x

Maziriri, E., Gapa, P., & Chuchu, T. (2020). Student perceptions towards the use of YouTube as an educational tool for learning and tutorials. *International Journal of Instruction*, 13(2), 119–138.

Tahmina, T. (2023). Students' perception of the use of YouTube in English language learning. *JOLLT Journal of Languages and Language Teaching*, 11(1), 151–159.

Post-Class Activities
This article:

> Kim, S., & Kim, H.C. (2021). The benefits of YouTube in learning English as a second language: A qualitative investigation of Korean freshman students' experiences and perspectives in the U.S. *Sustainability* 2021, *13*(13), 7365. https://doi.org/10.3390/su13137365

is available in open access. Ask students to read Section 3 **Use of Social Networking Sites among International Students**, which is part of the literature review. Students must then list the benefits for the use of Social Networking Sites (SNS) in their own words e.g.:

- Students are already familiar with these technologies.
- Students take charge of their own learning.
- These sites are user-friendly etc.

Once the students have listed the advantages, ask them to add the intext citation next to every advantage. The reference system used here is Vancouver, where numbers not names are used in the text. Students will need to use the article's reference list to complete the task. It is a good idea to expose students to different referencing systems.

Lesson 4: Bringing the Data Together

Time: 2 hours

Overview
In this lesson students will interact with the teacher and each other about the structure of the discussion essay. They will then use the data they have gathered in the previous two lessons to write the essay.

Purpose and Strategies

Purpose	Strategies
Writing the discussion essay	Students will be using the data they have gathered to inform the essay.
The structure of the essay	Students will discuss the structuring of the essay in class before they start writing.

Pre-Class Activities

⇒ *Teacher Notes*

Ask students to bring their notes from the previous lessons. Before they start writing the essay ask them about their findings. Here are a few prompts that might be useful:

- Were they surprised by anything they heard from other students?
- Were they surprised by anything they read in the literature?
- Has any of this input changed their opinions about using YouTube?
- Do they see trends emerging?
- Do they think the researchers have good insights into what happens in students' lives as far as learning English is concerned?

During Class

⇒ *Teacher Notes*

Exercise 1

Students now have data, both personal and from the literature, about the advantages and disadvantages of using YouTube to learn English. They will now use this data to write a discussion essay about using YouTube to help students learn English. A discussion essay covers a wide range of opinions and views using evidence to back up these views and opinions. One way to think of the discussion essay is to see it as an inverted pyramid. Students start with the general (what the literature says) before moving to the more specific (what the group of students think) and then on to the most specific (what the individual student thinks). When the student is referring to their own personal opinion, or to an opinion offered by the group, it would be good if this could be backed up by the literature. Here is a diagram to illustrate the concept.

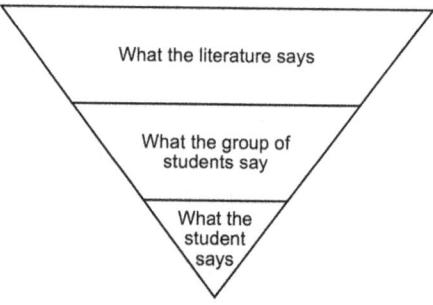

Just a quick word about the use of the first-person singular. In APA7, it is perfectly acceptable to use these pronouns (APA Style, 2022). It appears that even in the hard sciences the use of the first-person pronoun is becoming more acceptable (Brennan, 2024). I suggest you encourage students to use first person pronouns in the essay. It is far easier to write if they do.

For example:

I believe that the use of YouTube is the English classroom is not a good idea as students are too easily distracted by material that is not relevant to their English language learning.

OR

It is my opinion that YouTube should be employed in the language classroom.

Remind students to back up what they are saying by referring to the literature (Sacred Heart University Library, n.d.). In this case they will be referring to the literature on YouTube learning that has just been discussed. For example:

I believe that the use of YouTube is the English classroom is not a good idea as students are too easily distracted by material that is not relevant to their English language learning. This belief is backed up by the research of Julianto and Qamariah (2023) who note that it is very easy for students to click on links that have nothing to do with what is being taught.

OR

It is my opinion that YouTube should be employed in the language classroom as research indicates that using this video sharing platform increases student motivation to learn English.
(Wang & Chen, 2019)

They can also refer to the literature when they are discussing what their classmates said. For example:

The majority of the students believe that listening to YouTube clips helps them to improve their pronunciation. A study by Aldukhayel (2021) supports this belief.

It would probably be a good idea to mark this essay in full. However, if there are numerous grammatical errors you might, once again, want to focus on a few which you think are the most important. Examine the ideas that the students are communicating and congratulate them on thoughtful opinions and a good incorporation of the literature.

References

Aldukhayel, D. (2021). Vlogs in L2 listening: EFL learners' and teachers' perceptions, *Computer Assisted Language Learning*, 34(8), 1085–1104. https://doi.org/10.1080/09588221.2019.1658608

APA Style. (2022). *First-person pronouns*. https://apastyle.apa.org/style-grammar-guidelines/grammar/first-person-pronouns

Brennan, E.B. (2024). "I" versus "the author": The power of first- person voice when writing about science. *PNAS*, *121*(22), e2316966121. https://doi.org/10.1073/pnas.2316966121

Julianto, A., & Qamariah, Z. (2023). A Literature Study On The Negative Impact Of Youtube As An English Language Learning Media Qamariah. *Atmosfer*, *1*(3), 182–193. https://doi.org/10.59024/atmosfer.v1i3.232

Sacred Heart University Library. (n.d.). Organizing Academic Research Papers: 8. The Discussion. https://library.sacredheart.edu/c.php?g=29803&p=185933#:~:text=A%20good%20discussion%20section%20includes,relation%20to%20the%20overall%20study

Wang, H.-C., & Chen, C.W.-Y. (2019). Learning English from YouTubers: English L2 learners' self-regulated language learning on YouTube. *Innovation in Language Learning and Teaching*, *14*, 333–346. https://doi.org/10.1080/17501229.2019.1607356

Exercise 1

You will write an essay of between 500 and 600 words about the use of YouTube in learning English.

Essay:

Title	What title best summarises this essay?
Introduction	What are you going to be discussing?
Part 1	What do the experts in the field say about the advantages and disadvantages?
Part 2	The class's responses to the questionnaire.
Part 3	Your responses to the questionnaire.
Part 4	A comparison of your responses and the class responses.
Discussion	What have you learnt from the exercise? Remember to bring together the experts, your group's insights and your own opinions.
Conclusion	What are the most important points? What in the final analysis is YOUR opinion?

Post-Class Activities

⇒ *Teacher Notes*

A really useful activity would be to ask students to exchange essays. They would then comment on what the other person has written and make suggestions for improvements. If time permits, students should be allowed to make changes if they want to. This would be an excellent introduction for the next cycle which focusses on peer review.

Lesson 5: Misinformation and Disinformation

Time: 2 hours

Overview

It is becoming increasingly difficult to identify valid and reliable data. People find it hard to distinguish what is trustworthy and what is disinformation or misinformation. This lesson explores these concepts. Exercises in critical reading, paraphrasing, note taking and dealing with idiomatic language enable students to engage more closely with the topic. Finally, students are asked to write a very short essay using the information they have collected during the exercises.

Purpose and Strategies

Purpose	*Strategies*
Highlighting the importance of reliable sources	Passages and a video clip.
Reading critically	Analysing information provided.
Paraphrasing idiomatic language	Changing idiomatic language into acceptable academic writing.
Taking notes from a video	Processing information about accurate information gathering.
Rewriting notes in an essay form	Consolidating information gathered into a short essay.

Pre-Class Activities

⇒ *Teacher Notes*

The context of this lesson is mis/dis information. This short quiz serves as introduction to the lesson and allows students to explore their knowledge of the concepts of mis/disinformation. This quiz can be found on the worksheet.

1. What is *misinformation*?

| A lie told on purpose | FALSE INFORMATION SHARED BY MISTAKE | A secret message | Information from the government |

2. What is *disinformation*?

| A news story with too many facts | A report that needs checking | FALSE INFORMATION SHARED TO TRICK PEOPLE | A lie told by mistake |

3. Which of these is an example of misinformation?

| A FRIEND TELLS YOU SOMETHING THAT IS FACTUALLY INCORRECT, BUT THEY BELIEVE IT'S TRUE | A company makes a fake story to sell a product | A hacker makes a fake website | A news article has a headline that doesn't match the facts in the story |

4. Why is disinformation hard to stop once it spreads?

| It disappears quickly | People recognise it right away | IT SPREADS FASTER THAN CORRECTIONS AND PEOPLE IGNORE UPDATES | It's only shared in private chats |

5. What's one common strategy to spread disinformation?

| Telling personal stories | Creating fake news websites that look like real media outlets | USING BOTS OR FAKE ACCOUNTS TO MAKE IT LOOK POPULAR | Sharing only in newspapers |

6. A news story goes viral online, but no trusted news outlet reports it. What should you do?

| Share it to see if other people believe it | Wait until multiple trusted sources confirm the story before taking action | VERIFY IT THROUGH FACT-CHECKING WEBSITES AND CHECK IF ANY RELIABLE SOURCES ARE COVERING IT | Wait for a few days, then share if it's still popular |

7. Why do many disinformation stories use emotional topics like health, fear, or politics?

Emotional content is usually easier to disprove	People are less likely to share emotional content compared to neutral stories	EMOTIONAL REACTIONS MAKE PEOPLE SHARE QUICKLY WITHOUT VERIFYING FACTS	Emotional topics are always based on true, verified information

During Class
Exercise 1

⇒ *Teacher Notes*

The first exercise seeks to reinforce the importance of checking the validity of sources and the very serious consequences if that is not done in the academic world. The exercise gives students practice in paraphrasing and changing colloquial language into academic English.

Exercise 1

READING: MISINFORMATION AND DISINFORMATION

One important distinction that should be made is between misinformation and disinformation. Both these terms refer to inaccurate or misleading information, but misinformation is the *accidental* sharing of incorrect information. In other words, the person or persons sharing this information believe it is true. In contrast disinformation describes the sharing of information by people who know that this information is inaccurate, and in some cases has simply been made up (Armitage & Vaccari, 2021).

How can one then be sure that the information one is reading is as reliable as possible? Mislevy says reliability has to do with "the extent to which information can be trusted" (2004, p. 8). However, even experienced academics and experts can be misled.

This is a very serious issue as researchers base their own research on what others have done. Academics stand on the shoulders of others in developing their research. Scientific publications are the main source of this knowledge but unfortunately an increasing number of fake studies with manipulated and made-up data is being published (Wittau et al., 2024).

> Scientific fake papers, containing manipulated or completely fabricated data, are a problem that has reached dramatic dimensions… The main drivers of the fake paper flood are the pressure in academic systems and (monetary) incentives to publish in respected scientific journals and sometimes the personal desire for increased "prestige." Published fake papers cause substantial scientific, economic, and social damage.
> (Wittau & Seifert, 2024)

Academics are concerned that thousands of fake research papers are being published in journals. They believe that the situation is worsening every year (McKie, 2024). Some of these fake papers are exposed after publication – in 2023 over 10,000 papers were retracted by journals – but many in the academic world think these retractions are only the tip of the iceberg (McKie, 2024). There is particular concern that medical research is being compromised. Dorothy Butler, a professor at Oxford University, notes her concern arguing that "in many fields it is becoming difficult to build up a cumulative approach to a subject, because we lack a solid foundation of trustworthy findings" (McKie, 2024).

References

Armitage, R., & Vaccari, C. (2021). Misinformation and disinformation. In H. Tumber & S Waisbord (Eds.) *The Routledge companion to media disinformation and populism*, pp. 38–48. Routledge.

McKie, R. (February 3, 2024). 'The situation has become appalling': fake scientific papers push research credibility to crisis point. *The Guardian.* https://www.theguardian.com/science/2024/feb/03/the-situation-has-become-appalling-fake-scientific-papers-push-research-credibility-to-crisis-point

Mislevy, R.J. (2004). Can there be reliability without "reliability"? *Journal of Educational and Behavioral Statistics, 29*(2), 241–244. https://doi.org/10.3102/10769986029002241

Wittau, J., Celik, S., Kacprowski, T., Deserno, T., Seifert, R. (2024). Fake paper identification in the pool of withdrawn and rejected manuscripts submitted to Naunyn–Schmiedeberg's Archives of Pharmacology. *Naunyn-Schmiedeberg's Archives of Pharmacology, 397,* 2171–2181. https://doi.org/10.1007/s00210-023-02741-w

Wittau, J., & Seifert, R. (2024). How to fight fake papers: a review on important information sources and steps towards solution of the problem. *Naunyn-Schmiedeberg's Archives of Pharmacology 397,* 9281–9294. https://doi.org/10.1007/s00210-024-03272-8

1.1 The indented paragraph above starting "Scientific fake papers ..." is a direct quote from the article by Wittau and Seifert (2024). Rewrite this paragraph in your own words.

THE NUMBER OF ACADEMIC PAPERS THAT ARE BASED ON INACCURATE OR FALSE DATA HAS INCREASED CONSIDERABLY. THIS INCREASE IS HAPPENING BECAUSE ACADEMICS ARE UNDER PRESSURE TO PUBLISH. IN SOME CASES ACADEMICS ARE FINANCIALLY REWARDED IF THEIR RESEARCH IS PUBLISHED, PARTICULARLY IF IT IS PUBLISHED IN HIGHLY REGARDED JOURNALS. IN ADDITION, ACADEMICS WHO HAVE A GOOD PUBLICATION RECORD ARE WELL RESPECTED. HOWEVER, SUCH MISLEADING PUBLICATIONS ARE RESPONSIBLE FOR DAMAGING SCIENCE, THE ECONOMY AND SOCIETY.

1.2 McKie notes that the thousands of articles retracted by journals is "only the tip of the iceberg". What is meant by this expression?

THIS MEANS THAT ALTHOUGH THOUSANDS OF ARTICLES HAVE BEEN RETRACTED THERE ARE FAR MORE THAT ARE NOT BEING IDENTIFIED.

1.3 Rewrite Butler's warning in your own words. What idiomatic expression used earlier in the passage summarises her concern?

BUTLER WARNS THAT RESEARCHERS IN MANY DISCIPLINE AREAS ARE CONCERNED THAT THEY CANNOT SIMPLY ACCEPT THE FINDINGS OF THEIR PEERS AND BUILD ON THESE FINDINGS TO FURTHER RESEARCH BECAUSE THE RESEARCHERS CANNOT TRUST THAT THE FINDINGS ARE ACCURATE.

THE IDIOMATIC EXPRESSION IS "STAND ON THE SHOULDERS OF OTHERS".

Exercise 2

⇒ *Teacher Notes*

The TEDTalk used in this exercise is straightforward. The exercise could be done individually if the class is relatively confident. Students could listen to the talk, answer the questions and move straight onto the essay planning and writing in Exercise 3. If you believe the class lacks confidence or is struggling with the level of English you could ask them to work in groups. This would probably ensure that their answers will be more accurate and give them a more solid foundation for the writing exercise.

Exercise 2

Watch the following TEDTalk and then answer the questions. You will be using your answers to write a short essay describing the research discussed in the talk, and explaining how it came to be misrepresented.

https://www.ted.com/talks/joseph_isaac_why_people_fall_for_misinformation?subtitle=en

2.1 In 1902 David Hänig tried to find out how we taste what we put in our mouths. What did he find out about our ability to taste sweet, sour, bitter and salty?

HÄNIG FOUND THAT RECEPTORS AT THE TIP OF THE TONGUE WERE PARTICULARLY SENSITIVE TO SWEETNESS, RECEPTORS AT THE SIDES OF THE TONGUE TO SALTY AND SOUR, AND THOSE AT THE BASE OF THE TONGUE ALLOW US TO TASTE BITTERNESS.

2.2 What warning did Hänig give with regard to the different tasting areas of the tongue?

HE SAID EVERY SENSATION (SWEET, SALTY, SOUR AND BITTER) CAN BE TASTED ALL OVER THE TONGUE AND THE ABILITY TO TASTE SPECIFIC SENSATIONS IS ONLY SLIGHTLY INCREASED IN THE AREAS HE IDENTIFIED.

2.3 What, according to the talk, was responsible for the misrepresentation of Hänig's research?

HÄNIG'S RESEARCH WAS WRITTEN IN GERMAN SO THE ORIGINAL RESEARCH COULD ONLY BE READ IF ONE WAS FLUENT IN GERMAN. A READER WOULD ALSO HAVE HAD TO HAVE UNDERSTOOD HIS PARTICULAR AREA OF EXPERTISE.

2.4 Explain, in the context of the article, what is meant by the phrase "a game of telephone"?

WHEN INFORMATION IS NOT PROPERLY UNDERSTOOD ERRORS GROW AS PEOPLE PASS ON SOMETHING THEY DO NOT UNDERSTAND THEMSELVES.

2.5 What is nuanced consideration? How did people simplify Hänig's work? Why did they simplify it?

NUANCED CONSIDERATION MEANS THAT A PERSON MAKES A CAREFUL AND IN-DEPTH EXAMINATION OF A TOPIC. HÄNIG'S ORIGINAL DIAGRAMS WERE VERY COMPLEX AND THEY WERE CHANGED INTO SOMETHING MUCH MORE STRAIGHTFORWARD THAT UNFORTUNATELY DID NOT PRESENT AN ACCURATE PICTURE OF HIS RESEARCH. THIS WAS PROBABLY DONE BECAUSE PEOPLE LIKE DIAGRAMS TO BE CLEAR AND UNCOMPLICATED.

2.6 We are advised to maintain "healthy scepticism". According to Vogt (2022), the Greek word *skepsis* means investigation. Therefore a "sceptic" is an inquirer. How would you describe "healthy scepticism"?

HEALTHY SCEPTICISM MEANS THAT PEOPLE ASK FOR EVIDENCE BEFORE THEY MAKE THEIR MIND UP ABOUT AN ISSUE. THEY DO NOT JUST ACCEPT WHAT THEY ARE TOLD. THEY WANT PROOF.

2.7 Berentson-Shaw (2018) talks about the "myth of the knowledge gap" (p. 3). What they mean by this is that simply giving people evidence about why something is not true will very often not be accepted. People might well reject information if it conflicts with what they believe. How could this insight be important for Hänig's research?

PEOPLE MIGHT BE SHOWN THAT HÄNIG'S ORIGINAL RESEARCH DID NOT SUPPORT THEIR BELIEF ABOUT HOW WE TASTE. HOWEVER, SOMETIMES IF PEOPLE BELIEVE SOMETHING STRONGLY ENOUGH THEY WILL NOT ACCEPT THE EVIDENCE PRESENTED TO THEM. IN HÄNIG'S CASE THIS MEANS THAT TO A LARGE EXTENT HIS CAREFUL RESEARCH AND FINDINGS WILL BE MISREPRESENTED.

References

Berentson-Shaw, J. (2018). *A matter of fact: Talking truth in a post-truth world*. BWB Texts.

Vogt, K. (2022). Ancient skepticism. *The Stanford Encyclopedia of Philosophy* (Winter 2022 Edition), Edward N. Zalta & Uri Nodelman (eds.), https://plato.stanford.edu/archives/win2022/entries/skepticism-ancient/

Exercise 3

⇒ *Teacher Notes*

As indicated, this exercise builds on the work done in the two earlier exercises. If students are finding it hard to answer the questions you might want to talk through the answers with them in class before they attempt the short essay. Whether or not you provide them with the outline for the essay will depend on whether you believe they need this help. I suggest you mark this short piece of writing. If the student is not particularly strong, I suggest you focus on a few areas that need improvement such as linking paragraphs. Stronger students could have most of their mistakes highlighted with suggestions for improvement.

Exercise 3
Using the answers you have provided in Exercises 1 and 2, write a short essay 250 or 300 words on the topic of academic misrepresentation. Explain how Hänig's work is a good example of how

research can be misunderstood. Discuss the concepts of mis- and disinformation in your essay and explain why you believe or do not believe that we should maintain "a healthy scepticism". Plan your essay before you start and give it a title. Advice has been provided below but you might prefer to do it in your own way.

Introduction	What is academic mis/disinformation? How will it be explored in the essay?
Body paragraph 1	What was Hänig's research all about?
Body paragraph 2	Why was it misrepresented? How was it misrepresented?
Conclusion	What will happen to further research?

ACADEMIC MISREPRESENTATION: THE CASE OF DAVID HÄNIG

ACADEMIC MISREPRESENTATION MEANS THAT RESEARCH FINDINGS ARE NOT ACCURATELY PRESENTED. THE RESEARCH OF DAVID HÄNIG IS AN ILLUSTRATION OF ACADEMIC MISREPRESENTATION. THIS ESSAY WILL OUTLINE HÄNIG'S RESEARCH AND EXPLAIN HOW AND WHY IT WAS MISREPRESENTED. THE ESSAY WILL CONCLUDE WITH A BRIEF DISCUSSION OF THE SERIOUSNESS OF SUCH MISREPRESENTATION.

HÄNIG WAS A GERMAN SCIENTIST WHO WAS INTERESTED IN HOW HUMANS PERCEIVED THE DIFFERENT TASTE SENSATIONS OF SWEET, SALTY, BITTER AND SOUR. HE DISCOVERED THAT CERTAIN AREAS OF THE TONGUE WERE MORE RECEPTIVE TO THE DIFFERENT SENSATIONS THAN OTHERS. THE RECEPTORS AT THE TIP OF THE TONGUE WERE MORE SENSITIVE TO SWEET SENSATIONS, THE RECEPTORS AT THE BASE OF THE TONGUE RECORDED BITTERNESS THE BEST, WHILE THE SIDES OF THE TONGUE IDENTIFIED SWEET AND SALTY MORE EASILY. HOWEVER, HÄNIG MADE IT VERY CLEAR THAT EVERY SENSATION CAN BE TASTED ACROSS THE ENTIRE TONGUE, AND THE SENSATIONS ARE ONLY SLIGHTLY INCREASED IN THE AREAS INDICATED.

BECAUSE HÄNIG WAS GERMAN HE PUBLISHED HIS RESEARCH IN HIS NATIVE LANGUAGE. THIS MEANT THAT IT COULD ONLY BE READ BY PEOPLE WHO COULD READ GERMAN. IN ADDITION, ONLY THOSE WITH EXPERTISE IN HIS RESEARCH AREA COULD REALLY UNDERSTAND HIS FINDINGS. LATER HIS COMPLICATED DIAGRAMS WERE SIMPLIFIED TO MAKE THEM EASIER TO UNDERSTAND. THE SIMPLIFICATION IMPLIED THAT SENSATIONS COULD ONLY BE TASTED IN CERTAIN PARTS OF THE TONGUE. THIS IS WHAT PEOPLE CAME TO BELIEVE.

AS A RESULT OF THESE MISREPRESENTATIONS HÄNIG'S CAREFUL RESEARCH IS NOW WIDELY MISUNDERSTOOD. THIS MEANS THAT ANY RESEARCH BUILT ON THIS FALSE PREMISE WILL NOT HAVE ANY VALIDITY. (263 WORDS)

Post-Class Activity

⇒ *Teacher Notes*

> TED-Ed. (April 16, 2025). *What Earth in 2125 could look like. Iseult Gillespie* [Video]. https://www.youtube.com/watch?v=4UJTtk_2ly0

This short video clip (5:13) talks about using technology to create a sustainable world. It uses three cities, one in the US, one in Africa, and one in South America, to illustrate what can be done. Students could view the clip and write up the information they have acquired. You could also ask them to think of a city they know and how some of the ideas discussed in the clip could be profitably used to make these cities more sustainable.

Lesson 6: Thinking Critically about Sources

Time: 2 hours

Overview

In this lesson students are introduced to a system that helps them decide whether certain articles would be valuable in writing an essay. They will devise a series of questions to help establish this credibility and then test their questions on the material provided.

Purpose and Strategies

Purpose	Strategies
Thinking critically about evidence	Thinking critically about evidence.
Summarising information	Translating information into a table for considering and evaluating sources.
Considering sources	Using the table to consider the weight that should be given to articles.
Evaluating sources	Using the table to evaluate which texts are more useful than others.

Pre-Class Activities

⇒ *Teacher Notes*

Critical thinking is one of the most important skills in academic writing. Students are required to do far more than describe – they are expected to analyse and evaluate. In this introduction to the lesson it would be a good idea to point out to the class that it is not just in the academic world where these skills are important. We use critical thinking all the time. For example, if students are concerned about healthy eating, they might be attracted to products in the supermarket that claim to be sugar-free. However, if they read the small print on the package, they might find that while the item is low in sugar it is very high in salt, and that is not good for a healthy diet. Ask students about how they employ critical thinking in their day-to-day lives.

There is more information online that anyone could ever read in a lifetime; not all of it is trustworthy, however. Deciding what should be believed is difficult but students need to be able to discern what information is likely to be accurate and what should be regarded with scepticism (McGrew et al., 2024). As indicated, students make decisions about what to trust every day. However, when students go online, it is often difficult for them to know what they can trust. To introduce the lesson here are a few prompts:

- Do you always believe the labels on products at the supermarket?
- How do you verify the information about the items you want to buy?
- When it comes to politics, are there people whose opinions you trust more than others?
- If so, why?
- Which ones do you trust?
- If you saw a newspaper headline and you weren't sure if it was true, what would you do?

Reference

McGrew, S., Reynolds, E.C., & Glass, A.C. (2024). The problem with perspective: Students' and teachers' reasoning about credibility during discussions of online sources. *Cognition and Instruction, 42*(3), 399–425. https://doi.org/10.1080/07370008.2024.2340981

During Class
Exercise 1

⇒ *Teacher Notes*

As you have pointed out to your students, it is becoming increasingly difficult to decide what information available online is credible. It is important that students develop the skills to decide which information they should use in the assignments. This reading introduces the CRAAP test (outlined below) developed by a university librarian to help students decide if their sources are valid. The information should stand students in good stead in their academic careers. The material is quite demanding so it would probably be a good idea to explain briefly to them that the test for deciding how valid a source is, has five parts:

- Currency – how up to date the information is.
- Relevance – whether it is suited to the student's needs.
- Authority – where the information comes from.
- Accuracy – how reliable the information is.
- Purpose – what the reason is for the information's existence.

It might be an idea to ensure that the students understand the key terms before they embark on the reading. This would make a good group exercise. When they have finished, bring the class together to discuss their answers.

Exercise 1

READING: MAKING INFORMED CHOICES

To make informed choices you need to have information that is evidence-based. Making sure that the information we read online is accurate is becoming increasingly problematic (Armitage & Vaccari, 2021). Reputable academic journals try to ensure that the research they publish is accurate and reliable. They do this by using a system called peer review. Peer review means that before they are published academic articles are read by other experts in the field who judge whether the articles are good enough for publication. These reviews are usually caried out blind, which means that the reviewers do not know who the authors of the articles are.

It is important that you ensure the evidence you use in academic assignments is trustworthy. If it is not, this will raise doubts about the strength of your arguments. It is also important to keep an open mind about the data you encounter. An article that does not support your beliefs can be as valuable, if not more valuable, than one that confirms your opinions.

It is not always easy to decide whether data is reliable but there are ways to judge the reliability of information. One of these is the use of the CRAAP test. This test was developed by a librarian to help students decide whether their sources were reliable (University of Chicago Library, n.d). CRAAP stands for:

- Currency – how up to date the information is.
- Relevance – whether it is suited for the student's needs.
- Authority – where the information comes from.
- Accuracy – how reliable the information is.
- Purpose – what the reason is for the information's existence.

Currency is about when the information was posted or became available. What we accept as correct can change as more evidence is gathered. Generally, the most recent literature will be included (Leite, Padilha & Cecatti, 2019). The obvious question is what is meant by the term "most recent". Most academic writing advisors think that between 5 and 10 years should be the cut-off point. It will, of course, also depend on the discipline area. In many disciplines, it is accepted practice to restrict sources to those published within the last 5 years (Rasmussen University, 2024). In health sciences, for example, the use of older sources might mean that patients do not receive the best available options for their care (Rasmussen University, 2024). However, exceptions are made in all discipline areas for articles that are **seminal**. Seminal sources are studies that presented an idea of great importance or influence within a particular discipline. The authors of these studies are the researchers that everyone discusses whether they agree with their research or not (Rasmussen University, 2023). An example of a seminal article is *A Structure for Deoxyribose Nucleic Acid* by James Watson and Francis Crick. It was published in 1953 in the journal *Nature*. In the article, the authors describe the structure of DNA for the first time. These articles are also known as landmark articles (Pray, 2008).

Relevance is about whether the information is suited to its purpose. The original audience needs to be identified. We need to know if the article was written for experts or lay people. We need to weigh up whether it is sufficiently academic to be used in an academic assignment and whether the issues are covered in sufficient depth.

Authority is about who is responsible for the text. Where does the author work? Is the author qualified to write on the topic? Is there contact information such as an email address or a publisher? What about the URL? Academic URLs are the web addresses of universities, research centres or government departments. Examples are .edu, .ac (educational), .org (non-profit organisation), and .gov (government). Another URL widely used by journals is .com.

Accuracy is about where the information comes from. Again, it is a good idea to check to see whether the author is connected to a university, a research centre, a recognised organisation or a government department. Is the information backed up by reliable sources? Another important thing to look out for is the use of language. The language in the article should not have grammatical or spelling mistakes.

Purpose is about why the information exists. Very often in academic journals the information is there to inform the audience, for example an academic article that is presenting research findings. However, some large companies have publications that look like academic journals but are actually promoting their products (Hutson, 2009). Therefore it is important to decide what the author/s intentions are. There might be a desire to persuade the reader of something e.g. to buy a product. Perhaps the author/s wish to entertain rather than inform the reader. It is important too that the information is unbiased. An example of this is the idea that older people are a burden on society. Research indicates that older adults, as a group, provide more support to society through activities such as volunteering and care giving than they receive (Weir, 2023).

References

Armitage, R., & Vaccari, C. (2021). Misinformation and disinformation. In H. Tumber & S. Waisbord (eds.), *The Routledge Companion to Media Disinformation and Populism*. Taylor & Francis Group, pp. 38–48. 2021.

Hutson, S. (2009). Publication of fake journals raises ethical questions. *Nature Medicine, 15*, 598. https://doi.org/10.1038/nm0609-598a

Leite. D., Padilha, M., & Cecatti, J. (2019). Approaching literature review for academic purposes: The Literature Review Checklist. *Clinics, 74*, e1403. https://doi.org/10.6061/clinics/2019/e1403

Pray, L. (2008). Discovery of DNA structure and function: Watson and crick. *Nature Education, 1*(1), 100.

Rasmussen University. (2023). *What are seminal works and how do I find them?* https://rasmussen.libanswers.com/faq/270091

Rasmussen University. (2024). *Why do my sources need to be published within the last 5 years?* https://rasmussen.libanswers.com/faq/359297#:~:text=Answer,within%20the%20last%205%20years

Weir, K. (March 1, 2023). Ageism is one of the last socially acceptable prejudices. Psychologists are working to change that. *Monitor on Psychology, 54*(2). https://www.apa.org/monitor/2023/03/cover-new-concept-of-aging

1.1 Find two words in the text that are synonyms of "dependable". TRUSTWORTHY AND RELIABLE.

1.2 In the context of the passage, what is meant by the following words or phrases?
- Cut-off. POINT AT WHICH SOMETHING SHOULD STOP.
- An open mind. BEING WILLING TO CONSIDER NEW OR DIFFERENT IDEAS.
- Lay people. A PERSON WHO IS NOT AN EXPERT IN A PARTICULAR AREA.

1.3 Paraphrase the following:
An article that does not support your beliefs can be as valuable, if not more valuable, than one that confirms your opinions.
  ENCOUNTERING INFORMATION THAT GIVES DIFFERENT IDEAS AND INSIGHTS TO THE ONES WE CONSIDER CORRECT CAN BE VERY USEFUL.

Exercise 2

⇒ *Teacher Notes*

In this exercise the students are asked to take the information they have just read and create a chart that can be used to test whether an article should be used as source material. Students can continue in the same groups that tackled Exercise 1 or you might think it better to have them do the work in pairs. You could walk around the class and discuss what they are doing with them. Again, when students have finished get them together to compare their questions. They could talk about which ones are easiest to understand.

Exercise 2

The article you have just read contained a great deal of important information. However, it is often useful to have a brief summary or a list of questions you can use to check whether an article should be used or not. Use the reading to complete the table below in such a way that the questions could be used by students to check whether the articles/texts they have found are suitable to be used as sources for academic essays.

CRAAP Questions	
Currency	When did the article/information become available?
	IS IT A SEMINAL ARTICLE?
Relevance	WHO WAS THIS ARTICLE/TEXT WRITTEN FOR?
	IS IT ACADEMIC ENOUGH FOR AN ACADEMIC ESSAY?
	ARE THE ISSUES RAISED COVERED IN DEPTH?
Authority	WHERE DOES/DO THE AUTHOR/S WORK?
	Is the author/s qualified to write on the topic?
	IS THERE CONTACT INFORMATION, SUCH AS AN EMAIL ADDRESS OR A PUBLISHER?
	WHAT ABOUT THE URL?
	WHAT DOES IT TELL US ABOUT WHERE THE AUTHOR WORKS?
Accuracy	WHERE DOES THE INFORMATION COME FROM?
	IS THE AUTHOR/S CONNECTED TO A UNIVERSITY, A RESEARCH CENTRE, A RECOGNISED ORGANISATION OR A GOVERNMENT DEPARTMENT?
	IS THE INFORMATION BACKED UP BY RELIABLE SOURCES?
	Is the language use accurate?
	ARE THERE SPELLING OR GRAMMATICAL MISTAKES IN THE WRITING?
	IS THE LANGUAGE BIASED?
Purpose	WHY WAS THE ARTICLE WRITTEN?
	IS THE INFORMATION THERE TO INFORM THE AUDIENCE?
	DOES THE INFORMATION AIM TO GIVE THE READER NEW INSIGHTS?
	DOES THE INFORMATION AIM TO PERSUADE THE READER ABOUT SOMETHING?
	Does the article want to entertain the reader?
	DOES THE ARTICLE WANT TO SELL SOMETHING?
	DOES THE AUTHOR/S MAKE THEIR INTENTIONS CLEAR?
	DOES THE INFORMATION APPEAR IMPARTIAL AND OBJECTIVE?
	DO THERE APPEAR TO BE BIASES?

Exercise 3

⇒ *Teacher Notes*

This exercise asks students to put the questions they have developed to use. The students should do this exercise individually. When they have finished, ask them to get into groups to compare the answers. Ask the group to come up with an agreed list of most useful to least useful articles. If there is time a whole-group discussion would be a useful way to explore students' thinking on the issue. It is essential to note that there are no right or wrong answers. Students should be encouraged to discuss their choices. A possible answer has been provided, but this should not be taken as a model.

The sources listed below are all imaginary and were written for this exercise.

Exercise 3

You have been asked to write an essay about the advantages and disadvantages of having mandatory physical exercise classes in schools for school goers of all ages. Here is a list of sources that you have found. Using the questions you have developed discuss the merits of each of the articles based on the CRAAP principle. Then list the articles from 1–7, with 1 being the article you consider most valuable for your essay and 7 being the one that you consider would be least useful. There are no right or wrong answers – what is important is your justification for the selection of the evidence you will use.

NOTE: None of the sources really exist – they have been made up for this exercise.

A	"Physical Exercise as a mandatory school subject" is the name of an article written in the peer-reviewed journal *Physical Education Overview*. It is a highly ranked journal with a rigorous peer review process. The author, D. Major, was a professor at a prestigious US university. The article was published in 1912. It is a well-written article, giving a balanced overview of the advantages and disadvantages of physical exercise in the school system. It does not introduce new ideas but describes educational thinking at the time of writing.
B	Amanda Luxton and James Smith, who work at a well-known research institute, Research for Health and Wellbeing, published an article in 2024 in the highly ranked *International Journal of Wellbeing and Exercise*. The journal is peer-reviewed. The article, entitled "Healthy children and diet", does not focus on exercise but has interesting data on diet and wellbeing. However, the authors acknowledge the important role exercise plays in a healthy lifestyle.

(Continued)

C	The article entitled "Compulsory school physical activity and its effect on children's wellbeing" was published in 2023 in one of the top journals in the field of nutrition and physical activity, *Physical Activity*. The journal is peer-reviewed. The authors, B. Choo and L. Zhang, work at a top ranked Chinese university. The article deals with the most recent research in the field. The article only focuses on the Chinese system, but it covers all stages of schooling.
D	*School Health and Wellbeing* is the name of the journal that published the article "The link between physical activity and academic achievement in elementary school". The journal has only been in existence for a few years so it is not particularly well known, but the editorial board has a number of leading academics. The authors, M. Linden and P. Nielsen, received funding from the highly regarded Scandinavian Brain Foundation. Both authors are professors at one of the oldest Scandinavian universities. The article was peer-reviewed and published in 2022.
E	The first few lines of the abstract of this article read: This article represent research project carry out in a large number of schools in seven various countries. More than twenty researchers were involved in the research project that investigated the link between health and exercise in school attendees of all ages. The article was published in an online journal *Health and Wellbeing at School*. The article, which was not peer-reviewed, was published in 2023. The authors M. Macky, J. Langer and H. Sen work in an international organisation researching educational issues. The results raise a number of interesting questions for educators.
F	"Getting kids moving?" was published in the online *Journal of Movement* in 2014. The editorial covers the advantages and disadvantages of making exercise compulsory for school children. Editorials are not peer-reviewed. This one was written by J. Mountbank, a recognised expert in the field, and the Dean of the School of Medicine at one of the leading universities in the UK. The editorial has been cited numerous times.
G	*Focus on Physical Education* is an international journal that has been in existence for 30 years. The editorial board has a number of academics who are well known in the field. The article "Encouraging physical activity in senior secondary students" is the result of a collaboration by researchers from three leading Dutch universities. The work of all three authors, J. Poggenpoel, L. van der Waal and J. Grobbelaar, is respected. The article, which was peer-reviewed, was published in 2020.
H	"Physical exercise and young people's health" is the title of a well-written article about children and exercise. The article covers children from the time they enter school until they leave. The author, who originally worked at a large and well regarded university in Australia, is widely published and often asked to make keynote addresses at conferences. They now work as head of the research department at MOVE!, a company that manufactures sporting equipment. The article, which was published in a blog sponsored by the company, draws on the expertise of experts around the world, was made available in 2022.

Complete the table below:

Article	Currency	Relevance	Authority	Accuracy	Purpose
A	Very low because the article is over 100 years old.	It does cover relevant information but the relevance is questionable because of age. This does not appear to reach the criteria of a seminal article – it reviews other sources.	No problem in this area. The article is published in a respected journal and has been peer-reviewed.	For the time in which it was written it appears accurate.	Academic article giving findings.
B					
C					
D			The journal has not been in existence for long and is not well known but …		
E					
F	The article is more than 10 years old.				
G					
H					

CHOICE

THE **TOP** CHOICE WOULD BE C. THE ARTICLE IS RECENT AND IT HAS BEEN PUBLISHED IN A HIGHLY REGARDED JOURNAL. THE RESEARCHERS WORK AT A RESPECTED UNIVERSITY AND THEIR WORK HAS BEEN PEER REVIEWED. THE SUBJECT APPEARS TO BE RELEVANT TO THE ESSAY TOPIC. THE ONLY NEGATIVE ASPECT IS THAT THE ARTICLE ONLY FOCUSES ON CHILDREN IN CHINA. HOWEVER, IT IS LIKELY THAT THE INFORMATION WILL ALSO BE RELEVANT FOR CHILDREN IN OTHER PARTS OF THE WORLD.

MY **SECOND** CHOICE WOULD BE **D**. THERE ARE A FEW DRAWBACKS AS FAR AS THE ESSAY IS CONCERNED. THE ARTICLE FOCUSES ON YOUNGER CHILDREN, BUT THE AGE RANGE IS WIDER THAN ARTICLE G. THE JOURNAL IS NOT VERY WELL KNOWN BUT IT HAS A STRONG EDITORIAL BOARD, AND THE ARTICLE WAS PEER REVIEWED. THE AUTHORS WHO WORK AT A LEADING SCANDINAVIAN UNIVERSITY RECEIVED FUNDING FROM AN IMPORTANT RESEARCH ORGANISATION FOR THEIR WORK.

MY **THIRD** CHOICE WOULD BE **G** ALTHOUGH THERE ARE DRAWBACKS. THE ARTICLE FOCUSES ON ONLY A SMALL SECTION OF SCHOOL ATTENDEES, AND THE RESEARCH IS MORE THAN 5 YEARS OLD. HOWEVER, IT HAS BEEN PUBLISHED IN A JOURNAL THAT HAS BEEN IN EXISTENCE FOR MANY YEARS AND THE EDITORIAL BOARD HAS A NUMBER OF WELL-KNOWN ACADEMICS. THE AUTHORS ARE WELL REGARDED IN THE FIELD AND THE ARTICLE WAS PEER REVIEWED.

MY **FOURTH** CHOICE WOULD BE **F**. ALTHOUGH THE ARTICLE HAS NOT BEEN PEER REVIEWED THERE IS A GOOD REASON FOR THIS (IT IS AN EDITORIAL). THE AUTHOR IS A WELL-KNOWN EXPERT AND HOLDS A VERY SENIOR POSITION AT A LEADING UK UNIVERSITY. THE TOPIC OF THE ARTICLE IS RELEVANT TO THE ESSAY. HOWEVER, THE FACT THAT THE ARTICLE IS OVER 10 YEARS OLD IS A DRAWBACK.

MY **FIFTH** CHOICE WOULD BE **B**. THE ONLY REASON THAT THIS ARTICLE IS NOT HIGHER IS THAT IT MIGHT NOT BE VERY USEFUL FOR THE ESSAY. THE AUTHORS DO NOT FOCUS PRIMARILY ON EXERCISE BUT RATHER ON DIET. THE JOURNAL IS HIGHLY REGARDED AND THE ARTICLE WHICH WAS PUBLISHED RECENTLY WAS PEER REVIEWED. THE AUTHORS WORK AT A WELL KNOWN RESEARCH INSTITUTE.

MY **SIXTH** CHOICE WOULD BE **H**. ON THE SURFACE IT APPEARS TO BE A MORE USEFUL ARTICLE THAN SOME OF THE OTHERS ALREADY LISTED. IT COVERS THE ESSAY TOPIC AND IS WRITTEN BY A RECOGNISED EXPERT. IT IS ALSO MORE RECENT THAN SOME OF THE OTHER PUBLICATIONS. HOWEVER, IT WAS PUBLISHED IN A BLOG WITHOUT ANY REVIEW MECHANISM. THE BLOG IS SPONSORED BY THE COMPANY FOR WHICH THE AUTHOR NOW WORKS. THIS COMPANY SELLS SPORTING EQUIPMENT AND IT IS POSSIBLE THAT THE AUTHOR MIGHT BE PROMOTING PRODUCTS PRODUCED BY THEIR EMPLOYER.

MY **SEVENTH** CHOICE WOULD BE **E**. I WOULD BE CONCERNED ABOUT THIS ARTICLE BECAUSE IT HAS NOT BEEN PEER REVIEWED, AND NO INFORMATION IS PROVIDED ABOUT THE ONLINE JOURNAL. I WAS ALSO CONCERNED ABOUT THE LANGUAGE EMPLOYED IN THE ABSTRACT AS

THERE WERE A NUMBER OF ERRORS. "THIS ARTICLE REPRESENT.../MORE THAT TWENTY RESEARCHER WAS.../ THE LINK BETWEEN HEALTHY.../ AND EXERCISE ... ALTHOUGH THE DATA COULD BE VERY INTERESTING IT MUST BE APPROACHED WITH CAUTION AS THERE ARE QUALITY CONCERNS ABOUT THE ARTICLE.

MY FINAL CHOICE WAS A. THIS WAS NOT BECAUSE OF THE QUALITY OF THE ARTICLE. IT WAS WRITTEN BY A RECOGNISED ACADEMIC, PEER REVIEWED AND PUBLISHED IN A GOOD JOURNAL. IT COVERED THE AREA OF INTEREST. MY REAL CONCERN WAS THE AGE OF THE ARTICLE. SOCIETY HAS CHANGES SO MUCH IN THE LAST 100 YEARS THAT IT IS UNLIKELY THAT THE DATA WOULD BE RELEVANT. AT BEST IT COULD PROVIDE AN HISTORICAL CONTEXT.

Post-Class Activities

⇒ *Teacher Notes*

Students could be given copies of the questions finalised by the groups in Exercise 2. If the class is small, the questions of all the students could be used. With this list of possible questions and using the reading, students could be asked to draw up a short handout aimed at helping students identify reliable sources, that could be given out to first year students at the university who have not had academic writing training. The students would need to write a short introductory blurb for their handout explaining why it could be useful.

Cycle 4

Fast Fashion

Lesson 1 Circular Fashion

Time: 2 hours

Overview

The focus in this cycle is on fashion, particularly fast fashion. In this lesson students will be asked to critically examine material on the fast fashion industry. They will also be asked to translate some of the data into a diagram. Finally, students will examine how certain of the factors raised in the reading and the video play out in their own lives.

Purpose and Strategies

Purpose	Strategies
Collecting data from different sources	Students read a passage and view a short video clip.
Critical thinking skills	Students will answer questions set on the passage and the video clip.
Use data to draw a diagram	Students collect the relevant information from the data gathered and design a diagram to illustrate the concept.
Relating data to own observations	Students will relate the data raised in the lesson to their own lives.

Pre-Class Activities

⇒ *Teacher Notes*

This cycle will look at the fast fashion industry and the growing concerns about unethical and unsustainable business practices (Papasolomou et al., 2023). A class discussion around students' clothes buying habits would be a good way to introduce this cycle. Is fast fashion an addiction? An article in *Voice* (2024) claims that fast fashion consumption is as addictive as substance abuse and that when fast fashion addicts buy clothes, they have a temporary feeling of euphoria which is later followed by guilt and remorse. Psychologists also liken the addictive nature of fast fashion consumption to that of substance abuse, with individuals experiencing temporary euphoria followed by guilt and remorse. The Environmental Impact of Fast Fashion Statistics (2025) notes that nowadays clothing is worn only 7 to 10 times before being thrown away. The publication also notes that over 40% of young women feel pressurised not to wear the same outfit twice when they go out. It claims that young men feel less pressure and also shop less.

The following prompts might be useful:

- Do you think buying clothes could be addictive?
- Do you ever suffer from buyer's remorse when you buy clothes?
- If you do, why is this so?
- Do you think women feel pressurised not to wear the same outfit too often?
- Do you think there is less pressure on men to be fashionable?
- How often do you wear your clothes before you throw them out?
- Why do you throw them out if they are still wearable?

References

Environmental Impact of Fast Fashion Statistics. (2025). *Is Fast Fashion an addiction?* Uniform Market. https://www.fabricofchange.ie/articles/is-fast-fashion-an-addiction

Papasolomou, I., Melanthiou, Y., & Tsamouridis, A. (2023). The fast fashion vs environment debate: Consumers' level of awareness, feelings, and behaviour towards sustainability within the fast-fashion sector. *Journal of Marketing Communications, 29*(2), 191–209. https://doi.org/10.1080/13527266.2022.2154059

Voice. (2024). *Is Fast Fashion an addiction?* https://www.fabricofchange.ie/articles/is-fast-fashion-an-addiction#:~:text=Psychologists%20liken%20the%20addictive%20nature,followed%20by%20guilt%20and%20remorse

During Class
Exercise 1

⇒ *Teacher Notes*

This short reading is accompanied by a video clip (5:28). The reading sets out the environmental and social issues around the fast fashion industry that cause global concern. The video identifies ways in which people in the fashion industry are attempting to address these concerns. This is probably a good exercise to get students to do in pairs. When the class has finished, the exercise discuss the answers as a class exercise.

Exercise 1

READING: CONCERNS ABOUT THE FAST FASHION INDUSTRY

The world's interest in clothes is reflected in the fact that it is the third-biggest manufacturing industry in the world after cars and technology (Papasolomou et al., 2023). However, there is also a growing awareness that the clothing industry has a huge impact on the environment. Chang (2017) illustrates this by discussing the making of t-shirts. Over 2 billion t-shirts are made every year for use around the world. The cotton used in their making needs more pesticides than any other crop in the world. These pesticides put farm workers at risk because they are carcinogenic. According to the

Centre for Biological Diversity (Shedlock & Feldstein, 2023), the garment manufacturing process harms wildlife and pollutes soil and water. The fast fashion industry is a significant contributor to the climate crisis. Cotton crops, in particular, need large quantities of water – the cotton used in the average t-shirt needs 2700 litres. While the weaving of the cotton into fabric is largely mechanised, turning this material into t-shirts is done by millions of factory workers who are usually badly paid and have poor working conditions. In Bangladesh, the country that exported the most cotton t-shirts in 2023 (Workman, n.d.), garment workers who protest the conditions in which they are expected to work are often abused and physically attacked by factory owners (Shedlock & Feldstein, 2023).

Many in the fashion industry now wish to take responsibility for the problems.

REFERENCES

Chang, A. (2017). *The life cycle of a t-shirt.* https://www.youtube.com/watch?v=BiSYoeqb_VY

Papasolomou, I., Melanthiou, Y., & Tsamouridis, A. (2023). The fast fashion vs environment debate: Consumers' level of awareness, feelings, and behaviour towards sustainability within the fast-fashion sector. *Journal of Marketing Communications, 29*(2), 191–209. https://doi.org/10.1080/13527266.2022.2154059

Shedlock, K., & Feldstein, S. (2023). At what cost? Unravelling the harms of the fast fashion industry. *Centre for Biological Diversity.* https://www.biologicaldiversity.org/programs/population_and_sustainability/pdfs/Unravelling-Harms-of-Fast-Fashion-Full-Report-2023-02.pdf

Workman, D. (n.d.). T shirts by country. *World's Top Exports.* https://www.worldstopexports.com/t-shirt-exports-by-country/

Once you have finished the reading, watch this video to see what some companies are doing to tackle the problem.

https://www.youtube.com/watch?v=y78UVWd5PHE (5:28)

Now answer the following questions referring to both the reading and the video clip.

1.1 Explain, in your own words, the challenges facing workers involved in the production of cotton and the manufacturing of t-shirts.
FARM WORKERS ARE EXPOSED TO PESTICIDES THAT CAN CAUSE CANCER. THOSE WORKERS EMPLOYED IN THE MAKING OF T-SHIRTS ARE OFTEN VERY BADLY PAID AND WORK IN VERY POOR CONDITIONS. IN ADDITION, IF THEY PROTEST ABOUT THEIR WORKING CONDITIONS THEY ARE ABUSED AND PHYSICALLY ASSAULTED.

1.2 In the video mention is made of the "circular economy". What does this mean with regard to the clothing industry?
THIS MEANS THAT NO PIECE OF CLOTHING ENDS UP AS WASTE. THE CLOTHING IS ALL RECYCLED.

1.3 What is the ultimate goal of the clothing industry?
TO END WASTE.

1.4 In the video one of the founders of TeeMill identifies the two main problems of the fashion industry. What are they?
WASTAGE AND OVER-PRODUCTION.

1.5 How does this factory attempt to overcome these problems?
IT ONLY MAKES THE PRODUCTS AFTER THEY HAVE BEEN ORDERED.

1.6 How does TeeMill enact a circular economy? What do they do to ensure minimum waste? How do they encourage customers to participate?
EVERY T-SHIRT HAS A BAR CODE ON THE CARE LABEL. WHEN THE BUYER NO LONGER WANTS THE T-SHIRT THEY CAN SCAN THE BARCODE AND PRINT OUT A POSTAGE LABEL. THIS ENABLES

THEM TO RETURN THE GARMENT WITHOUT HAVING TO PAY FOR POSTAGE. IF CUSTOMERS RETURN CLOTHING THEY NO LONGER WANT THEY GET A DISCOUNT ON THEIR NEXT PURCHASE.

1.7 In the video clip the representative from Worn Again Technologies explains that they work to break down blended fabrics for recycling. What makes this process special?

IT IS MUCH HARDER TO RECYCLE BLENDED FABRICS.

1.8 Worn Again Technologies want to help other manufacturers recycle blended fabrics. What is the most important element in developing this recycling process? Why do they believe this?

THEY BELIEVE THE MOST IMPORTANT ELEMENT IS KEEPING THE COST OF THE PROCESS DOWN. OTHERWISE IT WILL BE PASSED ON TO THE CONSUMER.

1.9 The last manufacturer Brothers We Stand is also concerned about the environment. What do they do to address this concern?

THEY USE SUSTAINABLE AND RECYCLED MATERIALS. THEY ALSO MAKE THEIR GARMENTS TO LAST.

1.10 What problem do they have in common with TeeMill?

SUSTAINABLE MATERIALS ARE MORE EXPENSIVE THAN THEIR NON-SUSTAINABLE EQUIVALENTS.

Exercise 2

⇒ *Teacher Notes*

Quite often a really good way for writers to put their message across is by using a diagram. The way in which TeeMill tries to ensure that products are returned so that they can be recycled is a case in point. The students have already described what TeeMill does to promote a circular economy. They can now turn this into a labelled diagram. Buckley and Waring (2013) argue that despite the fact that diagrams are a good way to put across concepts they are underutilised in research. It is a good idea to encourage students to develop the skill of turning a concept into a diagram. Many people find these easier to understand than a description. In this context using a circular shape would probably make sense, but allow students to come up with their own interpretation. Once students have completed this exercise encourage them to exchange their diagrams. They could provide feedback to each other as to what they thought was good about the diagram and what could be improved.

Reference

Buckley, C. A., & Waring, M. J. (2013). Using diagrams to support the research process: examples from grounded theory. *Qualitative Research*, *13*(2), 148–172.

Exercise 2

Look at your answer to 1.6. Often a good way to put ideas across is by using a diagram. Turn your answer into a diagram to illustrate the circular fashion TeeMill is trying to promote.

POSSIBLE ANSWER

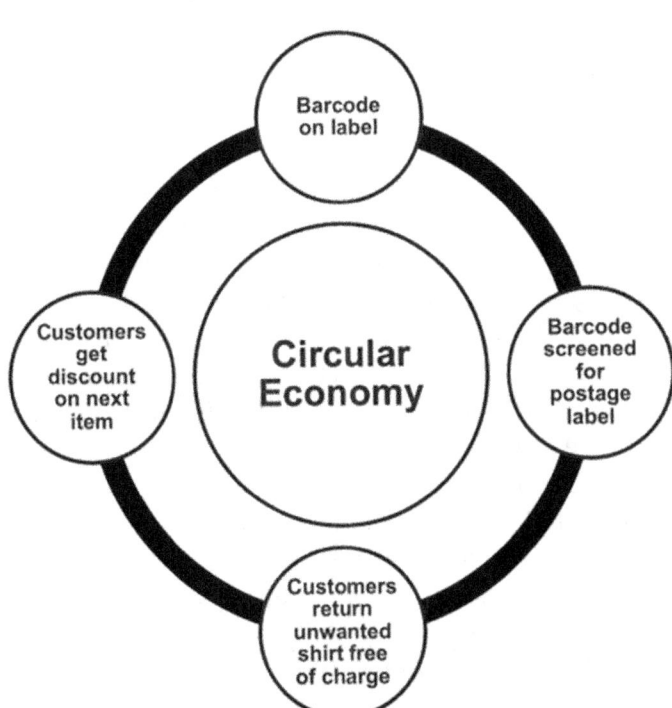

Exercise 3

⇒ *Teacher Notes*

In this cycle student will be asked to consider the concept of cognitive dissonance, that is the discomfort one feels when one doesn't act in accordance with one's beliefs. This will offer them an opportunity to demonstrate more nuanced writing. This exercise asks them to consider the factors that could affect their clothes-buying preferences. They are asked to write short notes about these preferences in preparation for an essay.

Exercise 3

Nowadays it is not strange for people to be torn between fashionable items that they want to buy and their concern for the environment. They realise that buying fast fashion items is not good for the planet and they are concerned about the working conditions and wages of people who work in the textile industry. At the same time, people want to look good. They want to wear the latest trends and fit in with what their friends are wearing.

Think about the following questions and write down your responses. Bring these to the next lesson.

3.1 Do you enjoy buying clothes? Are you quite neutral about it – it is something you have to do but it is not particularly enjoyable, or do you dislike clothes shopping? Describe your feelings.

3.2 Look at the list below. The items on this list have been identified as most influential when it comes to the purchase of clothing. Ones that influence clothing purchases are:
- Brands.
- What my friends are wearing.
- Whether it is fashionable.
- What I see on social media.
- If it suits me.
- My personal style.
- Price.

- ♦ If it is long-lasting.
- ♦ If the material it is made from is sustainable.
- ♦ If it was ethically manufactured (e.g. care was taken not to harm the environment and the workers involved were fairly treated).
- ♦ Influence of family.
- ♦ Influence of friends.

3.3 Choose the three factors that are most important to you when you are buying clothes. Explain why you have made this choice.

3.4 Then choose the three factors that are least important to you when you are buying clothes. Explain your choice.

Keep your answers as you will be using them in the next lesson.

Post-Class Activities

⇒ *Teacher Notes*

The article listed below is in the public domain so students can download it. The authors explore the idea that clothing overconsumption can be checked, or at least limited, by communication interventions. The article explores five short communications (less than 100 words in total) that it believed could be successful. Students will be asked to examine these short communications and explain what impact they would have on the students' attitudes towards clothes shopping.
Download this article:

> de Koning, J., Lavanga, M., & Spekkink, W. (2024). Exploring the clothing overconsumption of young adults: An experimental study with communication interventions. *Journal of Cleaner Production, 467,* 142970. https://doi.org/10.1016/j.jclepro.2024.142970

In this article the researchers explore ways that people can be discouraged from buying clothes. One idea is by exposing them to very short communications on the topic of how clothing overconsumption can be checked, or at least limited, by communication interventions. You will find these communications in Figure 5 in the article.

- Do you think these communications would be effective in your peer group? Give a reason for your answer.
- Do you think some of them would be more effective than others? Why?
- Which one would have the most effect on you? Why
- If an anti-waste organisation could only display one of these communications, which one would you suggest they choose? Why
- Try to come up with your own short communication (these range between 9 and 52 words) that you think might discourage people from overspending on their clothes.

Lesson 2: Attitudes Towards Fashion

Time: 2 hours

Overview
In this lesson students will compare notes and try to find consensus about their fashion choices. They will be introduced to the theory of cognitive dissonance and asked to demonstrate their understanding of the concept by using diagrams.

Purpose and Strategies

Purpose	Strategies
Comparing and evaluating data	Students compare notes and try to find consensus on views.
Introduction to an academic theory	Students introduced to the concept of academic dissonance.
Completing diagrams to share information	Students complete diagrams to illustrate their understanding of the concept.

Pre-Class Activities

⇒ *Teacher Notes*

This activity asks students to choose a partner whom they will be working with for the rest of the cycle. While it is often a good idea to give students autonomy in choosing a partner it is also a good idea for them to consider working with different people. All too often students simply work with the same person or group repeatedly, thus missing opportunities to hear new insights and opinions. They might be missing valuable input from other students with different perspectives. The work in this cycle will demand that each student exercises their judgement about their partner's work and also offers advice. Explain to the students that working with different people is often very productive. Choosing a partner can be done in different ways. Explain that there are three well-established ways of forming teams:

- Random selection.
- Student selection.
- Teacher selection.

All three ways have advantages and disadvantages. Ask them if they can think of what these are. (Random – quick and easy selection but might end up with combinations that do not work well; self-selection means people can choose partners they know they work well with but the consequence is that new combinations are never explored; teacher selection means the teacher can use their expertise and knowledge of students to choose good pairs – the problem is the teacher's knowledge of the students is probably limited. So these three methods all have advantages and drawbacks (Konieczna, 2024).)

Ask them if they can think of other ways to select partners. Then ask the class to decide which method they would like to employ. I suggest you accept the chosen method, even if you do not think it is the best option. If you do this, it is more likely that students will accept and take ownership of the resulting partnerships.

Reference

Konieczna, A. (2024). Criteria for selecting preferred and avoided partners for teamwork in the classroom and their contextual variability: An adolescent perspective. *e-mentor*, 4(106), 4–12. https://doi.org/10.15219/em106.1674

During Class
Exercise 1

⇒ *Teacher Notes*

This first exercise allows the pairs to discuss their attitudes towards fast fashion. If students are paired with peers they have not worked with before, this will give them an opportunity to get to know each other. They will be using the notes they made at the end of Lesson 1.

Exercise 1

In this lesson you will be considering your own attitude towards fashion.

Look at the notes you made in the last lesson and compare them with your partner. Do you feel the same way or are there differences? How do your reasons differ? Look at the three factors that each of you has ranked as most important to you. Again, are they similar? Are you surprised by what your partner has written? Has it given you food for thought? Then together try to agree on the 3 most important factors for buying and the 3 least important factors for buying. If you cannot reach an agreement, then each of you should choose one factor.

Together you should fill in the following table about your buying habits:

	Student 1	Student 2
Top 3 factors	1. 2. 3.	1. 2. 3.
Summary of reasons for choosing these 3		
Bottom 3 factors	1. 2. 3.	1. 2. 3.
Summary of reasons for choosing these 3		
	Students 1 and 2	
Jointly decided top 3 factors in decision to buy clothes	1. 2. 3.	
Jointly decided bottom 3 factors in decision to buy clothes	1. 2. 3.	
If you cannot agree	**Student 1**	**Student 2**
Top factor in decision to buy clothes		
Bottom factor in decision to buy clothes		

Exercice 2

⇒ *Teacher Notes*

In the last lesson we talked about how people are torn between environmental and humanitarian concerns, on the one hand, and wanting to dress well, on the other. There is a great deal of research about this (Taljaard, Sonnenberg & Jacobs, 2018). This difference between these two desires is called cognitive dissonance. Cognitive dissonance is the discomfort people feel when their behaviour does not align with their values or beliefs (MedicalNews, n.d.). It is the uncomfortable feeling they experience when they act in a way that does not live up to their values. For example, Alex might believe that it is wrong to kill animals to make fashion items. However, Alex sees an attaché case made out of pigskin which they really like. Alex decides to buy it. Alex's actions and thoughts/beliefs do not line up so they are uncomfortable. Alex tries to make themself feel better by reasoning that the case will last a lifetime so it was worth buying.

Share this diagram with the students – it has been set out on the worksheets. It shows what people do to relieve cognitive dissonance.

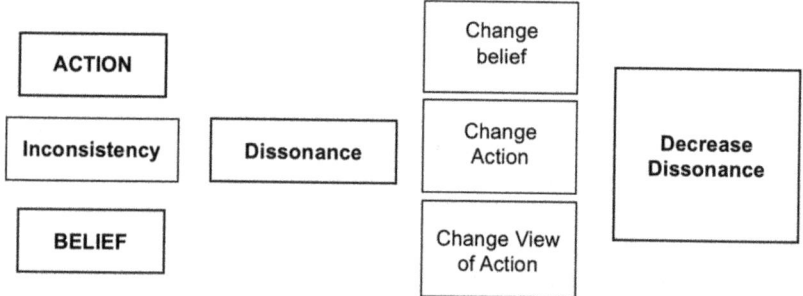

(Adapted from Cairns, Ritch & Bereziat, 2021)

The diagram below is also on the worksheet. Ask the students to explain what has been written in the boxes. This is a good way to check that they understand the concept.

So with Alex it would look like this:

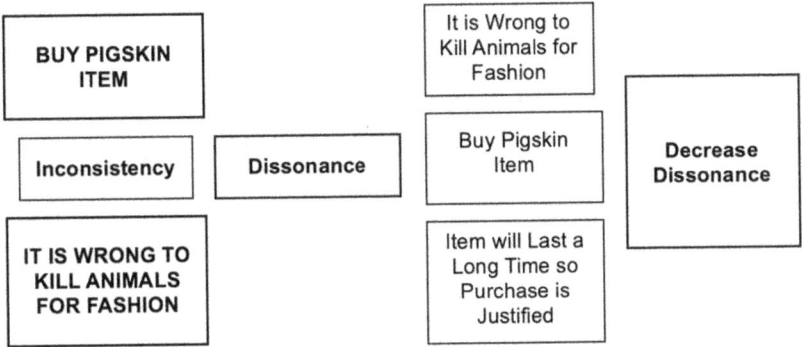

Here is an explanation:

Alex feels uncomfortable but still buys the pigskin case. What has changed is their view about buying the item. They feel it is not bad to use animal products if they last for a long time.

References

Cairns, H.M., Ritch, E., & Bereziat, C. (2021). Think eco, be eco? The tension between attitudes and behaviours of millennial fashion consumers. *International Journal of Consumer Studies, 46,* 1262–1277. https://doi.org/10.1111/ijcs.12756

MedicalNews. (n.d.). *What is cognitive dissonance?* https://www.medicalnewstoday.com/articles/326738

Taljaard, H., Sonnenberg, N. C., & Jacobs, B. M. (2018). Factors motivating male consumers' eco-friendly apparel acquisition in the South African emerging market. *International Journal of Consumer Studies, 42*(5), 461–468. https://doi.org/10.1111/ijcs.12441

Exercise 2

Look at the following examples. Draw up the diagrams that illustrate what Jay and Sam do to decrease dissonance.

2.1 Jay is very concerned about the environment and worried about the detrimental effect of fast fashion. However, Jay is a spokesperson for a big company and often has to make public appearances. Jay wants to look fashionable at these appearances and wear different clothes each time they appear in public. Nevertheless, they are feeling increasingly guilty every time they buy new clothes. They decide that they should ask their friends if they can borrow fashionable items for public events.

2.2 Sam really likes running shoes. Sam knows that the shoes are good for over 3000 kilometres but Sam gets bored with the same pair so they buy new running shoes regularly. Sam has read that making running shoes is bad for the environment so when Sam bought running shoes they didn't need Sam would feel guilty that they were causing damage to the planet. Then Sam came across a website that claimed that the data about the damage caused to the environment by shoe manufacturing is greatly exaggerated. Sam believes the website.

JAY CHANGES THEIR ACTION WHILE SAM CHANGES BELIEF.

2.3 Now fill in the diagram, using yourself as the subject. Can you think of fashion choices you have made/not made? Have you justified buying items that you do not feel comfortable about? Are you also uncertain or worried about your own fashion purchases? Perhaps you have changed your buying habits to alleviate your concern. Perhaps you believe current concerns are exaggerated. Once you have filled in the figure compare it with your partner.

Post-Class Activities

⇒ *Teacher Notes*

Give students this brief explanation of Jones and Podpadec's (2023) research.

Jones and Podpadec (2023) investigated the insights of 120 school children aged between 10 and 11 years on the future of fashion. To inform their input the children were shown the short video (6:04) *The lifecycle of a t-shirt* (Chang, 2017) https://www.youtube.com/watch?v=BiSYoeqb_VY

The children were asked to think of ways to lessen the impact of fast fashion on the environment. They came up with suggestions such as using less water and energy to clean clothes (e.g. line drying instead of tumble drying); redistributing outgrown or unwanted clothes and learning to sew so that clothes could be mended. The authors stopped the video at key points to discuss what was being shown.

Tell students that they too will design a lesson on fast fashion and the environment for a group of school goers. They can choose an age group and decide whether the school goers in their group are first- or second-language speakers of English. The students will use the same video as an aid to the lesson. They need to decide when they will pause the video to initiate a discussion. They can identify the moment by using the timing in the video e.g. 2:33. The students should then answer the following questions:

- How many times will you stop the video and when will you stop it?
- Why will you stop the video here?
- What points do you want to raise in the discussion?
- How will you introduce the discussion?
- What factors (e.g. language ability) will you consider?
- How will you address these factors?

References

Chang, A. (2017). *The lifecycle of a t-shirt*. TED-ED. https://www.youtube.com/watch?v=BiSYoeqb_VY

Jones, V., & Podpadec, T. (2023). Young people, climate change and fast fashion futures. *Environmental Education Research*, *29*(11), 1692–1708. https://doi.org/10.1080/13504622.2023.2181269

Lesson 3: Peer Reviewing

Time: 2 hours

Overview

In this lesson students are introduced to the concept of peer review and how it can contribute to their writing. Class and pair discussions as well as data from recent research will be used to help students examine the advantages and possible pitfalls of employing peer reviews in the essay writing process. Students will use the data gathered to write an essay.

Purpose and Strategies

Purpose	Strategies
Introducing peer review	Class discussion and a reading of the literature on the subject.
Critical thinking	In pairs, students are asked to consider pros and cons of peer review and strategies to solve/avoid problems.
Note taking	Students take notes from class/pair discussions and also from the reading.
Writing an essay	Students combine data from the literature and discussions to write an essay.

Pre-Class Activities

⇒ *Teacher Notes*

Research indicates overwhelmingly that peer feedback has a great deal to offer students in their writing (Huisman et al., 2018; Little et al., 2025; Lundstrom & Baker, 2009; Man et al., 2024; Wei & Liu, 2024). Tornwall et al. (2022) point out that if students recognise the value of the process they are more likely to invest time and effort into their reviewing. However, it is also clear that students need guidance as to how they can provide good feedback as students are often uneasy about providing such feedback

(Nurkhamidah et al., 2024). In the lesson students will explore the advantages (and disadvantages) of peer feedback. As an introduction to this activity ask students to think about their experiences with peer feedback. If they have not had any such experiences, perhaps peers with such experience can provide background.

Here are some prompts you might like to use:

- What is peer feedback?
- Have you had any experience of peer feedback?
- Do you think peer feedback is a good idea? Why? If you don't think it is a good idea, why not?

References

Huisman, B., Saab, N., van Driel, J., & van den Broek, P. (2018). Peer feedback on academic writing: undergraduate students' peer feedback role, peer feedback perceptions and essay performance. *Assessment & Evaluation in Higher Education*, 43 (6), 955–968. https://doi.org/10.1080/02602938.2018.1424318

Little, T., Dawson, P., Boud, D., & Tai, J. (2025). What does it take to provide effective peer feedback? *Assessment & Evaluation in Higher Education*. https://doi.org/10.1080/02602938.2025.2475059

Lundstrom, K., & Baker, W. (2009). To give is better than to receive: The benefits of peer review to the reviewer's own writing. *Journal of Second Language Writing*, 18, 30–43. https://doi.org/10.1016/j.jslw.2008.06.002

Man, D., Chau, M.H., Zainal, A.Z., & Rummy, J. T. (2024). Exploring the potential of brief peer review training in enhancing student feedback literacy. *International Review of Applied Linguistics*. https://doi.org/10.1515/iral-2023-0278

Nurkhamidah, N., Lustyantie, N., & Chaeruman, U.A. (2024). Peer feedback on academic writing: students' perspectives on learning and improvement. *Journal of English Language Teaching*, 11(2). https://doi.org/10.33394/jo-elt.v11i2.13330

Tornwall J., McGaughy M., & Schubert C. (2022). Peer review: factors that motivate students to provide supportive peer feedback. *Nurse Education, 47*(2), 114–119. https://doi.org/10.1097/NNE.0000000000001043

Wei, Y. & Liu, D. (2024). Incorporating peer feedback in academic writing: a systematic review of benefits and challenges. *Frontiers in Psychology, 15*, 1506725. https://doi.org/10.3389/fpsyg.2024.1506725

During Class
Exercise 1

⇒ *Teacher Notes*

In this exercise students will learn about the advantages and disadvantages of peer review as discussed in the literature. They will work with the partners chosen in Lesson 2 to consider the statements that follow the reading.

Exercise 1

READING: PEER REVIEW

Peer feedback is defined as a process in which "students critically assess the level, merit or quality of their peers' work" (Wei & Liu, 2024, Introduction). At a time when it is not always easy for university students to get feedback on their writing at university, there is great interest in using students as feedback providers (Little et al., 2025). Research shows overwhelmingly that such peer feedback can have a very positive effect (Huisman et al., 2018; Little et al., 2025; Lundstrom & Baker, 2009; Man et al., 2024; Wei & Liu, 2024). An important aspect of the process is allowing feedback givers and those receiving the feedback to have conversations about the feedback (Storch 2002). Interestingly, research indicates that giving feedback has a more positive effect on student writing than getting feedback. It appears to be better to give than to receive (Lundstrom & Baker, 2009). Students giving feedback are required to identify problems in the writing and suggest ways in which the problem can be overcome (Huisman et al., 2018).

As indicated, there are numerous advantages for students who take part in the peer feedback process. Research indicates that doing so improves students' academic writing skills and helps students understand the demands of academic writing. Students also learn to communicate their points of view more effectively and can improve their own knowledge of the shared discipline. Feedback promotes self-reflection and improves critical thinking and analytical skills. Importantly, the collaborative nature of the process encourages a sense of community among students which, in turn, can positively influence students' motivation and engagement in their own academic writing practices (Fan and Xu, 2020; Wei & Liu, 2024).

However, despite the benefits peer feedback offers students are often uneasy about engaging in the feedback process (Nurkhamidah, et al., 2024). In the first place students might not have enough knowledge to provide strong feedback; even if they are adequately equipped to do so, they might lack confidence in their own ability. Secondly, those receiving feedback might not value it, only trusting feedback supplied by teachers. Providing good feedback is a time-consuming process so students under time pressure might be reluctant to give up their time. If they do so reluctantly, the feedback might be superficial and the comments will not be particularly helpful. Finally, students are often concerned that if they give honest critical feedback they might offend their peers and thus disturb the harmony of the group (Tornwall et al., 2022; Wei & Liu, 2024). It is important to remember that peer feedback is a social activity that involves interactions with others (Little et al., 2025).

REFERENCES

Fan, Y., & Xu, J. (2020). Exploring student engagement with peer feedback on L2 writing. *Journal of Second Language Writing*, *50*, 100775. https://doi.org/10.1016/j.jslw.2020.100775

Huisman, B., Saab, N., van Driel, J., & van den Broek, P. (2018). Peer feedback on academic writing: undergraduate students' peer feedback role, peer feedback perceptions and essay performance. *Assessment & Evaluation in Higher Education, 43*(6), 955–968. https://doi.org/10.1080/02602938.2018.1424318

Little, T., Dawson, P., Boud, D., & Tai, J. (2025): What does it take to provide effective peer feedback? *Assessment & Evaluation in Higher Education.* https://doi.org/10.1080/02602938.2025.2475059

Lundstrom, K., & Baker, W. (2009). To give is better than to receive: The benefits of peer review to the reviewer's own writing. *Journal of Second Language Writing, 18*, 30–43. https://doi.org/10.1016/j.jslw.2008.06.002

Man, D., Chau, M.H., Zainal, A.Z., & Rummy, J.T. (2024). Exploring the potential of brief peer review training in enhancing student feedback literacy. *International Review of Applied Linguistics.* https://doi.org/10.1515/iral-2023-0278

Nurkhamidah, N., Lustyantie, N., & Chaeruman, U.A. (2024). Peer feedback on academic writing: students' perspectives on learning and improvement. *Journal of English Language Teaching, 11*(2). https://doi.org/10.33394/jo-elt.v11i2.13330

Storch, N. (2002). Patterns of interaction in ESL pair work. *Language Learning, 52*(1), 119–158.

Tornwall J., McGaughy M., & Schubert C. (2022). Peer review: factors that motivate students to provide supportive peer feedback. *Nurse Education, 47*(2), 114–119. https://doi.org/10.1097/NNE.0000000000001043

Wei, Y., & Liu, D. (2024). Incorporating peer feedback in academic writing: a systematic review of benefits and challenges. *Frontiers in Psychology, 15*, 1506725. https://doi.org/10.3389/fpsyg.2024.1506725

With your partner examine the following statements. How do you each feel about them?

- I feel that I can help my partner with their writing.
- I am happy for my partner to read my essay.

- I am embarrassed when my partner reads my essays.
- I think discussing the feedback is a good idea.
- I do not want to discuss feedback about my essays.
- I think it is the teacher's job to provide feedback.
- I think I can learn a lot from reading other people's work.

When you have considered the statements, draw up suggestions as to how you think the peer feedback process can be managed in a way that does not make people feel threatened or uncomfortable. Bring these suggestions to the group discussion.

Exercise 2

⇒ *Teacher Notes*

CLASS DISCUSSION

Ask students to take notes during the class discussion. Explain to them that they will be writing an essay about peer review and the reading they have just completed, and that the notes they will take during the discussion will inform the essay. In the discussion, encourage students to raise concerns and uncertainties. Tell them that there will be advice on feedback forms that could be useful but first you would like them to talk about their worries. It is true that peer feedback does not always help students. If the students *receiving* the feedback are unwilling to take it seriously it does not matter how good the feedback is. Secondly, if the person *giving* the feedback just gives superficial comments and doesn't really think about what the writer is saying the feedback will not be helpful. Sometimes students are worried that their partner will be offended by the feedback. That is why it is a good idea to allow students to have a conversation about the feedback. They should each have an opportunity to explain their ideas.

Ask students for suggestions as to how these issues can be dealt with – here are a few suggestions:

- Students giving feedback should start off by asking themselves how they can help the writer improve NOT by trying to find what is wrong.

- When suggestions are made to change the text the reviewer should provide reasons e.g. *If you provide a few examples your reader will understand the point you are making more easily.*
- It is good to be specific. Instead of just saying tense use is problematic, refer to specific instances in the text e.g. the discussion section starts off in the present tense *"In this section the advantages of peer review are analysed"* but in the next few paragraphs the past tense is employed *"It seemed that on the whole peer review was advantageous."* I think it would be better to use the present tense as this is your current view.
- Be careful about use of language. For example; *You must change this…* would be better expressed by saying *You might want to consider…*
- Give praise as well! But again, remember to be specific. Say *This idea has been very well explained. I found it easy to follow* rather than just saying *Good* where the writer is not sure what is good.

Exercise 3

⇒ *Teacher Notes*

In an essay entitled *The advantages and disadvantages of peer feedback* students will write between 500 and 600 words. Remind them that when they refer to the literature they must use intext citations and include a reference list.

Below is a framework that could be used to guide their writing. You might want to provide students with the full framework or part of the framework to assist them. You might decide, however, that they are able to complete the work without assistance. You will not mark this essay – it will be part of a peer-review exercise in the next lesson.

Introduction	Definition of peer review (Wei & Liu, 2024). How essay will unfold e.g. first exploration of advantages then disadvantages. Evaluating of pros and cons and the way forward.	± 100 words
Body: Part 1	Exploration of advantages.	± 150 words
Body: Part 2	Exploration of disadvantages.	± 150 words
Body: Part 3	Evaluation of the advantages and disadvantages. Include your own opinion backed up by the literature and the class discussion.	± 250 words
Conclusion	Summary of main points and the way forward	±150 words

You will need this essay for the work in Lesson 4.

Post-Class Activities

This short video gives one way that students could approach discussing a peer review. What is implied by the word actionable? Ask students to watch the video and decide whether or not they would like to implement the method suggested. Ask them to give reasons for their answers.

> Spencer, J. (2019). *How to get actionable peer feedback in 20 minutes* [Video] (YouTube). https://www.youtube.com/watch?v=jJJIY9DM-ts

Lesson 4: Putting Peer Reviewing into Practice

Time: 2 hours

Overview

Students will be offered opportunities to put peer review into practice. This will be done first with the help of a feedback form. The form will be discussed and then the pairs will review an essay provided for the purpose. Finally, the students will work with student-generated essays.

Purpose and Strategies

Purpose	Strategies
Looking at feedback guidelines	Students are given a feedback form to help them with peer reviews. The form is discussed in class.
Putting guidelines into practice in pairs	Students will be provided with an essay which they will then review with a partner.
Individual review of student generated essays	Students will then independently review their partner's essay.

Pre-Class Activities

⇒ *Teacher Notes*

It is important that students are able to identify bias in what they read and also in their own writing. Identifying bias and the words that demonstrate it could also be useful in their peer-review activities. The following passage is on a worksheet that you can share with your students. Ask the students to read through the passage and then discuss with them the questions that follow.

> Looking at Bias
> The fast fashion industry has rapidly expanded over the past two decades, offering consumers trendy clothing at prices that make shopping highly accessible. Companies have

cleverly capitalised on consumers' desire for affordable styles, producing garments quickly to meet ever-changing trends. Although critics argue that fast fashion fuels wastefulness and environmental degradation, many shoppers understandably prioritise price and convenience over long-term sustainability.

Workers in developing nations are often willing to accept low wages in exchange for steady employment opportunities offered by fast fashion production. Without these jobs, many individuals might face even harsher economic conditions. It is widely acknowledged that factory work can involve long hours and difficult conditions; however, the alternatives available to these workers are frequently worse. Therefore, some experts suggest that fast fashion manufacturing, while imperfect, plays a necessary role in the global economy.

From a consumer standpoint, affordable clothing options have democratised fashion, allowing people from all backgrounds to express themselves stylishly. While critics of fast fashion tend to focus narrowly on its negative externalities, they sometimes overlook the significant social benefits it provides to lower-income groups. In an ideal world, all clothing would be sustainably produced and ethically sourced, but such standards remain unrealistic for most consumers given current economic constraints.

What is the bias in the passage? THE PASSAGE IS BIASED IN FAVOUR OF FAST FASHION.

Whose interests does the writer appear to be promoting? THE WRITER APPEARS TO BE PROMOTING THOSE BUSINESSES RESPONSIBLE FOR MANUFACTURING AND SELLING FAST FASHION.

Look for phrases in the passage that show this bias.

- "cleverly capitalised" – THIS IMPLIES THAT MAKING MONEY OUT OF CONSUMER GREED IS PRAISEWORTHY.
- "understandably prioritise price" – THIS IS A SYMPATHETIC WAY OF LOOKING AT CONSUMER MOTIVES.

- ♦ "willing to accept" – MAKES IT SOUND AS IF WORKERS ARE HAPPY ABOUT LOW WAGES.
- ♦ "It is widely acknowledged" – THIS IS A CLAIM THAT HAS NO EVIDENCE. IF IT IS WIDELY ACKNOWLEDGED THERE SHOULD BE EVIDENCE.
- ♦ "alternatives ... frequently worse" – NO EXPLANATION IS OFFERED AS TO THESE ALTERNATIVES – NO EVIDENCE IS PROVIDED. HOW DO WE KNOW THEY ARE WORSE?
- ♦ "democratised fashion" – DEMOCRATISED COMES FROM THE WORD DEMOCRACY, WHICH IS USUALLY FAVOURABLY REGARDED. BY USING THIS WORD, THE WRITER IS TRYING TO MAKE FAST FASHION SOUND LIKE A GOOD THING.
- ♦ "critics ... tend to focus narrowly" – THIS IS AN ATTEMPT TO UNDERMINE PEOPLE WHO DO NOT AGREE WITH THE WRITER'S OPINION. ACCORDING TO THE WRITER, THEY ARE "NARROW" – A WORD THAT HAS NEGATIVE OVERTONES.
- ♦ "ideal world ... unrealistic" – THIS GIVES THE IMPRESSION THAT IT IS SILLY TO WORRY ABOUT THE BAD SIDE OF FAST FASHION. IT IS SIMPLY IMPRACTICAL TO DO SO.

During Class
Exercise 1

⇒ *Teacher Notes*

If students are to realise the benefits of peer review it is a good idea to allow them to practise the process in class and develop ways of offering constructive criticism. One important issue is the focus of the students' attention. Sometimes people differentiate between editing and proofreading. The former can be seen to concentrate more on the bigger picture:

- ♦ The logic of the argument – no contradictions in what is said.
- ♦ Whether it holds together.
- ♦ The structure of the essay.
- ♦ How easy it is to read and understand.
- ♦ The flow of the writing e.g. linking.

- Evidence-based writing.
- If literature is cited, it supports the argument.

Proofreading is seen as concentrating more on grammatical errors such as noun–verb agreement, spelling, punctuation etc. We do not want to give students the idea that proofreading is not important. It is important. It is unlikely that poor spelling will mean that the article is unintelligible, but it makes a very bad impression.

In this lesson a form has been developed to help students give feedback. In the first exercise the students will discuss the form.

An important point to stress to students is that feedback is most effective when it forms part of a dialogue. In other words, the ideal situation is when the reviewer and the writer can discuss the feedback. This enables the writer to clarify points that might have been unclear to the reviewer and allows the reviewer to explain why they have suggested changes. These dialogues can lead to far more coherent and interesting texts.

Exercise 1

In this lesson you will work in the pairs selected in Lesson 2.

Read through the feedback form together and then answer the following questions.

1.1 How many sections is the form divided into? FOUR.

1.2 Explain in your own words what each of these sections cover.

THIS STRUCTURE IS THE PLAN OF THE ESSAY. IN THIS SECTION THE REVIEWER WILL BE CHECKING TO SEE THAT THE ESSAY IS LAID OUT CLEARLY AND LOGICALLY. THE REVIEWER WILL LOOK AT THE LINKING STRATEGIES EMPLOYED. THEY WILL CHECK THAT THE POINTS RAISED HAVE BEEN DISCUSSED AND NOT JUST MENTIONED. THE REVIEWER WILL WANT TO SEE THAT THE INTRODUCTION AND CONCLUSION DO WHAT IS REQUIRED OF THESE SECTIONS OF THE ESSAY.

THE CONTEXT COVERS THE SUBJECT MATTER CONTENT OF THE ESSAY. THE REVIEWER WILL CHECK THAT THE POINTS RAISED HAVE BEEN PROPERLY EXPLAINED AND, WHERE APPROPRIATE, EXAMPLES HAVE BEEN GIVEN. IMPORTANTLY THE REVIEWER WILL

CHECK TO SEE THAT THE POINTS ARE SUPPORTED BY EVIDENCE AND THAT THIS EVIDENCE IS CREDIBLE. FINALLY, THE REVIEWER WILL LOOK FOR BALANCE IN THE ESSAY – HAVE BOTH SIDES OF THE MATTER UNDER DISCUSSION BEEN PRESENTED?

USE OF LANGUAGE IS A MORE TECHNICAL SECTION. THE REVIEWER WILL WANT TO MAKE CERTAIN THAT THE GRAMMAR IS ACCURATE AND THE ESSAY IS EASY TO READ. THE LANGUAGE NEEDS TO BE SUFFICIENTLY FORMAL, AND SPELLING AND PUNCTUATION MUST BE ACCURATE.

REFERENCING IS THE MOST TECHNICAL OF THE SECTIONS. THE REVIEWER MUST BE SATISFIED THAT THE REFERENCING AND INTEXT CITATION RULES HAVE BEEN PROPERLY APPLIED.

1.3 Which one/s do you think will be the easiest to review? Why?

REFERENCING WILL BE THE EASIEST TO REVIEW AS IT IS SIMPLY CHECKING THAT THE RULES HAVE BEEN FOLLOWED CORRECTLY. USE OF LANGUAGE IS PROBABLY THE NEXT AS IT INVOLVES CHECKING THAT THE RULES OF GRAMMAR HAVE BEEN APPLIED. HOWEVER, WORK AROUND FORMAL AND INFORMAL LANGUAGE AND SENTENCE STRUCTURE WILL BE MORE DEMANDING.

1.4 Which ones might be more difficult? Why?

STRUCTURE AND CONTEXT ARE MORE DEMANDING AS THE REVIEWER WILL NEED TO MAKE A NUMBER OF JUDGEMENT CALLS ABOUT THE LOGIC OF THE TEXT AND HOW WELL IT HANGS TOGETHER. THEY WILL ALSO NEED TO EXAMINE THE EVIDENCE PROVIDED AND DECIDE WHETHER IT IS CREDIBLE. THE EXAMPLES GIVEN MUST BE CONSIDERED TO SEE WHETHER THEY DO ILLUSTRATE THE POINTS MADE.

1.5 At this stage, are there any changes you would like to make? If so, what are those changes?

PEER FEEDBACK

Structure

Does the introduction state clearly what the essay will cover?

Is the essay set out in a logical way?

Does it follow the plan set out in the introduction?

Are the different sections linked?

(Continued)

PEER FEEDBACK

Does the body of the essay cover all the points raised?

Does it discuss these points?

Does the conclusion summarise the main points raised?

Does it indicate a direction that could be taken in response to the ideas raised?

Context

Are the points raised in the essay well-explained?

Are the points raised evidence-based?

Is this evidence credible?

Are examples provided?

Are these examples good illustrations of the points raised?

Does the author present a balanced picture?

Are possible solutions/new ideas raised?

Use of language

Is the vocabulary appropriate (sufficiently formal/no slang)?

Noun–verb agreement

Is it easy to read?

Are the sentences well structured? (not too long and rambling?)

Are appropriate linking words used?

Is the appropriate punctuation used?

Is spelling accurate?

Referencing

Are intext citations accurate?

If quotes are used, are they correctly inserted in the sentences?

Is the reference list set out alphabetically?

Are the references written up correctly according to the chosen referencing system?

Exercise 2

⇒ *Teacher Notes*

In Exercise 2 students will read through the essay in their pairs. When they have finished, ask them to complete the feedback form. Tell them that while they are filling in the form they should also be looking at the form itself and deciding how useful they think it is as a tool. When they have finished, go through the essay with the class and discuss changes suggested by the students.

Exercise 2

Read the essay below and then fill in the feedback form. Try to make your comments as constructive as possible and remember to be polite!

READING: ENVIRONMENTAL CONCERNS AND FAST FASHION – A YOUNG PERSON'S PERSPECTIVE

Humans are abusing the environment. Extreme weather conditions which are becoming more frequently have been linked to the damage humans has done to the environment (IPCC, 2021). One of the industries that has an awful effect on the environment is the fast fashion industry (Cairns et al., 2022). As a young person who is fashion conscious, I find these issues very troubling. I believe that fast fashion consumers need to face up to the damage caused by the industry and change their buying habits accordingly. In this essay I will discuss the issues.

People shouldn't be paid lousy wages or made to work in horrible broken-down old factories. It's bad that making fast fashion garments leads to a lot of waste. 92 million tons of waste is generated by the industry (Cairns et al., 2022). And it uses lots of water.

My friends and I like to wear the same kind of clothes because I need to be able to match their wardrobes. When I fit in with my friends, I feel great. If I didn't have the same clothes as they do it would be difficult for me to feel comfortable when I went out with them. I don't like to be seen with people who don't dress fashionably. When I look in the mirror and see a fashionable person I stop stressing about my looks and I believe that I can achieve anything I want.

I enjoy shopping for clothes but I don't have loads of cash, so I need to buy cheap items. Not having tons of clothes would make me unhappy so I would pester my parents for more money. This would cause friction between us as they are not wealthy. That would mean that I would have to work at a number of part time jobs to get the money I need. My studies would go downhill fast. Some people buy second hand clothing. I can see that this would lead to less waste but I find the idea gross.

I believe young people should buy what they want. I am going to buy stuff from vintage shops. I am sure scientists will find a solution to all the environmental problems we are facing.

REFERENCES

Cairns, H.M., Ritch, E., & Bereziat, C. (2021). Think eco, be eco? The tension between attitudes and behaviours of millennial fashion consumers. *International Journal of Consumer Studies, 46*, 1262–1277. https://doi.org/10.1111/ijcs.12756

Cairns, H.M., Ritch, E., & Bereziat, C. (2022). Think eco, be eco? The tension between attitudes and behaviours of millennial fashion consumers. *International Journal of Consumer Studies, 46*, 1262–1277. https://doi.org/10.1111/ijcs.12756

IPCC. (2021). *Climate Change 2021: The Physical Science Basis. Contribution of Working Group I to the Sixth Assessment Report of the Intergovernmental Panel on Climate Change.* Cambridge University Press https://doi.org/10.1017/9781009157896

POSSIBLE ANSWER

Humans are abusing the environment. THERE IS NO PROPER INTRODUCTION – WHAT IS THE ESSAY ABOUT? Extreme weather conditions which are becoming more *frequently* FREQUENT have been linked to the damage humans *has* NOUN–VERB AGREEMENT INCORRECT USE HAVE done to the environment (IPCC, 2021). One of the industries that has an awful COLLOQUIAL LANGUAGE – BETTER TO USE DETRIMENTAL/NEGATIVE effect on the environment is the fast fashion industry (Cairns et al., 2021). As a young person who is fashion conscious, I find these issues very troubling. I believe that fast fashion consumers need to face up to COLLOQUIAL LANGUAGE BETTER TO USE ACKNOWLEDGE the damage caused by the industry and change their buying habits accordingly. In this essay I will discuss issues THIS IS TOO VAGUE – WHAT ISSUES WILL BE DISCUSSED AND HOW WILL THEY BE DISCUSSED?

WHERE IS THE LINK BETWEEN THE PARAGRAPHS?

People shouldn't be paid *lousy* COLLOQUIAL LANGUAGE – BETTER TO USE POOR/INADEQUATE wages or made to work in *horrible broken down old* COLLOQUIAL LANGUAGE – BETTER TO USE DERELICT/RUN DOWN factories. *It's* NO ABBREVIATIONS IT IS *bad* COLLOQUIAL LANGUAGE – BETTER TO USE CONCERNING/ALARMING that making fast fashion garments leads to a great deal of waste. 92 million tons of waste is generated by the industry (Cairns et al., 2021). and it uses *lots of* COLLOQUIAL LANGUAGE – BETTER TO USE LARGE AMOUNTS /COPIOUS QUANTITIES water.

WHERE IS THE LINK BETWEEN THE PARAGRAPHS?

My friends and I like to wear the same kind of clothes, *because* INCORRECT LINKING WORD BETTER TO USE THEREFORE/SO I need to be able to match their wardrobes. When I fit in with my friends, I feel *great* COLLOQUIAL LANGUAGE – BETTER TO USE CONFIDENT/HAPPY. If I *didn't* NO ABBREVIATIONS DID NOT have the same clothes as they do it would be difficult for me to feel comfortable when I go out with them. I *don't* NO ABBREVIATIONS DO NOT like to be seen with people who *don't* NO ABBREVIATIONS DO NOT dress fashionably. When I look in the mirror and see a fashionable person I stop *stressing* COLLOQUIAL LANGUAGE – BETTER TO USE WORRYING about my *looks* COLLOQUIAL LANGUAGE – BETTER TO USE APPEARANCE and I believe that I can achieve anything I want.

I enjoy shopping for clothes but I *don't* NO ABBREVIATIONS DO NOT have *loads of cash* COLLOQUIAL LANGUAGE – BETTER TO USE A GREAT DEAL OF MONEY so I need to buy *cheap* COLLOQUIAL LANGUAGE – BETTER TO USE INEXPENSIVE items. Not having *tons of* clothes COLLOQUIAL LANGUAGE – BETTER TO USE A LARGE NUMBER would make me unhappy so I would *pester* COLLOQUIAL LANGUAGE – BETTER TO USE ANNOY MY PARENTS BY ASKING FOR my parents for more money. This would cause friction between us as they are not wealthy. That would mean that I would have to work at a number of part time jobs to get the money I need. My studies would *go downhill fast* COLLOQUIAL LANGUAGE – BETTER TO USE SUFFER AS A RESULT. Some people buy second hand clothing. I can see that this would lead to less waste but I find the idea *gross* COLLOQUIAL LANGUAGE – BETTER TO USE UNACCEPTABLE.

WHERE IS THE LINK BETWEEN THE PARAGRAPHS?

I believe young people should buy what they want. I am going to buy *stuff* COLLOQUIAL LANGUAGE – BETTER TO USE CLOTHES from vintage shops. THIS IS A CONTRADICTION. THE WRITER SAID IN THE PARAGRAPH ABOVE THAT THEY DO NOT WANT TO BUY SECOND HAND CLOTHES. I am sure scientists will find a solution to all the environmental problems we are facing. THIS IS NOT A PROPER CONCLUSION – THE MAIN POINTS HAVE NOT BEEN SUMMARISED AND THE SUGGESTION FOR FURTHER ACTION IS VERY LIGHTWEIGHT.

Exercise 3

⇒ *Teacher Notes*

When you and the students have finished reviewing the essay, ask them in their pairs to think about the feedback form and answer the questions provided. Then bring the class together to discuss the responses. This will give them an opportunity to hear what others feel with regard to the usefulness of the form. Then allow them time to make changes on the form that both partners agree on.

Exercise 3
You have now used the feedback form to critique an essay:

- Do you think it is fit for purpose?
- Do you find it easy to use?
- If not, what changes would you like to see?
- What difference do you think these changes will make?
- Do you think it is a good way of giving feedback to writers?
- Could it be improved?
- If so, what changes would you like to see?
- What difference do you think these changes will make?

Exercise 4

⇒ *Teacher Notes*

In Lesson 3, Exercise 3, students were asked to write a short essay about the advantages and disadvantages of peer feedback. They can now exchange essays and provide feedback using the guidelines outlined above. Ask them to bring the completed feedback to the next lesson.

Exercise 4
Use the guidelines that you and your partner have agreed on to provide feedback to each other on the essay *The advantages and disadvantages of peer feedback*. Keep the feedback to discuss in the next lesson.

Post-Class Activities
Ask students to return to the pre-class activity on bias. Bearing the class discussion in mind, ask students to rewrite the passage so that the bias is removed. Here is a possible answer.

> THE FAST FASHION INDUSTRY HAS EXPANDED SIGNIFICANTLY OVER THE PAST TWO DECADES, OFFERING CONSUMERS ACCESS TO INEXPENSIVE, TREND-DRIVEN CLOTHING. COMPANIES HAVE RESPONDED TO CONSUMER DEMAND FOR AFFORDABLE STYLES BY PRODUCING

GARMENTS RAPIDLY TO ALIGN WITH EVOLVING FASHION TRENDS. SOME SCHOLARS ARGUE THAT FAST FASHION CONTRIBUTES TO INCREASED TEXTILE WASTE AND ENVIRONMENTAL DEGRADATION, WHILE OTHERS NOTE THAT PRICE AND CONVENIENCE REMAIN IMPORTANT FACTORS FOR MANY CONSUMERS.

IN TERMS OF LABOR PRACTICES, FAST FASHION PRODUCTION PROVIDES EMPLOYMENT OPPORTUNITIES IN DEVELOPING NATIONS, OFTEN AT RELATIVELY LOW WAGE LEVELS. WHILE FACTORY WORK IN THESE CONTEXTS IS ASSOCIATED WITH LONG HOURS AND CHALLENGING CONDITIONS, PROPONENTS ARGUE THAT SUCH EMPLOYMENT CAN OFFER FINANCIAL STABILITY COMPARED TO OTHER AVAILABLE OPTIONS. HOWEVER, CONCERNS REMAIN REGARDING THE LONG-TERM EFFECTS OF SUCH WORKING CONDITIONS ON EMPLOYEE WELL-BEING AND REGIONAL ECONOMIES.

FROM A CONSUMER PERSPECTIVE, THE AVAILABILITY OF LOW-COST CLOTHING HAS EXPANDED ACCESS TO A WIDER RANGE OF FASHION CHOICES ACROSS DIFFERENT SOCIO-ECONOMIC GROUPS. ALTHOUGH CRITICS HIGHLIGHT THE ENVIRONMENTAL AND ETHICAL IMPLICATIONS OF FAST FASHION, SOME RESEARCHERS SUGGEST THAT AFFORDABLE CLOTHING OPTIONS HAVE PLAYED A ROLE IN INCREASING OPPORTUNITIES FOR SELF-EXPRESSION AMONG DIVERSE POPULATIONS. ACHIEVING WIDESPREAD SUSTAINABLE AND ETHICAL PRODUCTION PRACTICES REMAINS A SIGNIFICANT CHALLENGE GIVEN CURRENT PRODUCTION COSTS AND GLOBAL ECONOMIC CONDITIONS.

Lesson 5: Evidence-Based Writing

Time: 2 hours

Overview

In this lesson, students will discuss and respond to the reviews of their peers. They will describe why they have chosen or not chosen to implement suggested changes. Using the guidelines provided, students will work through an academic article to find evidence for an essay. They will use the data they have collected thus far in the cycle to plan an essay.

Purpose and Strategies

Purpose	Strategies
Dialogue between writers and reviewers	Students will use the reviews they wrote in the last lesson for the dialogue.
Implementing/not implementing reviewer's suggestions	After a discussion, students will decide whether or not to implement the suggestions. They will be required to provide reasons.
Evidence-based writing	Using guidelines, students will work through an academic article to find data for an essay.
Planning an essay	Students will use the data collected in this cycle to develop an essay.

Pre-Class Activities

Students have done a fair amount of work around peer review so it is probably a good idea to think about the importance of peer review in the academic world. Ask them to complete the following short quiz.

1. How does peer review contribute to the credibility of academic research?
    A. It allows friends to give advice on the paper's topic.
    B. It reduces the number of people who can access the research.
    C. IT ENSURES THAT RESEARCH IS EXAMINED BY QUALIFIED SCHOLARS BEFORE PUBLICATION.
    D. It guarantees the author receives a high grade.

2. Which of the following best describes a *limitation* of peer review?
   A. Reviewers are always biased and unqualified.
   B. THE PROCESS CAN BE SLOW AND SOMETIMES INCONSISTENT.
   C. It replaces the need for any future research.
   D. All papers automatically pass peer review with no changes.
3. Why might a peer-reviewed article be considered more reliable than a blog post on the same topic?
   A. It is written in longer sentences.
   B. It contains personal opinions and informal language.
   C. IT HAS UNDERGONE CRITICAL EVALUATION BY EXPERTS IN THE FIELD.
   D. It is easier to understand for the general public.
4. Which of the following is a recognised ethical concern in the peer review process?
   A. REVIEWERS MAY ACT UNFAIRLY DUE TO PERSONAL OR PROFESSIONAL CONFLICTS.
   B. Peer reviewers are allowed to publish the paper if they like it.
   C. Reviewers are paid by authors for good feedback.
   D. Reviewers must always agree with the author's conclusions.
5. What is one of the responsibilities of a peer reviewer?
   A. To promote the author's university.
   B. To fix all grammar and spelling mistakes.
   C. TO EVALUATE THE CONTENT, METHODS, AND LOGIC OF THE RESEARCH.
   D. To accept all papers that seem interesting.

During Class
Exercise 1

⇒ *Teacher Notes*

Students will bring to class the essay that they wrote in Lesson 4 and the review they wrote of their partner's essay. Research (Zhu & Carless, 2018) indicates that when receivers of peer feedback were asked to write down what they thought of the feedback, this exercise actually improved their writing. What is particularly important about this is the feedback on the reviews appears to lead to a productive dialogue between reviewer and writer. Zhu and Carless (2018) observed and interviewed students at a university in South China who were using dialogue in the peer-review process. One student remarked:

> Face-to-face communication allows the interaction between receiver and reviewer. Problems and related suggestions are explained promptly. Sometimes when receiving written feedback, we feel puzzled or may not agree with the reviewer. Through face-to-face oral response we can convey our confusion and reviewers can provide rationales for the feedback while receivers can explain their writing intention.
>
> (p. 890)

Another important point made in Zhu and Carless's research was that teacher guidance is essential if students are to successfully comment on complex features like content and structure. They argue that teachers need to provide feedback on student reviews.

In this exercise allow students time to read the feedback each has written. Then ask each to draw up a short written response. This response could include:

- Requests for clarification of points raised by reviewer.
- Explanations of concerns raised by reviewer.
- Acknowledgement of comments of reviewer.
- Requests for help from reviewer.

The students will then use these written responses to inform a dialogue about the essays each wrote. Approaching student reviews in this way seems to be a good strategy to ensure that students gain maximum benefit from the peer-review system. While students are working in pairs, it would be a good idea to move around the classroom and offer your assistance if students appear to need it. This might be where the students have different opinions about an issue raised and need you to provide advice. Once the students have been given sufficient time to discuss the essays and suggested corrections, ask students to indicate briefly which suggestions they intend to adopt and which they will not use. Ask them to provide brief answers for their decisions.

Although this is a rather cumbersome marking exercise it will be beneficial for the students. For each student you will need to read the original essay, the review of that essay and the writer's response to the review. So you will read Student A's essay, Student B's review of the essay and Student A's response to the review. In total, you will mark three pieces of work from each student. This will not only give them insight into their essay writing but also provide guidance on their reviewing ability and how to best respond to a review.

Reference

Zhu, Q., & Carless, D. (2018) Dialogue within peer feedback processes: clarification and negotiation of meaning. *Higher Education Research & Development*, 37(4), 883–897. https://doi.org/10.1080/07294360.2018.1446417

Exercise 1
Exchange your peer review with your partner and read through the comments you have received. Then write a brief response to the comments. This response could include:

- ♦ Requests for clarification of points raised by reviewer.
- ♦ Explanations of concerns raised by reviewer.
- ♦ Acknowledgement of comments of reviewer.
- ♦ Requests for help from reviewer.

Once you have done this you and your partner should discuss the respective reviews. See if you can reach agreement about the points of difference. If you have difficulties agreeing, ask your teacher for assistance. Once you have finished your discussion complete the following form. Examples (in italics) have been inserted to show you what is required.

Student comments on feedback

Questions	Examples of replies
List the comments you have accepted and the changes you will make to your essay as a result of the feedback.	The introduction does not give enough information as to how the essay will be structured. Changes: In this essay I will explore the advantages and disadvantages of peer feedback. Then these advantages and disadvantages will be evaluated. Finally I will suggest how the peer review system could be implemented successfully in the academic writing classroom.
List the changes you will NOT make to your essay.	According to the reviewer the sentence "I am not confident about my writing ability and I am not happy to share my writing with other students" should be rewritten "I lack self-confidence and therefore am reluctant to share my writing with my peers".
Why have you rejected this feedback?	I do not agree with this. My lack of confidence is only about my writing, and I do not see why I cannot say other students. Why should I use "peers"?
Will some of the feedback be useful for you in the rest of your writing? Give details if this is the case.	I realise that my introductions have not provided sufficient information for the reader.

Exercise 2

⇒ *Teacher Notes*

A really important skill that students need to develop is providing evidence for their assertions. In this exercise students will be guided through an academic article that they can use as evidence for their own essays which they will be writing later. These essays will explore the pros and cons of the fast fashion industry. This article is in the public domain.

> Williams, E. (2022). Appalling or advantageous? Exploring the impacts of fast fashion from environmental, social, and economic perspectives. *Journal for Global Business and Community, 13*(1). https://doi.org/10.56020/001c.36873

This article spells out clearly the advantages and disadvantages of the fast fashion industry but it differs from the other texts students have read by presenting a far more balanced picture of the industry. Below is a guideline to help find the information from the article that the students will need to complete an essay they will be writing. Part of the data has been filled in (in places where the students might struggle with the language) but most of the information gathering has been left to the students. This exercise can be handled in a number of ways. If the pairs are working well they could tackle the exercise together. However, if you believe a change in pace is advisable it can be completed as a whole-class exercise, or in groups, or individually. You might want to employ more than one approach. For example, start it off as a whole-class exercise and then ask students to complete the exercise in groups, pairs or individually.

Exercise 2

Filling in this table should help you with the writing of your essay. However, before you start filling in this table you should read through the entire article. The final column indicates whether the data cited can be seen as an advantage (**AD**) or a disadvantage (**DIS**).

Introduction	Provides a definition of fast fashion. (This should be paraphrased.)	
Findings Environmental impacts	There are no environmental benefits associated with the fast fashion industry.	
1. Clothing waste	Great deal of clothing goes to landfill.	**DIS**
	CLOTHING CAN REMAIN IN LANDFILL FOR OVER 200 YEARS.	
	CHEMICALS AND DYES CAN POISON THE GROUND.	
	EVEN RESELLING/DONATION OF CLOTHING DOESN'T SOLVE PROBLEM.	
2. Water use and pollution	Uses a great deal of water	**DIS**
	INDUSTRY USES AS MUCH WATER IN ONE YEAR AS 5 MILLION PEOPLE NEED.	
3. Plastic in the ocean	APPROX 60% OF MATERIAL MADE INTO CLOTHING IS PLASTIC. Manufacture and washing of clothes means that plastic makes its way into the oceans.	**DIS**
4. Carbon emissions	Manufacture of fast fashion results in the emission of between 2% and 8% of the global total.	**DIS**

(Continued)

Social impacts	There are a number of negative aspects about the fast fashion industry.	
1. Poor working conditions	DANGEROUS FACTORIES, EXPOSURE TO HAZARDOUS CHEMICALS, FIRES.	DIS
2. Child labour	OFTEN FORCED TO WORK IN POOR CONDITIONS. BADLY PAID. NOT PROVIDED WITH PROPER EDUCATION.	DIS
3. Feminisation of the workforce	Women paid less than men. Lack of rights such as bathroom breaks. Incidents of sexual harassment. Discriminated against when they are pregnant	DIS
Consumer impacts	How does this affect consumers?	
Mitigated classism	PEOPLE IN ALL SOCIAL CLASSES CAN NOW WEAR THE SAME FAST FASHION CLOTHES. THIS HELPS TO STOP DISCRIMINATION	AD
Economic impacts		
1. Growing industry	HELPS DEVELOPING COUNTRIES WHEN BUSINESSES OPERATE THERE – LEADS TO ECONOMIC GROWTH DEVELOP.	AD
2. More for less	IN DEVELOPED COUNTRIES BUYERS GET MORE CLOTHING FOR LESS MONEY.	AD
3. DEVELOPED COUNTRY ECONOMY	Manufacturing moved to developing countries – people lost jobs. Meant developed countries lost revenue.	DIS
4. DEVELOPING COUNTRY ECONOMY	OUTSOURCING CLOTHING MANUFACTURE WAS A BOON FOR THE ECONOMY OF DEVELOPING COUNTRIES. HELPED IN SOME CASES TO BRING MORE PEOPLE OUT OF POVERTY	AD
5. WAGES AND QUALITY OF LIFE	Because the wages paid are so low, in many ways the money does not provide a better way of life for workers in developing countries.	DIS
Conclusion	Summary of main points. What are they?	
	Environmentally, there are no advantages from the fast fashion industry	
	SOCIAL FACTORS POSITIVE AND NEGATIVE – POSITIVE FOR CONSUMERS BUT LARGELY NEGATIVE FOR WORKERS	
	ECONOMIC FACTORS – JOB LOSSES IN DEVELOPED COUNTRIES.	
	ECONOMIC DEVELOPMENT IN DEVELOPING COUNTRIES.	
	FAST FASHION MUST TAKE STEPS TO CONTROL ENVIRONMENTAL DAMAGE AND IMPROVE WORKING CONDITIONS. IT COULD THEN BE A POSITIVE FORCE.	
	Indicate the way forward.	

Exercise 3

⇒ *Teacher Notes*

Students will bring together all the data they have gathered during the course of Cycle 4. They will use this data to draw up a plan for an essay entitled:

Fast Fashion in the 21st Century – A Personal Dilemma?

Students have a great deal of information on which to draw for this exercise. Ask them to draw up a detailed plan for a 1500-word essay. At this stage you might want to leave students to design their own essay plan, but if you believe they require help here is a brief outline. The students will need to flesh this out.

Introduction	What essay will discuss and how e.g. exploration of why buying fast fashion is a moral dilemma and how this dilemma will be explored.
Body	What is fast fashion?
	Advantages and disadvantages of the industry in the global setting (environmental/social/economic).
	Personal dilemma.
	Discussion of how these factors interact and their effect on student's buying habits.
Conclusion	Summary of points raised and indications of further action both from industry and personal perspective.

Exercise 3

In this exercise you will bring together all the data you have gathered during Cycle 4 to plan an essay entitled:

Fast Fashion in the 21st Century – A Personal Dilemma?

- ♦ In Lesson 1 the environmental concerns in the fast fashion industry were discussed and you recorded your thoughts about what influences your fashion buying choices.
- ♦ In Lesson 2 you discussed your own attitude towards the industry and how many people are conflicted about their fashion choices.

♦ In Lesson 5 you discussed an academic article that reviewed the advantages and the disadvantages of the fast fashion industry.

Use this information to draw up a detailed plan for your 1500-word essay.

Post-Class Activities

⇒ *Teacher Notes*

Listed below are three articles discussing fast fashion. If students wish to do so, they could read the material contained in any or all of these articles and use it to expand their essays.

> Collective Fashion Justice. (n.d.). *Unsustainable consumption of fashion* https://www.collectivefashionjustice.org/mass-consumerism.
> Crumbie, A. (April 9, 2024). *What is Fast Fashion and Why is It a Problem?* Ethical Consumer. https://www.ethicalconsumer.org/fashion-clothing/what-fast-fashion-why-it-problem
> Lin, A. (August 5, 2022). *Driven to Shop: The Psychology of Fast Fashion.* Artists for the Earth. https://www.earthday.org/driven-to-shop-the-psychology-of-fast-fashion/

Lesson 6: Bringing it all Together

Time: 2 hours

Overview
In this lesson, students will write a 1500-word essay using the data they have gathered in this cycle. They will draw on feedback provided on their writing, as well as instruction on the appropriate use of language, the structuring of an essay and the provision of evidence to back up claims. In addition, they will be required to draw on their knowledge of referencing and in-text citations.

Purpose and Strategies

Purpose	Strategies
Synthesising data	Students will use the data collected during the cycle for their essay.
Putting feedback into practice.	Students will make use of the feedback provided by their partners on earlier essay writing attempts.
Accurate in-text citations and reference list	Students will draw on referencing and citation work done in the earlier cycles.

Exercise 1

⇒ *Teacher Notes*

In this lesson students will write a 1500-word essay on the topic:

Fast Fashion in the 21st Century – a Personal Dilemma?

They will have all the material they gathered in Lessons 1, 2 and 5. This essay should be marked in full. There are many good marking rubrics available, but one approach would be to adapt the peer-review form. A version of this can be seen below. Students should always write with the marking rubric in mind. Using a form with which they are already familiar will make it easier for students at this early stage of their writing careers. It would be a good idea to give students a copy of the rubric.

	FA	A	PA	NA	COMMENTS

STRUCTURE

The introduction states clearly what the essay will cover.

The essay is set out in a logical way.

The essay follows the plan set out in the introduction.

The different sections are linked.

The body of the essay covers all the points raised.

The body of the essay discusses these points.

Possible solutions/new ideas are raised.

The conclusion summarises the main points of the essay.

The conclusion indicates a direction that could be taken in response to the ideas raised.

CONTEXT

The points raised in the essay are well explained.

The points are backed up by evidence.

The evidence is credible.

Examples are provided.

The examples are good illustrations of the points raised.

USE OF LANGUAGE

The vocabulary is appropriate.

There is accurate use of grammar.

The sentences are well structured.

The essay is easy to read.

Spelling and punctuation are correct.

REFERENCING

In-text citations are correctly used.

Quotes are correctly inserted into sentences.

The Reference list is set out according to the rules of the chosen referencing system.

Note: FA = Fully achieved, A = Achieved, PA = Partly achieved, NA = Not achieved.

Exercise 1

Write a 1500-word essay on the topic:

Fast Fashion in the 21st Century – a Personal Dilemma?

In this essay you will explore the drawbacks and benefits of the fast fashion industry in today's world. Discuss the moral dilemmas that consumers face and then explore your own attitude towards the industry. Conclude your essay by summarising the main points and indicating possible solutions for the issues you have raised. Make sure your intext citations are accurate, and that if you have chosen to use direct quotes you have done so correctly. Make sure your reference list adheres to the rules of the particular system you are using.

Cycle 5

Artificial Intelligence (AI)

Lesson 1: The Benefits and Challenges of AI

Time: 2 hours

Overview

This lesson sets the tone for the rest of the cycle where the focus is on Artificial Intelligence (AI). Taking notes from videos and summarising skills are revised. Students are also required to look at other aspects of direct quotes, and practise paraphrasing more difficult passages.

Purpose and Strategies

Purpose	Strategies
Taking notes	Students are required to take notes from two videos discussing AI.
Comparing and contrasting data	Notes taken from two videos on AI. Students required to amalgamate information given in a summary.
Direct quotes (continuation of Cycle 2 Lesson 3)	Fitting direct quotes grammatically into a sentence.
Paraphrasing	Capturing the idea presented in a text in students' own words.

Pre-Class Activities

⇒ *Teacher Notes*

Here is a short quiz that you could give to the students to test their knowledge of Artificial Intelligence (AI). It was designed with AI help (OpenAI, 2025)! A worksheet for this activity has been provided.

1. Which of the following best defines Artificial Intelligence (AI)?

The study of how computers can be used to replace human workers	THE DEVELOPMENT OF COMPUTER SYSTEMS THAT CAN PERFORM TASKS REQUIRING HUMAN INTELLIGENCE	The process of automating mechanical tasks in factories	The use of advanced hardware to make computers faster

2. Which of these is an example of AI that improves over time through learning?

A SEARCH ENGINE THAT PROVIDES RESULTS BASED ON PREVIOUS SEARCHES	A basic calculator performing arithmetic operations	A car's windshield wiper system detecting rain	A GPS device showing static maps

3. What is Machine Learning?

A way of manually programming every machine action	A method where machines are physically trained by humans	A storage system for large amounts of data	A PROCESS WHERE MACHINES LEARN FROM DATA AND IMPROVE THEIR PERFORMANCE

4. Which of the following best demonstrates AI using pattern recognition to make predictions?

A VOICE ASSISTANT RECOGNISING DIFFERENT ACCENTS OVER TIME AND IMPROVING RESPONSES	A light sensor automatically adjusting brightness in a room	A vending machine dispensing the correct item when a button is pressed	A stopwatch measuring elapsed time accurately

5. Which of the following best describes Deep Learning?

A method of manually instructing machines step by step	A way to design faster computers	A TYPE OF AI THAT RELIES ON LARGE DATASETS AND NEURAL NETWORKS	A simple programming technique

6. What is the purpose of Natural Language Processing (NLP)?

To create new programming languages	TO HELP COMPUTERS UNDERSTAND AND PROCESS HUMAN LANGUAGE	To improve battery life in devices	To make graphics more realistic

7. How does AI typically play chess at a high level?

By memorising every possible move in advance	BY USING ALGORITHMS TO EVALUATE POSITIONS AND CALCULATE THE BEST MOVES	By copying the moves of human grandmasters exactly	By randomly selecting moves and hoping for the best

8. What is the main difference between weak AI and strong AI?

Weak AI is for entertainment, strong AI is for business	Weak AI is outdated, strong AI is modern	Weak AI is based on robotics, strong AI is based on software	WEAK AI PERFORMS SPECIFIC TASKS, STRONG AI HAS HUMAN-LIKE INTELLIGENCE

9. Which of the following is a major ethical concern in AI?

AI making smartphones more efficient	AI SYSTEMS REINFORCING SOCIETAL BIASES	AI improving gaming graphics	AI being used in movie special effects

10. What is a potential long-term risk of advanced AI systems?

AI REPLACING HUMAN CREATIVITY ENTIRELY	AI increasing global temperatures	AI requiring too much physical storage space	AI causing computer viruses to spread faster

Once the students have completed the quiz it would be a good idea to have a short discussion about AI. You could focus on their feelings toward the development and role that AI plays in our lives. Here are a few questions you might use:

- How do you feel about the role AI plays in our lives?
- What do you believe are the most important changes AI has made to modern society?
- How do you see AI influencing society in the future?

During Class
Exercise 1

⇒ *Teacher Notes*

In this next exercise students will watch two short videos featuring well-known computer experts. The first *"What's the difference: AI and AGI?"* is 4:37 minutes long and the second *"How will AI change the world?"* is 5:55 minutes long. Students will summarise the material in these videos.

The first features Bernard Marr, a well-known futurist and author. He explains the difference between AI and AGI (Artificial General Intelligence). Marr explains the differences between traditional AI and what it does and then describes the different ways in which AI learns and the results of this learning. Marr ends off by discussing the future, which he claims, will be the domain of AGI.

https://www.youtube.com/watch?v=Q0D37WWpvrs

The second video summarises the views of Professor Stuart Russell, a computer scientist. Russell is talking about how AI will change the world. He looks, in particular, at the differences in the way humans and AI will carry out commands. He explains why, at this point in time, humans still have a great advantage over computers.

https://www.youtube.com/watch?v=RzkD_rTEBYs

Students need to take notes while they are watching the videos. They can work in groups or individually.

Students were introduced to using direct quotes in Cycle 2 Lesson 3. In this exercise students are told how to quote words used in a video and reference them correctly.

Exercise 1

The two video clips you are going to watch feature two well-known computer scientists, Bernard Marr and Professor Stuart Russell. You will summarise the material presented in each video. In order to do this you will need make notes of each speaker's remarks while you are watching, With Marr, focus on the definitions he gives and the explanations of the different types of computer learning he provides. Remember to give a few examples.

https://www.youtube.com/watch?v=Q0D37WWpvrs

Russell looks at some of the challenges scientists encounter when developing AI. He explains some of the difficulties involved in giving instructions to AI. Explain these problems in your own words and provide examples. What do humans have that AI systems do not?

https://www.youtube.com/watch?v=RzkD_rTEBYs

Remember to indicate which scientist you are referring to. The in-text citation is simply Marr (2024) or Russell (2022).

Your summary should be between 300 and 350 words in length.

If you want to use some of the exact words in the video you should make use of a timestamp. The timestamp gives the time in the video when the words were spoken. For example, if you wanted to quote the words, "even if they have to kill everybody off in Starbucks" you would follow this with (Russell, 2022, 0:42) because the quote started 42 seconds into the video. The full references are in the reference list below.

⇒ *Teacher Notes*

Here is a possible answer for this exercise:

> IN HIS TALK MARR EXPLAINS HOW VARIOUS AI SYSTEMS ARE TAUGHT OR HOW THEY TEACH THEMSELVES. TRADITIONAL AI CAN MAKE RECOMMENDATIONS FOR USERS BASED ON PREVIOUS

INTERACTIONS WITH THOSE USERS. IN OTHER WORDS, THEY RELY ON PRIOR LEARNING. AI SYSTEMS SUBJECTED TO SUPERVISED LEARNING CAN COPY HUMAN BEHAVIOUR, WHILE UNSUPERVISED LEARNING ENABLES AI SYSTEMS TO IDENTIFY PATTERNS AND RELATIONSHIPS ON THEIR OWN. AI SYSTEMS EXPOSED TO REINFORCEMENT LEARNING LEARN THROUGH TRIAL AND ERROR. FOR EXAMPLE, SELF-DRIVING CARS ARE EXPOSED TO VARIOUS SIMULATED ENVIRONMENTS AND LEARN FROM THEIR OWN ACTIONS AND EXPERIENCES. GENERATIVE AI SYSTEMS SUCH AS CHATGPT CAN CREATE REALISTIC IMAGES, TEXTS AND VIDEOS. THEY OPERATE BY PREDICTING WHAT THE NEXT WORD OR PIXEL WILL BE, DRAWING ON THE DATA THAT HAS BEEN USED IN THEIR TRAINING. HOWEVER, THESE SYSTEMS DO NOT UNDERSTAND THE CONTENT THAT THEY CREATE. ARTIFICIAL GENERAL INTELLIGENCE OR AGI CAN OPERATE IN THE SAME WAY AS HUMANS. IT IS CAPABLE OF ABSTRACT THOUGHT, CAN PLAN SYSTEMATICALLY AND CAN EVEN EXPERIENCE EMOTIONS. HOWEVER IT STILL LACKS A DEEP UNDERSTANDING OF THE WORLD. AT THIS STAGE AGI DOES NOT EXIST.

IN CONTRAST TO MARR PROFESSOR RUSSELL EXPLORES HOW AI SYSTEMS AND HUMANS DIFFER IN THEIR PERFORMANCE OF A TASK. HUMANS UNDERSTAND THAT THERE ARE NUMEROUS FACTORS THEY NEED TO TAKE INTO ACCOUNT WHEN PERFORMING A TASK. FOR INSTANCE, IF SOMEONE IS ASKED TO BUY A TAKE AWAY COFFEE THEY MIGHT BE RELUCTANT TO DO SO IF THEY FEEL THAT THE PRICE ASKED IS TOO HIGH. AN AI SYSTEM, ON THE OTHER HAND, WILL CARRY OUT THE INSTRUCTION REGARDLESS OF OTHER FACTORS AS THEY ARE UNABLE TO TAKE THESE FACTORS INTO ACCOUNT. HUMANS WILL SEEK FURTHER GUIDANCE IF THEY ARE UNSURE AS TO THE WISDOM OF A CERTAIN ACTION WHILE AI SYSTEMS WILL NOT. THE DIFFERENCE MEANS THAT GREAT CAUTION MUST BE EXERCISED IN INSTRUCTING SUCH SYSTEMS. AGI WOULD BE CAPABLE OF TAKING THESE FACTORS INTO ACCOUNT BUT RUSSELL DOES NOT BELIEVE THAT THE EMERGENCE OF AGI IS IMMINENT. (330 WORDS)

References

Marr, B. (2024). What's the difference: AI and AGI? [Video] YouTube. https://www.youtube.com/watch?v=Q0D37WWpvrs

Russell, S. (December 20, 2022). How will AI change the world? [Video] Ted Conferences https://www.youtube.com/watch?v=RzkD_rTEBYs

Exercise 2

⇒ *Teacher Notes*

This next exercise also talks about direct quotations and expands the work already done on summarising. You might want to remind students of the rules governing direct quotes:

- Direct quotes must be used sparingly.
- They must match the original source in all ways.
- You must be very careful to indicate that you are using a direct quote.
- The quote must fit in the sentence grammatically.
- You must provide sufficient details for the quote to be easily found.

This exercise reminds students of the way in which direct quotes must be identified when there are no page numbers.

Exercise 2

Read the passage below and answer the questions that follow.

Open AI is an artificial intelligence (AI) research laboratory that seeks to develop AI in ways "that will benefit humanity as a whole" (Rudolph et al., 2023, p. 343). The founders of the research laboratory maintain that the focus is on assisting humans rather than replacing them. One of the tools that this laboratory has developed is ChatGPT. The tool is trained using massive amounts of data. This data has allowed the tool to learn language patterns and associations. When the tool is given a command it responds very quickly, "presenting information verbally in human-like text" (Lingard, 2023, p. 262). According to Oates and Johnson (2025), these tools have become very popular in education. The tools can alter their responses to suit the needs of the users. For example, a student who is struggling to understand a difficult concept will be given a detailed explanation, while another who simply wants a summary will be provided with an overview of the concept. Their value therefore "lies in their adaptability and responsiveness" (Oates & Johnson, 2025, Introduction).

However, the introduction of new education technology "often engenders strong emotions, ranging from doomsday predictions to unbridled euphoria" (Rudolph et al., 2023, p. 343). Weissman (2023, Title) for example has called it "a plague upon education". However, many researchers argue that managing "disruptive education technologies" (Rudolph et al., 2023, p. 353) is part and parcel of the work of educators and policy makers and that these AI tools have much to offer students. Oates and Johnson argue that the new technology is not used simply:

> for the sake of modernization but has brought tangible benefits. Students can now access resources from any corner of the globe, teachers can tailor learning experiences to individual student needs, and educational administrators can streamline operations, all thanks to the capabilities provided by educational technology.
> (Oates & Johnson, 2025, Introduction)

What is not disputed is the fact that students need assistance to make the most of tools such as ChatGPT. "Educators play a pivotal role in guiding learners on the judicious use of AI, not as a dependency, but as a supplement" (Oates & Johnson, 2025, Introduction). Levine et al. (2024) believe than rather than attempting to punish students who make use of the new technology teachers "may find it more productive and fulfilling to focus their energy on guiding students to use generative AI responsibly as opposed to attempting the difficult task of detecting cheating – or even defining it – in this new era of AI" (Levine et al., 2024, Conclusion).

Please note that there are far more direct quotes in the above passage than one would normally find in a piece of academic writing. This had been done simply for the purposes of this exercise.

2.1 When direct quotes are used in academic writing one of the requirements is that the page number must be supplied. This has proved problematic as more research is published online and page numbers are not used. Other means must therefore be found to identify where, in the article cited, the reader can find the quotation. In the passage above there are four examples where this technique has been used. Find these examples:

OATES AND JOHNSON, 2025, INTRODUCTION.
WEISSMAN, 2023, TITLE
OATES & JOHNSON, 2025, INTRODUCTION
LEVINE ET AL., 2024, CONCLUSION

2.2 One of the requirements for using quotes in academic writing is ensuring that these quotes fit into the writing grammatically. Look at the sentences below. The quotes have not been grammatically inserted into the sentences. Change the sentences so that they are grammatical. Do not change the quotes.

2.2.1 Lingard argues that these AI tools perform a good function because "presenting information verbally in human-like text" (2023, p. 262).

2.2.2 Researchers who argue that these tools have much to offer students are supported by Oates and Johnson, who point out that they are useful "lies in their adaptability and responsiveness" (Oates and Johnson, 2025, Introduction).

2.2.3 Supporters of AI have high hopes of its benefits "that will benefit humanity as a whole" (Rudolph et al., 2023, p. 343).

2.2.4 However there is also concern that these tools are encouraging students to become lazy and should be carefully vetted "a plague upon education" (Weissman, 2023, Title).

HERE ARE POSSIBLE ANSWERS BUT THEY ARE NOT THE ONLY ONES THAT CAN BE PROVIDED.

2.2.1 LINGARD ARGUES THAT THESE AI TOOLS PERFORM A GOOD FUNCTION BECAUSE THEY PRESENT "INFORMATION VERBALLY IN HUMAN-LIKE TEXT" (2023, P. 262).

2.2.2 RESEARCHERS WHO ARGUE THAT THESE TOOLS HAVE MUCH TO OFFER STUDENTS ARE SUPPORTED BY OATES AND JOHNSON WHO POINT OUT THAT THEIR USEFULNESS "LIES IN THEIR ADAPTABILITY AND RESPONSIVENESS" (OATES AND JOHNSON, 2025, INTRODUCTION).

2.2.3 SUPPORTERS OF AI HAVE HIGH HOPES THAT ITS USE "WILL BENEFIT HUMANITY AS A WHOLE" (RUDOLPH et al., 2023, p 343).

2.2.4 HOWEVER THERE IS ALSO CONCERN THAT THESE TOOLS ARE ENCOURAGING STUDENTS TO BECOME LAZY AND SHOULD BE CAREFULLY VETTED. WEISSMAN DESCRIBES THEM AS "A PLAGUE UPON EDUCATION" (2023, TITLE).

3. Usually it is far better to paraphrase what an author has said. Rewrite the following quotations in your own words. Be careful to reflect their meaning accurately.

3.1 The new technology is not used simply "for the sake of modernization but has brought tangible benefits. Students can now access resources from any corner of the globe, teachers can tailor learning experiences to individual student needs, and educational administrators can streamline operations, all thanks to the capabilities provided by educational technology" (Oates & Johnson, 2025, Introduction).

3.2 Levine et al. (2024) believe than rather than attempting to punish students who make use of the new technology teachers "may find it more productive and fulfilling to focus their energy on guiding students to use generative AI responsibly as opposed to attempting the difficult task of detecting cheating – or even defining it – in this new era of AI" (Levine et al., 2024, Conclusion).

POSSIBLE ANSWERS:

3.1 OATES AND JOHNSON (2025) ARGUE THAT THE NEW TECHNOLOGY HAS PROVED USEFUL TO STUDENTS, TEACHERS AND ADMINISTRATORS. IT HAS ALLOWED STUDENTS ACCESS TO RESOURCES FROM ALL OVER THE WORLD. IT PROVIDES TEACHERS WITH AN OPPORTUNITY TO REDESIGN THEIR TEACHING SO THAT THEY CAN HELP ALL STUDENTS. THE NEW TECHNOLOGY ALSO MEANS THAT ADMINISTRATORS CAN WORK MORE SWIFTLY AND EFFICIENTLY.

3.2 LEVINE et al. (2024) BELIEVE THAT TAKING A PUNITIVE APPROACH TO STUDENTS WHO USE AI SYSTEMS IS UNWISE. THEY ARGUE THAT CURRENTLY IT IS DIFFICULT TO DEFINE

WHAT CHEATING IS, AND IT IS VERY HARD TO IDENTIFY STUDENTS WHO MIGHT BE USING AI IN WAYS THAT TEACHERS DISAPPROVE OF. A BETTER APPROACH WOULD BE TO WORK WITH STUDENTS TO ENSURE THAT AI IS USED IN WAYS THAT ARE USEFUL AND PRODUCTIVE.

References

Levine, S., Beck, S., Mah, C., Phalen, L., & Pittman, J. (2024). How do students use ChatGPT as a writing support? *Journal of Adolescent & Adult Literacy*. https://doi.org/10.1002/jaal.1373

Lingard L. (2023). Writing with ChatGPT: An illustration of its capacity, limitations & implications for academic writers. *Perspectives on Medical Education, 12*(1), 261–270. https://doi.org/10.5334/pme.1072

Oates, A., & Johnson, D. (2025). ChatGPT in the classroom: evaluating its role in fostering critical evaluation skills. *International Journal of Artificial Intelligence in Education.* https://doi.org/10.1007/s40593-024-00452-8

Rudolph, J., Tan, S., & Tan, S. (2023). ChatGPT: Bullshit spewer or the end of traditional assessments in higher education? *Journal of Applied Learning & Teaching, 6*(1), 342–363. https://doi.org/10.37074/jalt.2023.6.1.9

Weissman, J. (February 9, 2023). ChatGPT is a plague upon education. *Inside Higher Ed*. https://www.insidehighered.com/views/2023/02/09/chatgpt-plague-upon-education-opinion

Post-Class Activities

Ask students to find a short video clip about AI. Suggest a maximum length – say 10 minutes – and ask student to summarise the main points in a series of bullets. Each bullet should also include a brief direct quote illustrating the point being made. The brief quotes must be correctly cited. Students could exchange their work with each other. The quotes could be checked, and students could perhaps select the most interesting of the videos to circulate in class.

Lesson 2: Artificial Intelligence and Education

Time: 2 hours

Overview

In this lesson students will read a passage about the pros and cons of using chatbots in the higher education sector. They will be introduced to de Bono's thinking strategy and asked to analyse the text using the approaches advocated in the strategy.

Purpose and Strategies

Purpose	Strategies
Introduction to the use of AI in writing	Reading to introduce class to role of AI in academic writing.
Thinking critically	Weighing up advantages and disadvantages of using chatbots in academic writing.
Thinking creatively	Thinking of solutions for problems with AI in academic writing.
Using a thinking strategy	Students introduced to De Bono's six hat thinking strategy and asked to apply it to a problem.

Pre-Class Activities

⇒ *Teacher Notes*

Ask students about their experiences with chatbots. Probably most of them will be familiar with ChatGPT and might have used it to help with assignments. According to TechTarget (2025), ChatGPT is still the most popular chatbot but others, such as Microsoft Copilot, Google Gemini and Claude, are also becoming popular. So what do people use chatbots for? According to Brandtzaeg and Følstad (2017), the top uses are:

- ♦ To obtain information.
- ♦ To get assistance.
- ♦ For entertainment.

- To talk to someone.
- To try something new.

Chatbots are used to answer questions and to give advice on things such as travel. Some of the respondents said they found chatting with the chatbots fun and mentioned that they were often humorous. Others found companionship when they were lonely and other groups used them simply out of curiosity to find how they worked.

You might like to put questions like these to the class to get the discussion going:

- Do you use AI? (You might want to remind them that the editorial tools in Word are AI!)
- What do you know about chatbots?
- Which ones are you familiar with?
- How do you use them?
- How do you think other people use them?
- What do you think are the pros and cons?
- How do you think they will affect our lives in the future?

References

Brandtzaeg, P.B., & Følstad, A. (2017). Why People Use Chatbots. *Lecture Notes in Computer Science, 10673*. https://doi.org/10.1007/978-3-319-70284-1_30

TechTarget. (January 22, 2025). *The best AI chatbots for 2025: Compare features and costs*. https://www.techtarget.com/searchenterpriseai/tip/The-best-AI-chatbots-Compare-features-and-costs

During Class
Exercise 1

⇒ *Teacher Notes*

This is quite a long passage (911 words). It serves as a backdrop to the rest of the cycle, pointing out the pros and cons of the use of chatbots in education. In addition, it will be used as an exercise in putting a thinking strategy into practice. During the reading students should take brief notes. These notes should focus on what AI can offer and what the drawbacks are.

READING: THE ADVANTAGES AND DISADVANTAGES OF USING CHATBOTS IN EDUCATION

Artificial Intelligence (AI) refers to systems that are able to carry out tasks that would normally be performed by humans. Using AI in the area of languages has led to the development of chatbots that can understand and produce language (Farrokhnia et al., 2023). One of the most popular of these chatbots is Chat Generative Pre-Trained Transformer commonly known as ChatGPT. This chatbot was released in November 2022 and had soon gained over a million subscribers (Farrokhnia et al., 2023). Currently it is believed that over 400 million people use the chatbot weekly (Duarte, 2025).

The rapid technology advancements of this century have affected all sectors of society and the education sector is no exception (Oates & Johnson, 2025). It is therefore essential that educators evaluate the strengths and weaknesses of technological innovations to ensure that the use of these innovations will be of benefit to the student population.

Oates & Johnson (2025) note that ChatGPT is able to have meaningful conversations with its users. This means that students can engage in conversations with the chatbot, enabling the students to clarify issues. They can even use the chatbot to help them brainstorm ideas. Farrokhnia et al. (2023) highlight ChatGPT's ability to improve itself. The chatbot can remember earlier conversations and use these in its later responses. It can also customise the way it responds depending on the user's preferences and needs. For example, a student who is struggling to understand a difficult concept will be given a detailed explanation, while another who simply wants a summary will be given a brief overview (Oates & Johnson, 2025).

These personalised responses are very important in education. Students face different challenges in their studies and according to Oates & Johnson (2025), chatbots like ChatGPT can analyse student input and address individual problems. Their advice can be tailored to the needs and the interests of individual students. Unlike human tutors they are available 24 hours a day and the responses are very swift (Farrokhnia et al., 2023).

In addition, due to time constraints most human tutors are not able to provide feedback on numerous drafts, but writing is a process that requires drafting, reviewing and rewriting. ChatGPT can provide continuous feedback (Oates & Johnson, 2025). Also, AI can lessen lecturers' workload by providing feedback on student work (Farrokhnia et al., 2023). This frees academic staff up to engage in other activities that are beneficial to students.

Despite these impressive advantages the use of ChatGPT in the education sector also has serious drawbacks. Firstly, the chatbot does not understand the words it uses – it can identify patterns and deliver responses that sound correct but that does not mean that it understands the words it is using. What makes it worse is that ChatGPT does not have a world model (Farrokhnia et al., 2023) which means it does not fully understand the physical and social world we live in.

Significantly for researchers and students the accuracy of the information it provides has been called into serious doubt (Borji, 2023; Farrokhnia et al., 2023). Another significant concern for educators is that the chatbot appears to encourage plagiarism.

Plagiarism, according to Burton (2002), is the inclusion of another person's published words or ideas without acknowledgement. Research has shown that the latest ChatGPT models can generate "unique, coherent, and accurate responses that can evade text-matching software" (Elkhatat, 2023, Conclusion). The student can therefore submit work as their own although they have had no hand in creating it apart from providing a prompt to the software. Lecturers often find it difficult to distinguish between a student's writing and that of ChatGPT. Apart from the dishonesty of the act educators are also concerned that they will not be able to assess whether the student actually understands the material they need to master (Cotton et al., 2023).

Added to this is the concern that students might become too reliant on AI (Oates & Johnson, 2025) and this in turn could lead to a decline in their ability to reason and problem solve (Farrokhnia et al., 2023).

Then there is concern that the use of chatbots might lead to unfair discrimination against some student cohorts. ChatGPT, for example, is trained using data from Western European students (Farrokhnia et al., 2023) and might not be as useful for students from other cultural and ethnic groups.

Students themselves appear to be cautious about the use of chatbots in Higher Education. In a survey of almost 6000 students in Sweden (Stöhr et al., 2024) the researchers found that there was almost a fifty/fifty split between those who were positive about the use of chatbots in education and those who expressed reservations. While the students acknowledged that the chatbots could be very useful a large number were concerned about the impact they would have on education in the future. A study by Güner et al. (2024) of 88 students at a Turkish university indicated that most of the students felt positive about the use of chatbots but there were concerns that the use of the chatbots might promote dishonesty and plagiarism. They were also concerned that the use of ChatGPT could have a negative impact on students' ability to think creatively.

In summary it appears that that the emergence of chatbots is a mixed blessing. If they are to help academics and students reach their potential, they must be used in a way that is both accountable and transparent.

REFERENCES

Borji, A. (2023). A categorical archive of ChatGPT failures. arXiv. https://doi.org/10.21203/rs.3.rs-2895792/v1

Burton, I. (2002). *An Interactive Approach to Writing*. John Wiley & Sons.

Cotton, D.R., Cotton, P.A., & Shipway, J.R. (2023). Chatting and cheating: Ensuring academic integrity in the era of ChatGPT. *Innovations in Education and Teaching International*, 4(61). https://doi.org/10.1080/14703297.2023.2190148

Duarte, F. (2025, August 19). Number of ChatGPT users (July 2025). *Exploding Topics*. https://explodingtopics.com/blog/chatgpt-users

Elkhatat, A.M. (2023). Evaluating the authenticity of ChatGPT responses: a study on text-matching capabilities. *International Journal for Educational Integrity*, 19(15). https://doi.org/10.1007/s40979-023-00137-0

Farrokhnia, M., Banihashem, S.K., Noroozi, O., & Wals, A. (2023). A SWOT analysis of ChatGPT: Implications for educational practice and research. *Innovations in Education and Teaching International*, 61(3), 460–474. https://doi.org/10.1080/14703297.2023.2195846

Güner, H., Er, E., Akçapinar, G., & Khalil, M. (2024). From chalkboards to AI-powered learning. *Educational Technology & Society*, 27(2), 386–404. https://www.jstor.org/stable/48766180

Oates, A., & Johnson, D. (2025). ChatGPT in the classroom: evaluating its role in fostering critical evaluation skills. *International Journal of Artificial Intelligence in Education*. https://doi.org/10.1007/s40593-024-00452-8

Stöhr, C., Ou, A. W., & Malmström, H. (2024). Perceptions and usage of AI chatbots among students in higher education across genders, academic levels and fields of study. *Computers and Education: Artificial Intelligence*, 7. https://doi.org/10.1016/j.caeai.2024.100259

Exercise 1: Thinking Critically and Creatively

⇒ *Teacher Notes*

It is not possible to give students all the information they will need for their studies and the careers that will follow. Information is expanding so rapidly – it is estimated that 90% of the world's data was generated in the last two years alone (Duarte, 2025a, 2025b) – that it is impossible for students to *know* a subject. Therefore, it is important that we encourage critical and creative thinking. Critical thinking requires students to be analytical and logical. They are expected to question and critique. Creative thinking asks students to find solutions for problems. Various programmes exist to encourage the development of critical and creative thinking. One of the best known of these is the "six hats" model developed by Edward de Bono in 1994 (Karadağ et al., 2009). This model helps people think in a specific way for a period of time. The various "ways" of thinking are then combined to help people come up with solutions to problems.

With de Bono's six hat approach the idea is that a person metaphorically puts on a different hat and then approaches a problem using the type of thinking the hat represents (Kivunja, 2015).

The six hats are different colours – representing different ways of thinking. The table below explains the different ways of thinking and the questions that are associated with the thinking:

Hat	Type of thinking	Questions to ask
White	Objective thinking – looking for information	♦ What information is available? ♦ What information is missing? ♦ What information do we need to solve the problem? ♦ How can we get this information?
Yellow	An optimistic approach to solving the problem	♦ What are the good aspects of the situation? ♦ Who can benefit from this? ♦ What are the strengths we can use to solve problems?

(*Continued*)

Hat	Type of thinking	Questions to ask
Red	Draws on personal feelings	◆ How do I feel about this? ◆ What feels right? ◆ Am I excited/worried? ◆ Have my feelings changed as I learnt more?
Black	Critical – looks at problems. De Bono called this the most important hat	◆ What are the disadvantages of this? ◆ What harm could it do? ◆ Who will not benefit from this? ◆ Why could it not work? ◆ What problems could it create?
Green	Looking for new ideas and alternatives	◆ What haven't we thought about? ◆ What is interesting about this idea? ◆ Are there alternatives? ◆ What are they?
Blue	Turning it into action	◆ Where are we now? ◆ Where do we want to be? ◆ How do we get there?

Give students the worksheet where they can look at this table. Explain the purpose of the six hat approach and ask them what they think about it. Then work through the example below with the students. Ask them to add or change any of the suggested answers they feel could be improved. Stress that there are no right or wrong answers and that what is important is looking for innovative ways of solving problems.

References

Duarte, F. (February 24, 2025a). *Amount of data created daily.* https://explodingtopics.com/blog/data-generated-per-day

Duarte, F. (March 1, 2025b) *Number of ChatGPT users (Feb 2025).* https://explodingtopics.com/blog/chatgpt-users

Karadağ, M., Saritaş, S., & Erginer, E. (2009). Using the 'six thinking hats' model of learning in a surgical nursing class: sharing the experience and student opinions. *Australian Journal of Advanced Nursing, 26*(3), 59–69.

Kivunja, C. (2015). Using de Bono's six thinking hats model to teach critical thinking and problem solving skills essential for success in the 21st century economy. *Creative Education, 6*, 380–391. https://doi.org/10.4236/ce.2015.63037

Exercise 1

The library at X university is a very beautiful building but it is not really fit for purpose. It was built more than a 100 years ago and does not have the study space students require. It is also quite dark and gloomy, and expensive to heat in winter. However, it is an iconic building and well loved by staff and students. A decision has to be made as to whether a new library should be built. The old building will have to be demolished to make way for the new one. The committee that makes the decision has decided to use the six hat strategy. Read the points that have been raised below. Can you think of others that could be added?

Should the old library be demolished and a new library built?

White hat:

- The university will need to find a way to pay for the new building.
- The cost to heat the old building will double over the next ten years.
- Maintenance costs for old building will escalate dramatically over time.
- A number of old trees will have to be cut down if a new building is erected.

Yellow hat:

- The new library will be equally beautiful, just in a different way.
- Students are more likely to use the library if the study rooms are warm and well lit.
- Maintenance costs in the new building will be far lower.
- Students will be able to say what they would like in a library.

Red Hat:

- The old building is so beautiful and adds greatly to the atmosphere on the campus.

- The oak trees that will be cut down if a new building is erected are over two hundred years old.
- The current study rooms are small and poky and often cold and damp.
- The library always feels crowded and noisy.

Black hat:

- The university will struggle to find the money to fund the new building.
- There will be protests about pulling down the old building and cutting down the trees.
- What will happen in the interim between the opening of the new library and the closing of the old? Where will students find the resources they need and places to work?

Green hat:

- Perhaps parts of the old building could be incorporated in the new building.
- It might be possible to build around the trees, making courtyards and open spaces.
- Perhaps the new library could include accommodation for students – that would bring in funding to help cover construction costs.
- The trees might be moved to another part of the campus.

Blue hat:

- The main issues are the old building is dark, cold and too small.
- It is expensive to maintain in its current state.
- What is needed is more suitable study space for students, and a warmer lighter building.
- To achieve this the costs of renovation and rebuilding must be compared and the historic significance of the old building must be kept in mind.
- The feasibility of moving the trees elsewhere or incorporating them into a new design needs to be explored.

Exercise 2

⇒ *Teacher Notes*

Ask the students to get into groups. There are a few ways that these groups could be configured. If you have six in each group this gives students the option to assign a hat to each member, but that will mean that students only explore one aspect of the dilemma. Another approach might be to ask each group member to take a turn wearing each hat and jot down their findings and ideas. Once the group members have completed this task, they could get together to compare notes before filling in the table. Alternatively, the group could work together from the start and work through each approach to the problem as a whole group.

The question:

> *How can we ensure that the use of chatbots in education is beneficial for students?*

Examples have been included to help but you need to stress again that there are no right and wrong answers. Students could well put information in different boxes. As long as they can justify what they are doing that is not a problem. *NOTE*: Ask students to record their own thoughts – not just the material available in the passage.

Exercise 2

Use the six hat approach to come up with answers to the following question:

> *How can we ensure that the use of chatbots in education is beneficial for students?*

Use the table to record your answers. Examples have been provided.

Hat Type of thinking	
White Objective thinking –looking for information	Chatbots are very popular (over 400 million users weekly). CAN DO WORK NORMALLY ONLY DONE BY HUMANS. CAN HAVE MEANINGFUL CONVERSATIONS WITH USERS. CAN TAILOR CONVERSATIONS FOR INDIVIDUAL USERS.
Yellow An optimistic approach	Available to everyone with internet access. MAKES ALL TYPES OF INFORMATION EASILY ACCESSIBLE TO MILLIONS OF PEOPLE. CAN ACT AS A PERSONAL TUTOR FOR EVERY STUDENT. CAN SUMMARISE DIFFICULT ARTICLES FOR STUDENTS SO THAT THEY UNDERSTAND THE MATERIAL. IT IS AVAILABLE 24/7 TO HELP STUDENTS. ANSWERS ARE SUPPLIED VERY QUICKLY. CHATBOTS CAN CRITIQUE STUDENT WRITING AND IDENTIFY PROBLEMS. MULTIPLE DRAFTS CAN BE SUBMITTED FOR CRITIQUE. CHATBOTS CAN HELP STUDENTS IMPROVE THEIR WRITING.
Red Draws on personal feelings	It might be unfair if rich students can afford to use upgraded models to get good essays. PART OF ME WELCOMES CHAT GPT BUT I AM NOT SURE HOW GOOD IT WILL BE IN THE FUTURE. WILL STUDENTS CHEAT MORE? WILL I BE TEMPTED TO CHEAT? WILL THIS INTERFERE WITH A POSITIVE LEARNING EXPERIENCE?
Black Critical – looks at problems.	Chatbots don't really understand the world we live in. CHATBOTS DON'T REALLY UNDERSTAND THE WORDS THEY ARE USING. THE RESOURCES THEY PROVIDE MIGHT NOT BE ACCURATE. THEY MIGHT ENCOURAGE STUDENTS TO CHEAT. STUDENTS MIGHT BECOME TOO RELIANT ON THEM. STUDENTS MIGHT LOSE THEIR ABILITY TO REASON AND SOLVE PROBLEMS.

(Continued)

Hat Type of thinking	
Green Looking for new ideas and alternatives	Perhaps students could write exams in the classroom and just use chatbots to help them understand material. STUDENTS COULD HAND IN THREE VERSIONS OF AN ASSIGNMENT – ONE WRITTEN UNAIDED, ONE WRITTEN BY A CHATBOT, AND A FINAL ONE (FOR GRADING) THAT COMBINED BOTH EFFORTS.
Blue Turning it into action	At the moment it seems that chatbots can be very useful but there are serious issues with their use. Would it be an idea to try to get academics to agree on how they should be used? DO WE NEED MORE RESEARCH ABOUT CERTAIN ASPECTS – IF SO WHICH? EDUCATORS COULD CO-OPERATE WITH AI DEVELOPERS TO ENSURE THAT CHATBOTS ENHANCE STUDENT EDUCATION.

Post-Class Activities

⇒ *Teacher Notes*

1. Students could discuss the six hat thinking strategy and discuss how useful (or not) they found it. They could compare this strategy with the more common approach of simply looking at the advantages and disadvantages of certain options. The question that could be posed: *Is the six hat thinking approach more useful for writing an argumentative essay than analysing the pros and cons?*
2. Students can reflect on their own interactions with ChatGPT. What regulations (if any) would they like to see in place in their tertiary institutions? Why would they want these particular rules? If they don't believe that the use of chatbots should be regulated, how do they think the institutions should monitor plagiarism?

Lesson 3: Can Chatbots Be Trusted?

Time: 2 hours

Overview

This lesson provides students with an opportunity to determine the limitations of ChatGPT as well as its advantages. It also provides an opportunity to introduce students to Google Scholar, which is a very useful tool in finding articles and readings to help students write their assignments.

Purpose and Strategies

Purpose	Strategies
Testing reliability of chatbots	Class ask ChatGPT to write an essay of their choosing using academic references.
Introducing students to Google Scholar	Explain the importance of Google Scholar for evidence gathering.
Checking references	Students then use Google Scholar to check references.
Looking at structure of ChatGPT essay	Students use the framework from Cycle 4 Lesson 4 to identify strengths (and possible weaknesses) in the structure of AI essay.

Pre-Class Activities

⇒ *Teacher Notes*

Ask students to focus their attention on their own use of chatbots in their studies. How do they use chatbots? Research indicates that students use chatbots to:

- Develop their skills.
- Get immediate feedback.
- Get answers to academic questions.
- Access personalised learning.
- Obtain guidance through complex material (Labadze et al., 2023; Richter et al., 2024).

It might also be an idea at this stage to ask them to talk about the downsides of using chatbots in an educational setting.

References

Labadze, L., Grigolia, M., & Machaidze, L. (2023). Role of AI chatbots in education: systematic literature review. *International Journal of Educational Technology in Higher Education*, *20*(56). https://doi.org/10.1186/s41239-023-00426-1

Richter, S., Bate, G., Kishore, S., Inna Piven, I., & Dodd, P. (November 29, 2024). *What do students want from AI chatbots?* https://www.auckland.ac.nz/en/news/2024/11/29/what-do-student-want-from-ai-chatbots-.html

During Class
Exercise 1

⇒ *Teacher Notes*

AI has a great deal to offer students as they attempt to tackle challenges in their academic career. However, there are also numerous pitfalls in relying too heavily on their use. The following exercise has been designed to alert students to the dangers. In this introductory exercise I have chosen to use Google Scholar because it is free to access and provides a comprehensive and reliable service for checking academic articles (Martín-Martín et al., 2020).

In this exercise you will work with the students to show them how to check the references in a ChatGPT text. There are a number of ways that you might choose to approach this exercise:

- Adopt a whole-class approach with the teacher demonstrating how to use Google Scholar to check the references.
- Divide class into groups and allow the groups to check the references in their groups. This could work well with students who are familiar with Google Scholar. Another option would be to work through the first example with

the whole class and allow the groups to check the second example.
- ♦ Instead of groups, students could work in pairs or individually to check the references.

Example to use:
ChatGPT 4 March 2025
Seaweed is rich in essential nutrients, including proteins, fibres, vitamins, and minerals (Mata et al., 2018). It is particularly noted for its high content of iodine, calcium, magnesium, and iron, which are often lacking in plant-based diets. Additionally, seaweed contains bioactive compounds, such as polyphenols and carotenoids, which have antioxidant and anti-inflammatory properties.

Google Scholar can be opened and the reference typed in e.g.:

> Cui, Y., Yang, X., & Liang, X. (2020). Nutritional value and health benefits of seaweed. *Food Science & Nutrition, 8*(1), 5–15. https://doi.org/10.1002/fsn3.1369
>
> Mata, L., Martins, A., & Nunes, M. (2018). Seaweed: An alternative sustainable food source. *Food Research International, 109*, 79-85. https://doi.org/10.1016/j.foodres.2018.03.003

The students will then be able to check if the citation is accurate.
If the full citation, Cui et al., (2020) is entered; the article does not appear. If only the doi is typed in this is what comes up:

> Wang L., Chen Z., Han, B., Wu, W., Zhao, Q., Wei, C., & Liu, W. (2020). Comprehensive analysis of volatile compounds in coldpressed safflower seed oil from Xinjiang, China. *Food Science Nutrition, 8*, 903–914. https://doi.org/10.1002/fsn3.1369

Ask students if they can see why this article came up in Google Scholar. The answer is that the doi is the same. This would seem to indicate that the article cited by ChatGPT does not exist. Remind them that the doi can be used to as a shortcut to search for an article. Simply entering the doi in a search engine should lead to the article. However, there are other ways to search for this article. Ask students to try using the journal name. This will show them that this is indeed a journal with this title. It is an open access journal so they can search for the article. If they go to the journal website and enter Browse they will be able to see all the publications in the journal. They know that this particular publication is supposed to be in volume 8 Issue 1. Volume 8 was indeed published in 2020. There are a large number of articles in the issue, but not the one cited above.

The same holds good for Mata et al., 2018. What comes up is:

> Oliveira, D., Ares, G., & Deliza, R. (2018). The effect of health/hedonic claims on consumer hedonic and sensory perception of sugar reduction: Case study with orange/passionfruit nectars. *Food Research International, 108,* 111–118. https://doi.org/10.1016/j.foodres.2018.03.003

Again, the journal exists as does this volume and issue but not this article.

References

Martín-Martín, A., Thelwall, M., Orduna-Malea, E., & López-Cózar, E.D. (2020). Google Scholar, Microsoft Academic, Scopus, Dimensions, Web of Science, and OpenCitations' COCI: a multidisciplinary comparison of coverage via citations. *Scientometrics, 126,* 871–906. https://doi.org/10.1007/s11192-020-03690-4

Mata, L., Martins, A., & Nunes, M. (2018). Seaweed: An alternative sustainable food source. *Food Research International, 109,* 79–85. https://doi.org/10.1016/j.foodres.2018.03.003

Exercise 2

⇒ *Teacher Notes*

In this exercise students will work with their own material. Again, you could ask students to work in groups, pairs or individually.

Students will ask ChatGPT to write a 750-word essay on a title of their choice. Alternatively, you might want to give the essay title to them. If they all enter the same topic, it would then be possible to compare the different responses generated! The choice is yours. If you decide to allow them to select their own topics they can look to the worksheets they have already completed for inspiration e.g.:

- The potential of seaweed as a sustainable food source.
- Fast fashion in the 21st century.
- Using peer evaluation in the English classroom.
- The advantages and disadvantages of using AI to teach academic writing.
- Robot companions – curse or blessing?
- YouTube as an educational tool.

The wording of the prompt to ChatGPT is important. Here is an example:

Write a 750-word essay on the following topic: *Robot companions – curse or blessing?* Provide evidence for the claims in the essay by referring to at least five academic journals. Make use of APA 7. Make sure the articles cited really exist.

List the references and then explain whether they are accurate or not providing details as to what the problems are. Remind them to check:

- Journal title.
- Article title.
- Year of publication.
- Doi.
- Volume and issue number.
- Authors.

Here is an example of what students should do.

Reference provided:

Kasyanov, I., Sokolov, I., & Shevchenko, I. (2019). Humanoid robots in social interaction: A study on emotional engagement. *Journal of Robotics and Autonomous Systems, 113*, 121–130. https://doi.org/10.1016/j.robot.2018.11.004

Journal Title: This journal is simply called *Robotics and Autonomous Systems*.

Article title: There does not appear to be an article with this title.

Year of publication/volume and issue number/page numbers: *Robotics and Autonomous Systems* does have Volume 113 but there is no issue number. In this issue the article "'Fast finger design automation for industrial robots" is found on pp. 120–131.

Doi: The doi number belongs to an article entitled "Deep reinforcement learning with smooth policy update: Application to robotic cloth manipulation". This article is found in *Robotics and Autonomous Systems* but it is not the work of these authors.

Authors: These authors do not appear to have collaborated in the writing of any articles.

Did the AI tool give any warning about the content of the essay?

Students can then challenge the AI tools about non-existent references. Quite often the tool will return with assurances that the problems have been sorted. What appears to happen is that some of the references are genuine but a number are still fake.

Exercise 2

Ask ChatGPT to write a 750-word essay on a title of your choice. The wording of the prompt to ChatGPT is important. Here is an example:

Write a 750-word essay on the following topic: *Robot companions – curse or blessing?* Provide evidence for the claims in the essay by referring to at least five academic journals. Make use of APA 7. Make sure the articles cited really exist.

Read through the essay briefly, but focus primarily on the references. List the references and then decide whether they are accurate or not. If they are not accurate provide detail as to what the problems are. Check:

- Journal title.
- Article title.
- Year of publication/volume and issue number/page numbers.
- Doi.
- Authors.

Did the AI tool give any warning about the content of the essay?
Here is an example of what you are required to do:
Reference provided:

> Kasyanov, I., Sokolov, I., & Shevchenko, I. (2019). Humanoid robots in social interaction: A study on emotional engagement. *Journal of Robotics and Autonomous Systems*, 113, 121–130. https://doi.org/10.1016/j.robot.2018.11.004
> Journal Title: This journal is simply called *Robotics and Autonomous Systems*.
> Article title: There does not appear to be an article with this title.
> Year of publication/volume and issue number/page numbers: *Robotics and Autonomous Systems* does have Volume 113 but there is no issue number. In this issue the article 'Fast finger design automation for industrial robots is found on pp. 120–131.
> Doi: The doi number belongs to an article entitled "Deep reinforcement learning with smooth policy update: Application to robotic cloth manipulation". This article is found in *Robotics and Autonomous Systems* but it is not the work of these authors.
> Authors: These authors do not appear to have collaborated in the writing of any articles.

Exercise 3

⇒ *Teacher Notes*

As indicated earlier, there is much to recommend the use of AI in student writing and it is a good idea to make students aware of how they can put chatbots to positive use. In this exercise students will make use of part of the peer-review feedback form introduced in Cycle 4 Lesson 4. They will use this to critique the structure of the essay they instructed ChatGPT to write.

While it is impossible to provide a model answer for this question students will be expected to answer along the lines indicated below.

FEEDBACK on AI ESSAY

Structure	Reasons
Does the introduction state clearly what the essay will cover?	YES – THE INTRODUCTION TELLS THE READER THAT THE ADVANTAGES AND DISADVANTAGES OF USING ROBOTS AS COMPANIONS WILL BE LAID OUT.
Is the essay set out in a logical way?	YES – FIRST THE ADVANTAGES ARE EXPLORED THEN THE DISADVANTAGES AND FINALLY THE TWO ARE WEIGHED UP AGAINST EACH OTHER. FINALLY RECOMMENDATIONS ARE MADE AS TO THEIR USE.
Does it follow the plan set out in the introduction?	YES – THIS WAS THE PLAN OUTLINED IN THE INTRODUCTION.
Are the different sections linked? Provide examples where possible.	YES – FOR EXAMPLE IN THE INTRODUCTION WE ARE TOLD THAT THE ADVANTAGES WILL BE DISCUSSED AND THEN THE DISADVANTAGES. THE FIRST PARAGRAPH AFTER THE INTRODUCTION STARTS OFF BY SAYING *AS INDICATED IN THE INTRODUCTION THE ADVANTAGES OF ROBOT COMPANIONS WILL BE EXPLORED.* THIS SECTION ENDS BY SAYING *IN THE NEXT SECTION THE DISADVANTAGES OF HAVING SUCH COMPANIONS WILL BE DISCUSSED.*
Does the body of the essay cover all the points raised?	YES – IN THE INTRODUCTION THE READER IS TOLD THAT THE ADVANTAGES OF ROBOT COMPANIONS WILL BE DISCUSSED AND COMPARED AND THAT RECOMMENDATIONS TO IMPROVE THEIR USE WILL BE PROVIDED. THIS HAS BEEN DONE.
Does it discuss these points?	ALL THE POINTS ARE DISCUSSED ALTHOUGH MORE DETAILS ARE PROVIDED ABOUT THE ADVANTAGES THAN THE DISADVANTAGES.

(Continued)

FEEDBACK on AI ESSAY	
Structure	Reasons
Are possible solutions/new ideas raised?	YES – IT WAS SUGGESTED THAT PEOPLE SHOULD NOT JUST RELY ON ROBOTS AS COMPANIONS BUT THAT HUMAN COMPANIONS SHOULD BE PROVIDED AS WELL. IT WAS ALSO SUGGESTED THAT THESE ROBOTS COULD USE THE VOICES OF PEOPLE THAT ARE CLOSE TO THE PERSON USING THE ROBOT.
Does the conclusion summarise the main points raised?	YES – THE ADVANTAGES AND DISADVANTAGES ARE BRIEFLY SUMMARISED AND THE WARNING ABOUT RELYING TOO GREATLY ON ROBOTS TO PROVIDE COMPANIONSHIP IS STRESSED.
Does it indicate a direction that could be taken in response to the ideas raised?	YES – IT WAS SUGGESTED THAT MORE FUNDING BE PROVIDED FOR RESEARCH INTO DEVELOPING ROBOTS THAT ARE CAPABLE OF RESPONDING BETTER TO THE NEEDS OF USERS, AND FOR RESEARCH INTO FINDING OUT FROM USERS WHAT THEY WOULD LIKE THEIR COMPANIONS TO BE ABLE TO DO.

In groups, students could then discuss the advantages and disadvantages of using AI in writing essays.

Exercise 3

Exercise 2 demonstrated that you need to exercise care when you make use of ChatGPT for research purposes. However, ChatGPT can be very useful in providing examples of good writing. Use the peer-review feedback form introduced in Cycle 4 Lesson 4 to critique the structure of the essay you asked ChatGPT to write.

FEEDBACK on AI ESSAY	
Structure	Reasons
Does the introduction state clearly what the essay will cover?	
Is the essay set out in a logical way?	
Does it follow the plan set out in the introduction?	
Are the different sections linked? Provide examples where possible.	
Does the body of the essay cover all the points raised?	
Does it discuss these points?	

(Continued)

FEEDBACK on AI ESSAY	
Structure	Reasons
Are possible solutions/ new ideas raised?	
Does the conclusion summarise the main points raised?	
Does it indicate a direction that could be taken in response to the ideas raised?	

Post-Class Activities

- If students are interested, they can return to the table in Exercise 2 and challenge the chatbot about false citations. Often the chatbot will offer to rewrite the essay with genuine references, but for the large part these references too are fake. Students can have quite illuminating discussions with the chatbot about the problems. This could reinforce the message that information from these sources must be treated with care.
- Students could take a piece of earlier work and ask a chatbot to comment on the structure. Students could ask for a friendly approach or a more critical approach. This would allow them to see which of the two they prefer.

Lesson 4: AI and Plagiarism

Time: 2 hours

Overview

This lesson and the exercises are designed to help students identify plagiarism and provide them with strategies to avoid being accused of plagiarising. Students are given an explanation of what needs to be cited and what does not. Students are then required to put this knowledge into practice.

Purpose and Strategies

Purpose	Strategies
What is plagiarism?	Discussing the derivation of the word.
How do people plagiarise?	A simple explanation of the most common forms of plagiarism. A number of exercises are included to help students understand what plagiarism looks like in practice.
What doesn't need to be cited?	Explanation of what students don't need to cite with examples.
Revision of summarising and direct quoting	Students download an open access article and use a small section to practise summarising and direct quotes.

Pre-Class Activities

⇒ *Teacher Notes*

Research indicates that one of the leading causes of plagiarism is ignorance of what plagiarism is. This ignorance is found on two levels:

- ◆ A lack of understanding of the concept of plagiarism.
- ◆ A lack of understanding of plagiarism policies at the educational institution they are attending (Nabee et al., 2020).

A basic understanding of what constitutes plagiarism and how they can avoid it will stand your students in good stead. Certainly, there will always be students who will plagiarise intentionally, some because they lack the academic writing skills they need to successfully complete their assignments (Ayton et al., 2021). However, providing them with information about plagiarism and giving them the opportunity to develop skills to avoid it, either purposefully or inadvertently, will greatly assist your students.

Before you explore these materials with your class, it might be a good idea to explore their understanding of plagiarism. Here are a few questions you might use in the discussion:

- Do you know what plagiarism is?
- How would you explain this concept to people who do not know the word?
- Do you think plagiarism is widespread? Why do you think so?
- Do you think the average student understands what plagiarism is?
- Do you think students plagiarise without meaning to?

References

Ayton, D., Hillman, C., Hatzikiriakidis, K., Tsindos, T., Sadasivan, S., Maloney, S., & Illic, D. (2021). Why do students plagiarise? Informing higher education teaching and learning policy and practice. *Studies in Higher Education, 47*(9), 1921–1934. https://doi.org/10.1080/03075079.2021.1985103

Nabee, S.G., Mageto, J., & Pisa, N. (2020). Investigating predictors of academic plagiarism among university students. *International Journal of Learning, Teaching and Educational Research, 19*(12), 264–280. https://doi.org/10.26803/ijlter.19.12.14

During Class
Exercise 1

⇒ *Teacher Notes*

This exercise would probably be best tackled in groups. The purpose of the reading is to help students gain insight into what plagiarism is and the most common forms of plagiarism. Once the students have read the passage they can work on Exercise 1.

READING: WHAT IS PLAGIARISM?

Plagiarism comes from the Latin word *plagiarius* meaning kidnapper. This word, in turn, came from the Latin word *plag* which referred to a net used by hunters. The use of the word was later broadened to include a person who stole someone's words rather than their children (Merriam-Webster, n.d.). Gullifer and Tyson also talk about plagiarism as an "act of theft" (2010, p. 463).

Crème and Lillis explain it simply:

> One of the rules of academic writing is that you always attribute ideas that "belong" to somebody else. Put another way you must never try to pass off as your own, ideas that "belong" to somebody else and did not originate from you, particularly if they are published ideas.
>
> (2003, p. 63)

Citation therefore "is the practice of giving credit to others in one's work" (Lim, 2024, p. 387). If students do not have a sound understanding of what plagiarism is they might plagiarise unintentionally (Prashar et al., 2023); therefore it is important that students understand the concept. Unfortunately, it seems education institutions, on the whole, do not explain the concept well. Students are simply given a list of rules and told of the dire consequences of plagiarising. A better approach would be to stress that when students use citations they are demonstrating that their writing is based on "on a sound foundation of evidence" (Gullifer & Tyson, 2010, p. 472).

The most common forms of plagiarism include the following:

- Copying a text word for word without acknowledging the author.
- Copying a text making only minor alterations such as different verbs.
- Copying a text but leaving out a few sentences or parts of sentences.
- Changing the order of the sentences in a text.
- Rewriting a text in your own words but not acknowledging the author.
- Using someone else's diagrams, charts, illustrations pictures without acknowledgement.
- Getting another person to write the assignment for you. This includes paying someone to do your work.
- Getting someone to help you with an assignment and not acknowledging the help.
- Using material that you have submitted in one assignment in another assignment (Aronson, 2024; Swales & Feak, 2007).

REFERENCES

Aronson, J. (2024). When I use a word… Academic fraud – plagiarism. *British Medical Journal, 387*, q2627. https://doi.org/10.1136/bmj.q2627

Crème, P., & Lea, M. (2003). *Writing at University: A guide for students.* (2nd ed.).Open University Press.

Gullifer, J., & Tyson, G. A. (2010). Exploring university students' perceptions of plagiarism: a focus group study. *Studies in Higher Education, 35*(4), 463–481. https://doi.org/10.1080/03075070903096508

Hutson, J. (2024). Rethinking plagiarism in the era of generative AI. *Journal of Intelligent Communication, 3*(2). http://ojs.ukscip.com/index.php/jic

Lim, W.M. (2024). A pragmatic view of citations. *Activities, Adaptation & Aging, 48*(3), 387–392. https://doi.org/10.1080/01924788.2024.2379157

Merriam-Webster. (n.d.). Plagiarism. In *Merriam-Webster.com dictionary*. Retrieved February 26, 2025, from https://www.merriam-webster.com/dictionary/plagiarism

Nabee, S.G., Mageto, J., & Pisa, N. (2020). Investigating predictors of academic plagiarism among university students. *International Journal of Learning, Teaching and Educational Research, 19*(12), 264–280. https://doi.org/10.26803/ijlter.19.12.14

Prashar, A., Gupta, P., & Dwivedi, Y.K. (2023). Plagiarism awareness efforts, students' ethical judgment and behaviors: a longitudinal experiment study on ethical nuances of plagiarism in higher education. *Studies in Higher Education, 49*(6), 929–955. https://doi.org/10.1080/03075079.2023.2253835

Swales, J., & Feak, C. (2007). *Academic Writing for Graduate Students*. University of Michigan Press.

Exercise 1

⇒ *Teacher Notes*

Tight's article is available online. Students can download it themselves, but you could also print off the two pages (917–918) and give them to students to use.

> Tight, M. (2024). Challenging cheating in higher education: a review of research and practice. *Assessment & Evaluation in Higher Education, 49*(7), 911–923. https://doi.org/10.1080/02602938.2023.2300104

Students read the sections indicated and then answer the questions that follow.

1.1 Universities respond to issues such as dropout and non-completion by identifying at risk students (Tight, 2024). THIS IS PLAGIARISM AS THE WRITER HAS SIMPLY REARRANGED THE SENTENCES AND SUBSTANTIALLY USED THE SAME WORDS.

1.2 Tight (2024) argues that students would benefit if assessments were less numerous and better designed. THIS IS NOT PLAGIARISM. THE CONCEPT HAS BEEN REWORDED AND ACKNOWLEDGMENT PROVIDED.

1.3 Many universities now require students to submit their assignments through plagiarism detection software (Tight, 2024). THIS IS PLAGIARISM AS THE WRITER HAS NOT INDICATED THAT THESE WORDS ARE TAKEN DIRECTLY FROM TIGHT'S ARTICLE. THERE SHOULD BE QUOTATION MARKS AND THE PAGE NUMBER. "MANY UNIVERSITIES NOW REQUIRE STUDENTS TO SUBMIT THEIR ASSIGNMENTS THROUGH PLAGIARISM DETECTION SOFTWARE" (TIGHT, 2024, P. 918).

1.4 In his discussion of how the assessment system can be improved, Tight (2024, p. 917) argues that encouraging the development of "more meaningful assessments" would be a good step. THIS IS NOT PLAGIARISM – THE CONCEPT HAS BEEN REWORDED AND THE DIRECT QUOTE ACKNOWLEDGED.

Exercise 1

Download this article:

Tight, M. (2024). Challenging cheating in higher education: a review of research and practice. *Assessment & Evaluation in Higher Education, 49*(7), 911–923. https://doi.org/10.1080/02602938.2023.2300104

Read the two sections: *Identifying at risk students* and *Use of technology* (917–918) and then look at the passages that follow. Which ones have been plagiarised? Give reasons for your answers.

1.1 Universities respond to issues such as dropout and non-completion by identifying at-risk students (Tight, 2024).

1.2 Tight (2024) argues that students would benefit if assessments were less numerous and better designed.

1.3 Many universities now require students to submit their assignments through plagiarism detection software (Tight, 2024).

1.4 In his discussion of how the assessment system can be improved, Tight (2024, p. 917) argues that encouraging the development of "more meaningful assessments" would be a good step.

Exercise 2

⇒ *Teacher Notes*

In this exercise students are asked to summarise an author's ideas in their own words and then give their own opinion. The open access article is:

> Hutson, J. (2024). Rethinking plagiarism in the era of generative AI. *Journal of Intelligent Communication*, 3(2). https://ojs.ukscip.com/journals/jic/article/view/220/202

The extract is on p. 23, the section starting "However, concepts of academic integrity… teachers are expected to recognize these texts as part of common knowledge" (approximately 11 lines).

This is probably better as an individual exercise. However, when students have completed their answers exchanging what they have written with a partner would be useful. They could be asked to scrutinise each other's work in three ways:

1. See whether they believe that the author's ideas have been accurately summarised.
2. See whether the student's opinion is logical and well argued.
3. See whether the technical requirements have been met:
   a. Is the summary too close to the original?
   b. Is the quote well chosen?
   c. Does the quote fit grammatically into the summary?

HERE IS JUST ONE WAY STUDENTS COULD ANSWER:

> HUTSON (2024) NOTES THAT THE UNDERSTANDING OF PLAGIARISM DIFFERS AROUND THE WORLD. AMERICANS, WHO ARE STRONGLY INDIVIDUALISTIC, SEE IT AS STEALING ANOTHER PERSON'S IDEAS. HOWEVER, OTHER COUNTRIES DIFFER IN THEIR UNDERSTANDING. EAST ASIAN COUNTRIES OFTEN VIEW KNOWLEDGE AS SOMETHING THAT BELONGS TO SOCIETY, THAT IDEAS DO NOT BELONG TO ONE PERSON, SO "THIS NEGATES THE NEED FOR INDIVIDUAL ATTRIBUTION" (HUTSON, 2024, P. 23). SIMILARLY, AS HUTSON NOTES, MIDDLE EASTERN STUDENTS VIEW RELIGIOUS AND POLITICAL TEXTS AS BEING SO WELL-KNOWN NO CITATION IS NECESSARY.
> I BELIEVE CARE NEEDS TO BE TAKEN THAT STEREOTYPING DOES NOT BECOME AN ISSUE WITH CERTAIN STUDENT COHORTS. WHILE THERE ARE CLEARLY CULTURAL DIFFERENCES BETWEEN GROUPS, STUDENTS ARE ABLE TO UNDERSTAND THAT UNIVERSITIES IN OTHER COUNTRIES HAVE DIFFERENT REGULATIONS, AND THEY SHOULD ADJUST THEIR ASSIGNMENTS ACCORDINGLY.

Exercise 2

Download the PDF of this article:

> Hutson, J. (2024). Rethinking plagiarism in the era of generative AI. *Journal of Intelligent Communication*, 3(2). https://ojs.ukscip.com/journals/jic/article/view/220/202

Turn to p. 23 and read the section starting "However, concepts of academic integrity... teachers are expected to recognize these texts as part of common knowledge" (approximately 11 lines).

Rewrite this passage in your own words. You may use one short direct quote. Give your own opinion of the ideas in this passage, and how they could impact on ESL students.

Change exercises and read what your partner has written.

1. Has your partner summarised the author's ideas accurately?
2. Is the summary too close to the original?
3. Does the quote fit grammatically into the summary?
4. Is the quote well chosen?
5. Is their opinion logical and well argued?

Exercise 3

⇒ *Teacher Notes*

This exercise focuses on plagiarism involving the use of other people's words. Students are asked to identify the type of plagiarism and how it could be corrected so that the text is acceptable. Students could do the work in pairs or individually for this assignment. Each pair must complete the table below. They need to indicate the kind of plagiarism identified and then explain how it could be corrected. Once the students have finished, they could be given a copy of the model answer provided below and asked to compare this with their own attempts. It is important to stress that the model provides just one way to complete the exercise, and students should be encouraged to make suggestions as to different answers. Comparing the model answer to what students have written would provide the basis for a good class discussion. The article used is:

> Rospigliosi, P. 'asher.' (2023). Artificial intelligence in teaching and learning: what questions should we ask of ChatGPT? *Interactive Learning Environments*, 31(1), 1–3. https://doi.org/10.1080/10494820.2023.2180191

Type of plagiarism	Original text	Text in plagiarised version	How to correct the plagiarism
COPYING TEXT WORD FOR WORD WITHOUT ACKNOWLEDGING THE AUTHOR.	"The purpose of ChatGPT is to interact through conversation, which involves a series of questions from users and responses from the app."	The purpose of ChatGPT is to interact through conversation, which involves a series of questions from users and responses from the app.	ROSPIGLIOSI (2023) NOTES THAT "THE PURPOSE OF CHATGPT IS TO INTERACT THROUGH CONVERSATION, WHICH INVOLVES A SERIES OF QUESTIONS FORM USERS AND RESPONSES FROM THE APP" (P. 1).

(Continued)

Type of plagiarism	Original text	Text in plagiarised version	How to correct the plagiarism
COPYING A TEXT MAKING ONLY MINOR ALTERATIONS SUCH AS DIFFERENT VERBS.	"ChatGPT's ability to respond to follow-up questions allows students to challenge and clarify information."	ChatGPT is able to answer follow-up questions which allows students to challenge and ask questions about the information provided.	STUDENTS ARE ABLE TO MAINTAIN A DIALOGUE WITH CHATGPT. AS A RESULT, THE INFORMATION PROVIDED BY THE CHATBOT IS OPEN TO SCRUTINY AND CHATGPT CAN BE CALLED UPON TO EXPLAIN THIS INFORMATION (ROSPIGLIOSI, 2023).
COPYING A TEXT BUT LEAVING OUT A FEW SENTENCES, OR PARTS OF SENTENCES.	"The recent release of ChatGPT, a flexible and accessible form of artificial intelligence, raises a multitude of questions for those of us interested in interactive learning environments. The purpose of ChatGPT is to invite questions, but many of the questions being asked in relation to teaching and learning tend to focus on the potential risks of students misusing ChatGPT, for example by using it to write essays."	The release of ChatGPT, a flexible and accessible form of artificial intelligence, raises a multitude of questions about interactive learning environments. The purpose of ChatGPT is to invite questions, but the questions being asked in relation to teaching tend to focus on the potential risks of students misusing ChatGPT.	THE EMERGENCE OF CHATGPT IN THE TEACHING AND LEARNING ENVIRONMENT HAS LED TO NUMEROUS QUESTIONS BEING RAISED. THESE QUESTIONS TEND TO FOCUS ON CONCERNS THAT STUDENTS MIGHT USE CHATBOT DISHONESTLY (ROSPIGLIOSI, 2023).

(Continued)

Type of plagiarism	Original text	Text in plagiarised version	How to correct the plagiarism
CHANGING THE ORDER OF THE SENTENCES IN A TEXT.	"With ChatGPT, students can ask questions in their own words and receive responses tailored to their specific formulations. The ability to engage in a sequence of questions, follow-ups, and clarifications allows students to personalise the information they receive, making it their own."	The ability to engage in a sequence of questions, follow-ups, and clarifications allows students to personalise the information they receive, making it their own. With ChatGPT, students can ask questions in their own words and receive responses tailored to their specific formulations.	USING CHATGPT ALLOWS STUDENTS TO FORMULATE THEIR OWN QUERIES AND RECEIVE FEEDBACK IN A WAY THAT IS UNDERSTANDABLE TO THEM. THIS TYPE OF INTERACTION IS MORE LIKELY TO GIVE THEM A FEELING OF OWNERSHIP OF THE MATERIAL (ROSPIGLIOSI, 2023).
REWRITING A TEXT IN YOUR OWN WORDS BUT NOT ACKNOWLEDGING THE AUTHOR.	"As artificial intelligence becomes increasingly integrated into new learning environments such as the metaverse, it is essential that we consider the ethical implications and potential risks associated with its use …"	Because AI has become an important part of tertiary education there is an onus on educators to consider the dangers and ethical issues that arise with its use.	BECAUSE AI HAS BECOME AN IMPORTANT PART OF TERTIARY EDUCATION THERE IS AN ONUS ON EDUCATORS TO CONSIDER THE DANGERS AND ETHICAL ISSUES THAT ARISE WITH ITS USE (ROSPIGLIOSI, 2023).

Exercise 3

This exercise focuses on plagiarism involving the use of other people's words. You must decide whether the extract has been plagiarised or not. If it has, you must identify the type of plagiarism. For example, the writer might have copied the text word for word without acknowledging that they have done so. You must then show how the plagiarism could be corrected so that the text is acceptable.

Type of plagiarism	Original text	Text in plagiarised version	How to correct the plagiarism
	"The purpose of ChatGPT is to interact through conversation, which involves a series of questions form users and responses from the app."	The purpose of ChatGPT is to interact through conversation, which involves a series of questions form users and responses from the app.	
	"ChatGPT's ability to respond to follow-up questions allows students to challenge and clarify information."	ChatGPT is able to answer follow-up questions which allows students to challenge and ask questions about the information provided.	
	"The recent release of ChatGPT, a flexible and accessible form of artificial intelligence, raises a multitude of questions for those of us interested in interactive learning environments. The purpose of ChatGPT is to invite questions, but many of the questions being asked in relation to teaching and learning tend to focus on the potential risks of students misusing ChatGPT, for example by using it to write essays."	The release of ChatGPT, a flexible and accessible form of artificial intelligence, raises a multitude of questions about interactive learning environments. The purpose of ChatGPT is to invite questions, but the questions being asked in relation to teaching tend to focus on the potential risks of students misusing ChatGPT.	

"With ChatGPT, students can ask questions in their own words and receive responses tailored to their specific formulations. The ability to engage in a sequence of questions, follow-ups, and clarifications allows students to personalise the information they receive, making it their own."

"As artificial intelligence becomes increasingly integrated into new learning environments such as the metaverse, it is essential that we consider the ethical implications and potential risks associated with its use…."

The ability to engage in a sequence of questions, follow-ups, and clarifications allows students to personalise the information they receive, making it their own. With ChatGPT, students can ask questions in their own words and receive responses tailored to their specific formulations.

Because AI has become an important part of tertiary education there is an onus on educators to consider the dangers and ethical issues that arise with its use.

Post-Class Activities

⇒ *Teacher Notes*

Ask students in pairs to find an open access article and then draw up their own exercise based on the table they have just used. Different pairs could exchange and complete each other's exercises.

Lesson 5: What Students Think of Plagiarism

Time: 2 hours

Overview
In this lesson students look at summaries of four research studies into why students plagiarise. They are then asked to collect and table the relevant data. They will compare and contrast the research findings and give reasons for prioritising some of the findings. This lesson underscores the importance of providing evidence for claims and insights. In addition, it will provide students with an opportunity to explore their own feelings towards plagiarising.

Purpose and Strategies

Purpose	Strategies
Collecting data from different sources	Data is provided in a graph, bullet point text and paragraphs.
Tabling data from different sources	Students need to collate the data in a table.
Analysing data and giving own opinion	Students then assess the data and decide which they think are the most salient aspects. These are recorded in a table with justifications.
Revising own interpretation of the data	After a discussion with peers students are asked to consider revising their initial responses and recording the changes in the original table. Students then write a paragraph explaining their views.

Pre-Class Activities

⇒ *Teacher Notes*

Class Discussion on Cheating
Research into cheating indicates that the practice is widespread in universities. What is also clear is that the concept of collective cheating plays an important part in students' decision as to whether they should cheat (Grenness, 2022; Zanetti & Butera,

2025). Collective cheating is defined as "breaking the rules with several people" (Zanetti & Butera, 2025, p. 67). Basically, this can be summarised as students excusing their behaviour because "everyone does it". It appears, too, that certain types of cheating are seen as less serious than others. For example, the students in Grenness's study (2022) argued that plagiarism is not a serious form of cheating because it doesn't hurt anyone. This, of course, can be disputed. Clearly, it is detrimental to students who don't cheat! Another belief appears to be that it is not cheating if a student does not benefit from the action. If Student A allows Student B to copy an assignment, Student B is viewed as cheating but not Student A. One aspect that appears to be regarded seriously is contract cheating where a student gets another person to write the assessment. However, this is also open to interpretation – what if a student receives some help? How much help is too much? There is also concern that students are cheating themselves – that is that by not completing the tasks required of them they are not deriving the full benefit of what tertiary study has to offer.

This lesson deals with student perceptions of cheating and their motivation to cheat. A class discussion around the topic would be a good way to set the scene and allow teachers and students the opportunity to discuss the matter in a non-judgemental environment.

Possible questions:

- Do you think some forms of cheating are more serious than others? If so, what do you regard as serious cheating and what do you classify as less serious cheating?
- Do you think students are more likely to cheat if they know other students are cheating? Why do you think so?
- Do you think cheating hurts people? Who gets hurt? Why do you think this?
- If Student A lets Student B copy their assessment is Student A cheating?
- What is worse – paying someone to write your essay for you or getting an essay through ChatGPT? Are they both equally bad? Why do you think so?

- Do you think students get away with cheating? If you do think so, do you think this makes students more likely to cheat?

References

Grenness, T. (2022). "If You Don't Cheat, You Lose": An explorative study of business students' perceptions of cheating behavior. *Scandinavian Journal of Educational Research*, 1–15. https://doi.org/10.1080/00313831.2022.2116479

Zanetti, C., & Butera, F. (2025). Detecting collective cheating culture in academic contexts. *Educational Psychology*, 45(1), 67–86. https://doi.org/10.1080/01443410.2025.2449976

Exercise 1

⇒ *Teacher Notes*

In this exercise students are given the findings of four studies; two of these studies have been summarised into paragraphs, one is reported using bullets and in the first article a graph provides the necessary data. Students are required to table the reasons that the students in these studies gave for cheating. Students are also required to identify the reasons that are mentioned in more than one study and record the information from the most commonly cited reason to the least cited reason. In this exercise one factor (time pressures) is common to all the studies. The language in the summaries is accessible and students should not experience difficulties reading them. An example of what is required is provided in the table. If you think it is necessary, you could help students identify the reason given in all the studies. An answer is provided below.

This exercise can be done individually or in pairs.

Reason paraphrased	Kalicharan (2024)	Ayton et al. (2022)	Bennett (2005)	Awdry et al. (2020)
KALICHARAN DIFFERENTIATES BETWEEN THE DIFFICULTIES STUDENTS EXPERIENCED IN COPING WITH THEIR ASSESSMENTS AND THE OTHER DEMANDS IN THEIR LIVES. AYTON ET AL. SIMPLY COMMENTED ON STUDENTS' INADEQUATE TIME MANAGEMENT SKILLS. BENNETT REFERS TO THE FACT THAT STUDENTS HAVE TO SPEND A GREAT DEAL OF TIME IN MEETING THE DEMANDS OF THEIR ACADEMIC PROGRAMS. AWDRY ET AL. ALSO RAISES LACK OF TIME AS A REASON FOR PLAGIARISING.	ASSESSMENT WORKLOAD. BUSY SCHEDULE.	STUDENTS DO NOT ALLOW THEMSELVES SUFFICIENT TIME TO COMPLETE ASSIGNMENTS.	UNDER ACADEMIC PRESSURE.	LACK OF TIME.
Three studies identified student laziness as one explanation for plagiarism. Kalicharan gives laziness as a reason for plagiarising. Ayton et. al think that students are too lazy to cite their sources correctly. Awdry et. al also note that laziness appears to be a cause of plagiarism.	Laziness.	Lazy or lack motivation.		Laziness.
AYTON ET AL., BENNETT AND AWDRY ET AL. BELIEVE THAT THE FACT THAT STUDENTS DO NOT HAVE SUFFICIENT MASTERY OF ENGLISH CAN LEAD TO PLAGIARISM.		ENGLISH IS POOR.	ESL STUDENTS CAN ENCOUNTER LANGUAGE DIFFICULTIES.	STUDYING IN A SECOND LANGUAGE CAN LEAD TO PLAGIARISM.
TWO STUDIES HIGHLIGHT THE FACT THAT MANY STUDENTS HAVE A POOR UNDERSTANDING OF ACADEMIC WRITING AND CITATION.	STUDENTS DO NOT KNOW HOW TO CITE.	DO NOT HAVE NECESSARY ACADEMIC WRITING SKILLS.		
KALICHARAN ARGUES STUDENTS MIGHT NOT UNDERSTAND THE SUBJECT MATTER THEY ARE ASKED TO DISCUSS. AWDRY ET AL. AGREES WITH THIS REASONING.	DO NOT UNDERSTAND THE ASSESSMENTS THEY ARE REQUIRED TO WRITE.			DO NOT UNDERSTAND THE TOPIC.

BENNETT AND AWDRY ET AL. BOTH SAY THAT THERE IS ALSO A BELIEF THAT VERY FEW INCIDENTS OF PLAGIARISM ARE ACTUALLY UNCOVERED BY AUTHORITIES.		DO NOT BELIEVE THEY WILL BE CAUGHT.	PLAGIARISM WILL NOT BE DETECTED.
AWDRY ET AL. MAINTAIN THAT STUDENTS PLAGIARISE BECAUSE THERE IS PRESSURE ON THEM TO GET GOOD GRADES. BENNETT AGREES.		WANT TO OBTAIN GOOD GRADES.	PRESSURE TO OBTAIN GOOD GRADES
BENNETT SUGGESTS THAT IF STUDENTS FEEL SOCIALLY ISOLATED IN ACADEMIC INSTITUTIONS, THEY ARE MORE LIKELY TO PLAGIARISE. AWDRY ET AL. ALSO VIEW DISSATISFACTION WITH THE INSTITUTION AS A POSSIBLE REASON FOR PLAGIARISM.		ARE NOT HAPPY AT THEIR INSTITUTIONS.	DISSATISFACTION WITH THE TEACHING AND LEARNING ENVIRONMENT.
KALICHARAN IS THE ONLY RESEARCHER WHO ARGUES THAT STUDENTS MIGHT FIND IT DIFFICULT TO FIND DATA TO COMPLETE THEIR ASSIGNMENTS.	DIFFICULTY FINDING SOURCES.		
KALICHARAN POINTS OUT THAT STUDENTS MAY STRUGGLE TO IDENTIFY WHAT IS REQUIRED OF THEM IN THE ASSIGNMENT BECAUSE INSTRUCTIONS ARE NOT CLEAR.	DO NOT UNDERSTAND ASSIGNMENT INSTRUCTIONS.		
AYTON ET AL. SUGGEST THAT STUDENTS DO NOT RECEIVE ENOUGH GUIDANCE IN THE FEEDBACK ON THEIR ASSIGNMENTS TO HELP THEM AVOID PLAGIARISM.	DO NOT RECEIVE FEEDBACK ON ASSIGNMENTS THAT HELPS COMBAT PLAGIARISM.		
BENNETT BELIEVES THAT THE INTERNET HAS MADE IT MUCH EASIER FOR STUDENTS TO FIND MATERIAL TO PLAGIARISE.		EASIER TO PLAGIARISE.	
AWDRY ET AL. ARGUE THAT THERE IS OFTEN A BELIEF AMONGST STUDENTS THAT PLAGIARISM IS COMMONLY PRACTISED.			EVERYONE DOES IT.

Exercise 1

Study the data from the four research studies below.

Which reasons for student plagiarism are listed in the four studies? Begin by identifying the reason/s that are listed in all the studies, then in three of the studies, then two and finally reasons that are raised in only one study. Remember to explain the reasons in your own words. An example is supplied in the table.

First source:

> Kalicharan, L. (2024). Understanding Perceptions of Undergraduate Students on Academic Plagiarism. *European Journal of Contemporary Education and E-Learning*, 2(3), 9–17 https://doi.org/10.59324/ejceel.2024.2(3).02

Kalicharan (2024) conducted a study at a university in Guyana which she asked 278 first and second year students about plagiarism. She asked them why they thought students plagiarised.

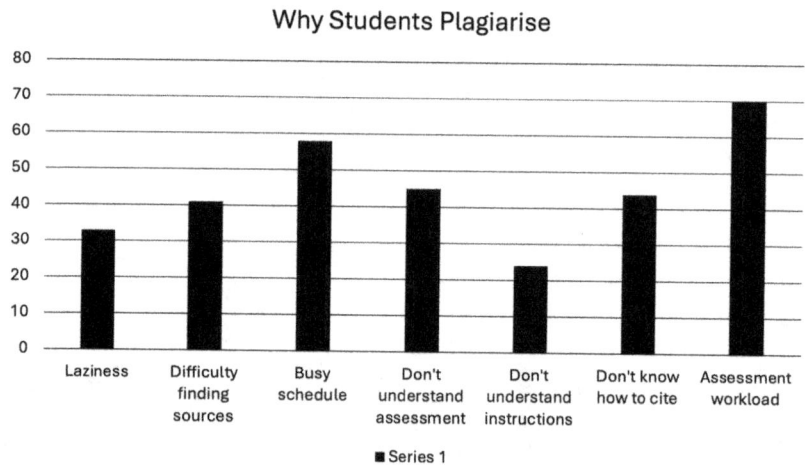

Second source:

> Ayton, D., Hillman, C., Hatzikiriakidis, K., Tsindos, T., Sadasivan, S., Maloney, S., … Illic, D. (2021). Why do students plagiarise? Informing higher education teaching and

learning policy and practice. *Studies in Higher Education*, 47(9), 1921–1934. https://doi.org/10.1080/03075079.2021.1985103

Ayton et al. (2021) sought to explore the views of undergraduate university students on the same topic at a university with campuses in Australia and Malaysia. The following areas were highlighted as possible causes for plagiarism:

1. Students did not have a strong understanding of what plagiarism is.
2. They did not have the necessary academic writing skills.
3. Sometimes students' English was poor.
4. Students did not receive helpful feedback about their assignments, so it was difficult to improve their writing and referencing.
5. Students may be lazy or lack motivation.
6. Students did not allow themselves sufficient time to complete assignments.

Third source:

Bennett, R. (2005). Factors associated with student plagiarism in a post-1992 university. *Assessment & Evaluation in Higher Education*, 30(2), 137–162. https://doi.org/10.1080/0260293042000264244

Bennett (2005) made an extensive survey of the literature on plagiarism and suggested a number of possible causes. Firstly, it has become much easier to plagiarise. Using the Internet students can access material from many sources. Secondly, students do not believe that educational institutions police plagiarism actively and the students believe they will not be caught. Thirdly, Bennett believes that students plagiarise because they want to obtain good grades. Fourthly, students appear to be under pressure because they have heavy academic workloads. This pressure might encourage students to plagiarise. Fifthly, students who are not first-language speakers of English and who encounter language difficulties appear to be more likely to plagiarise. Finally, Bennett noted that students who at not happy at their institutions and do not feel that they fit into academic life are more likely to plagiarise.

Fourth source:

> Awdry, R., & Ives, B. (2020). Students cheat more often from those known to them: situation matters more than the individual. *Assessment & Evaluation in Higher Education*, 46(8), 1254–1268. https://doi.org/10.1080/02602938.2020.1851651

In their article Awdry and Ives examine the literature to find reasons for student plagiarism. There are a number of factors, they argue. At a time when the number of people attending tertiary institutions has grown dramatically there are those who are dissatisfied with the teaching and learning environment in which they find themselves. Those who are studying in a second language might find assignments particularly challenging and this could provide an incentive to plagiarise. Nor, do the authors argue, is it simply a matter of not understanding the language. Research indicates that many students simply do not understand the topics of the assessments. Students are also under pressure to complete a number of assessments in a limited amount of time. Added to this is the fact that many students feel under pressure to obtain good grades and plagiarising will, they believe, help them achieve this. Some, of course, are lazy and there is also a belief that it is unlikely that their plagiarism will be detected. Finally, there appears to be an attitude on some campuses that "everyone does it", so students might feel that they will be disadvantaged if they do not plagiarise as well.

Which reasons for plagiarising are listed in the four studies? Begin by identifying the reason/s that are listed in all the studies, then in three of the studies, then two and finally reasons that are raised in only one study. Remember to explain the reason in your own words. An example is supplied.

Reason paraphrased	Kalicharan (2024)	Ayton et al. (2022)	Bennett (2005)	Awdry et al. (2020)
Four studies identified …				
Three studies identified student laziness as one explanation for plagiarism. Kalicharan gives laziness as a reason for plagiarising. Ayton et Al. think that students are too lazy to cite their sources correctly. Awdry et Al. also notes that laziness appears to be a cause of plagiarism.	Laziness	Lazy or lack motivation		Laziness
Complete the table.				

Exercise 2

⇒ *Teacher Notes*

This exercise should be done individually. Students will have different opinions as to what the main reasons for plagiarism are. Even if students choose the same options explanations will vary. Exercise 2.2 allows students to compare their choices and explanations with their peers.

Exercise 2

2.1 Now select the four reasons from the ones listed above that you believe are the main ones that cause students to plagiarise. Explain your choice briefly in your own words. An example has been provided:

Reason	Explanation	Changes/no changes after discussion
Students do not understand assignment instructions Kalicharan (2024).	I believe this is an important reason for students to plagiarise. Often students do not understand the vocabulary of the assessments. They do not know what words like "justify" mean and are thus uncertain as to what they should do.	
1.		
2.		
3.		
4.		

2.2 Once you have completed the first two columns of the table above, get together with a partner or in small groups and compare your answers. Have you chosen the same reasons? If you have chosen different reasons, listen to the explanations given by fellow students and then reconsider what you have selected. Would you make any changes? If so, what would you change and why? If not, why do you think differently to your peers?

Exercise 3

⇒ *Teacher Notes*

Encourage students to record their responses clearly and accurately. Tell them that they will be relying on the notes they make in this lesson for the assignment they will complete in Lesson 6. You might want to walk around the classroom while they are busy. You could ask a student about a particular reason they have chosen and get them to explain this to you orally. Often students find it easier to write when they have explained their ideas orally. Remind students to keep their summaries.

Exercise 3

Summarise briefly the four main reasons you believe students plagiarise and your explanation for this selection. This work will help you write the essay required in Lesson 6.

Post-Class Activities

⇒ *Teacher Notes*

This lesson has allowed students to explore the concept of cheating and the reasons provided by their peers for cheating. A short discussion at the end of the lesson would provide students with an opportunity to reflect on the practice. You could ask them if what they have read and heard has changed their mind about cheating.
Possible questions:

- Have you changed your mind about any aspects of cheating because of what you have read and heard? If so, in what why and how? If not, why not?
- Do you think tertiary institutions give enough information about cheating, and particularly plagiarism, to students?
- What information would you like?

Lesson 6: Writing an Essay about Plagiarism

Time: 2 hours

Overview
In this lesson students will draw on the data collected during earlier lessons, in particular Lessons 4 and 5, to write a 1500-word assignment. In addition, students will be asked to read the Discussion section of an academic article and incorporate the data in this article into their work. There is no introductory activity as students will need time to complete the essay.

Purpose and Strategies

Purpose	Strategies
Reading an academic article for data	Students will read the Discussion section of an open access article to find data for their essay.
Planning an essay	Students will be required to draw up a plan for their essay and hand it in for feedback.
Write 1500-word essay	Students will write a 1500 word article with intext citations and a reference list using the data they have gathered.

During Class
Exercise 1

⇒ *Teacher Notes*

In this lesson students will write a 1500-word essay on the following topic:

> Plagiarism in modern higher education: The student experience

In the essay students will define the concept and discuss the effect of plagiarism in higher education. They will examine student reasons for plagiarising and what factors appear to play an important role in the decision to plagiarise. They will then offer solutions to the issue. As in earlier essays, students have data collected during the cycle. Lessons 2 and 3 gave background information on the role of AI, particularly chatbots in education, while Lesson 4 focused on defining and explaining the concept of plagiarism. Lesson 5 explored student perceptions of plagiarism.

In addition, before they start writing the essay students will be asked to look at the following open access article:

de Lima, J.A., Sousa, A., Medeiros, A., Misturada, B., & Novo, C. (2022). Understanding undergraduate plagiarism in the context of students' academic experience. *Journal of Academic Ethics*, 20, 147–168. https://doi.org/10.1007/s10805-021-09396-3

The authors of this article surveyed 427 undergraduate students at a higher education institution in Portugal about plagiarism. Their research indicates that there is a relationship between individual factors (e.g. gender – men are more likely to plagiarise than women) and situational factors (e.g. students who are experiencing difficulties with their courses are more likely to plagiarise than those who are not experiencing the same problems). The article is an interesting read for those students who are willing to undertake it, but what is particularly relevant for students is the Discussion section (pp.162–165). Students will find material relevant to their essays in this section. They should read the relevant pages and incorporate the data into their own essays.

Before they start writing their essays students must draw up a plan. This must be handed in with the essay. When you mark this essay it would be a good idea to have the essay plan at hand. If there are problems in the essay, such as poor structure, look at the plan to see if the fault lies there or with the implementation of the plan. Good planning is a great help in ensuring logical coherent writing. You might want to make use of the same marking rubric you used in the last cycle.

Remind students that they must use intext citations and provide a reference list.

Exercise 1

During the course of Cycle 6 you have explored the role of AI, particularly chatbots, in modern higher education. You have also investigated the concept of plagiarism and student perceptions of this concept. You are now asked to write a 1500-word essay on the following topic:

Plagiarism in modern higher education: The student experience

In this essay you will define the concept and discuss the effect of plagiarism in higher education. You will examine student reasons for plagiarising and what factors appear to play an important role in the decision to plagiarise. You will then offer possible solutions to the issue. An additional source for your essay is the following article:

de Lima, J.A., Sousa, A., Medeiros, A., Misturada, B., & Novo, C. (2022). Understanding undergraduate plagiarism in the context of students' academic experience. *Journal of Academic Ethics*, 20, 147–168. https://doi.org/10.1007/s10805-021-09396-3

The article is accessible online.

The authors of this article surveyed 427 undergraduate students at a Higher Education institution in Portugal about plagiarism. Their research indicates that there is a relationship between individual factors (e.g. gender – men are more likely to plagiarise than women) and situational factors (e.g. students who are experiencing difficulties with their courses are more likely to plagiarise than those who are not experiencing the same problems). The article is an interesting read but what is particularly relevant for you is the Discussion section (pp. 162–165). In this section you will find data that you can use in your essay.

Before you start writing, draw up a plan. You will hand this in with your essay. Remember to use intext citations and provide a reference list.

7

Conclusion

Introduction

Assessment is necessary in all language programs. It provides students with an opportunity to demonstrate what they have learnt and what they are able to do with their newly acquired knowledge. Tests give teachers an insight into student progress and help them identify areas where the students need more assistance (Rauff & McCallum, 2020). The assessments discussed in this chapter are classroom assessments, designed as an aid to teaching and learning. They are not intended to be used to measure student achievement for administrative purposes. Hopefully they will provide teachers with information about issues in student learning which will enable the teachers to adjust their teaching strategies if necessary (Rauff & McCallum, 2020). While teachers acknowledge the importance of evaluating students, many are uncertain about designing tasks to perform this function (Rauff & McCallum, 2020). This chapter aims to help teachers set up class tests.

On the whole EAP programs seek to determine students' ability to cope in mainstream English Medium of Instruction classes (Douglas, 2013). Boud (2000) maintains that assessments need to do "double-duty" (p. 160). They must not only equip students to deal with the demands of their current writing studies but should also prepare students "to meet their own future learning needs" (Boud & Soler, 2016, p. 401). If assessments fulfil this criteria Boud describes them as sustainable, building as they do on the concept of assessment *for* learning rather than simply the assessment *of* learning.

To put it another way, assessment for learning can be seen as formative while assessment of learning is summative (Mahshanian et al., 2019). This is not to decry the role of summative assessment. Mahshanlan et al.'s study suggests that a combination of formative and summative assessments can lead to higher achievement than either formative or summative assessment separately. However, summative assessments are customarily high-stakes evaluations, used at the end of a teaching period to measure the outcome of student learning. In this particular context, students' admission to tertiary courses may well depend on these results (Kibble, 2017).

Sambell et al. (2012) have developed criteria for Assessment for Learning (AfL). They believe that lecturers should focus on what they want students to achieve and should not choose assessment types simply because they are easy to assess (e.g. multiple choice tests) or are what has traditionally been done in the discipline area (traditional essays). Secondly, they believe that lecturers should create opportunities for practice. Boud and Soler (2016) agree pointing out that encountering new tasks in assessment conditions is disconcerting for students and is not conducive to effective learning.

Sambell et al. (2012) believe that it is important that informal feedback is provided during formative assessment. They argue that providing feedback once the assessment has been completed does not maximise learning opportunities. This informal feedback could be dialogue with peers and teachers (Sambell et al., 2012). Students should be required to react to feedback (Gibbs, 2006). They are at liberty to disagree with what has been suggested, but they need to explain why they are rejecting suggestions for improvement. An approach incorporating these principles is discussed in an article by Seviour (2015).

Seviour reported on an assessment used in a pre-sessional English for Academic Purposes (EAP) writing course in the United Kingdom. The assessment was a single 2500-word essay written over a period of six weeks. At various stages during the course the students submitted draft plans for feedback. The final plan received 15% of the course mark. The students then submitted a draft of the essay which was marked and received another 15%. The final essay had a 70% weighting. The very real advantage of this approach is that students were working continually on a piece of writing and being given both written and oral feedback from their teachers. It is an interesting idea which will be explored in more detail later in the chapter.

One of the key principles of this book is that the lessons provided are sequenced and scaffolded. It is important, therefore, that the assessments designed to be used in conjunction with the lessons adhere to this principle. Students should be tested on what they have been taught. At the end of the course evaluations should cover the skills that have been built up over the five cycles. Students should be in a position to write a 1500 word essay which has been carefully planned and researched.

In the next section we look at using assessments in the classroom. The first assessment designed to be used at the end of Cycle 1 is discussed in detail below. The other assessments (Cycles 2, 3, 4 and 5) are available online. You can access them by visiting the book product page: https://www.routledge.com/9781032889801 (or search for the book title on https://routledge.com).

Assessment at the End of Cycle 1

This is a test that could be administered to students at the end of Cycle 1. However, it needs to be stressed that the assessment presented here is not designed to be a summative assessment and no marks have been allocated. The assessment provides an opportunity for teachers and students to identify what the students do well and where there might be challenges. The "test" could also be an opportunity for students to discuss their learning. It might, therefore, be a good idea to discuss each question in class once the question has been completed. Informal feedback from the teacher and other students might prove useful to all.

The assessment could be done individually or in groups or pairs. Again, you might decide to ask students to tackle some of the questions on their own and some with their peers.

Question 1

⇒ *Teacher Notes*

The passage in question 1 informs much of the test. At this stage it might be an idea to allow students to take control of the reading. If they are uncertain as to the meaning of words you could encourage them to try and infer the meaning from the context. If they are still at a loss you might want to allow the use of an online dictionary. However, point out to them that this option will probably not be available to them in formal test situations.

READING: ONLINE MENUS

Online food delivery platforms such as UberEats and Deliveroo have become popular particularly since the pandemic, when people could not visit restaurants.

Menus, as the first communication tool for customers, are very important for restaurants. This is particularly true when customers are ordering online. During the COVID-19 pandemic when people could not visit restaurants, getting people to order food online was a lifeline for restaurants. Even now, when people no longer have to stay at home, ordering food online has remained very popular. Customers find these online menus attractive because of their ease and speed of use. In turn, restaurants have experienced an upturn in profitability.

Research indicates that as far as the design of a good online menu is concerned, there are three important points. Firstly, the menu must be visually appealing; secondly, the menu must be informative; finally, ordering the food must be easy.

Visual Appeal

The online menus should have attractive images of the food to entice people to order. Not only should the food look appealing, but it should be attractively arranged on the plate. Customers are also influenced by factors such as background, text colours, fonts and dialogue boxes. However, restaurateurs must be careful that the photos accurately reflect the food that the purchasers will receive. Photos must be of the actual food made in the restaurant.

Information

Digital menus allow restaurants to provide a great deal of information inexpensively. This is important as people want to know what is in the food and how it was cooked. People are also interested in the health benefits of the food they are ordering. For example, it is a good idea to stress that a spinach salad is rich in iron. Research also shows that people are more likely to buy food that is described in a way that makes it sound tasty so words like "crispy", "tender" and "creamy" are useful. The names of the food items are also important. Consumers are more likely to order a Mouthwatering Melting Mouthful than just a cheeseburger. Next the price of the item must be shown clearly. This should also indicate what is included. For example, does the cost of the Mouthwatering Melting Mouthful include the fries and onion rings shown in the picture?

Convenience

People are concerned about convenience. Modern technology makes it possible for people to place orders through restaurant websites, via platforms such as Facebook or Instagram or through online food ordering services. People also want to be able to choose how they pay so there must a number of safe payment options. Finally, delivery should be fast. People do not want to have to wait for a long time when they are hungry.

REFERENCES

Bai, Y., Jung, S., & Behnke, C. (2024). Judging food by its description: a text mining approach examining the most influential words on restaurant menus. *Journal of Foodservice Business Research, 27*(2), 157–172. https://doi.org/10.1080/15378020.2022.2072153

Brewer, P., & Sebby, A.G. (2021). The effect of online restaurant menus on consumers' purchase intentions during the COVID-19 pandemic. *International Journal of Hospitality Management, 94*. https://doi.org/10.1016/j.ijhm.2020.102777

Gopal, S., Gil, M.T., Cydel Salian, B., & Baddaoui, J. (2024). Optimizing digital menus for enhanced purchase intentions: insights from India's restaurant industry in the post-COVID-19 era. *Cogent Business & Management, 11*(1). https://doi.org/10.1080/23311975.2024.2432536

Le, T.T., Bui Thi Tuyet, N., Le Anh, T., Dang Thi Kim, N., Trinh Thi Thai, N., & Nguyen Lan, A. (2023). The effects of online restaurant menus on consumer purchase intention: evidence from an emerging economy. *British Food Journal, 125*(7), 2663–2679. https://doi.org/10.1108/BFJ-10-2022-0916

Mao, W., Ming, L., Rong, Y., Tang, C.S. & Zheng, H. (2025). Faster deliveries and smarter order assignments for an on-demand meal delivery platform. *Journal of Operations Management, 71*, 220–245 https://doi.org/10.1002/joom.1354

McCall, M., & Lynn, A. (2008). The effects of restaurant menu item descriptions on perceptions of quality, price, and purchase intention. *Journal of Foodservice Business Research, 11*(4), 439–445. https://doi.org/10.1080/15378020802519850

Vocabulary

⇒ *Teacher Notes*

The first exercise is familiar to students and should assure them that they can cope with the assessment.

   1.1   Find one word in the passage that means the same as the following:

something which provides help or support	LIFELINE
things that can be chosen from a number of possibilities	OPTIONS
boost	UPTURN
something that produces good results	BENEFITS
tempt	ENTICE
cheaply	INEXPENSIVELY

   1.2   Paraphrasing

⇒ *Teacher Notes*

This exercise is also familiar to the students. Students could discuss the various options in pairs.
Read the following paragraph:

> Researchers studied the impact of a menu design on consumer perceptions. They found that the appropriate images can elicit a strong feeling of craving. In addition, they found that people respond to the name and description of a particular dish and that they anticipate the enjoyment they will experience.
> (Adapted from: Le et al., 2023)

Which of the following best paraphrases this extract? Choose a reason for your choice.

Paraphrases:

1. People who buy food from pictures on the menu are influenced by good images.
2. Researchers examined the impact of menu design on consumers' perceptions. Their findings show that appropriate pictures can bring about a strong craving. They also discovered that people respond to particular dishes and anticipate their enjoyment.
3. Research has found that while people appreciate menus with good images of the food with which they are familiar these pictures do not have a great impact on what they buy.
4. According to research, customers are influenced by pleasing images of the food portrayed on online menus. People report having a desire for certain foods after seeing these images. When they see the pictures of these dishes they think about how they will enjoy eating this food.

Possible reasons:

- There are too many words that are the same as the original text.
- This paraphrase does not capture the meaning of the original text.
- This paraphrase is too brief and does not contain all the information in the original text.
- This paraphrase is the best answer because it gives all the information in the original text but it does so in different words.

MODEL ANSWER

SENTENCE	√	X	REASON
1		X	1 IS BRIEF AND DOES CAPTURE THE MAIN IDEA. UNFORTUNATELY, IT IS TOO BRIEF AND DOES NOT CONTAIN ALL THE INFORMATION IN THE ORIGINAL TEXT – THERE IS NO MENTION OF PEOPLE DESIRING PARTICULAR DISHES.

(Continued)

SENTENCE	√ X	REASON
2	X	2 THERE ARE TOO MANY WORDS THAT ARE THE SAME AS THE ORIGINAL TEXT – E.G. CONSUMERS, PERCEPTIONS, CRAVING, ANTICIPATE.
3	X	3 CANNOT BE ACCEPTED BECAUSE IT HAS NOT CONVEYED THE INFORMATION IN THE ORIGINAL TEXT. IT IS SAYING THE COMPLETE OPPOSITE OF WHAT IS CONTAINED IN THE TEXT.
4	√	4 IS THE BEST ANSWER. IT GIVES ALL THE INFORMATION IN THE ORIGINAL TEXT BUT IT DOES SO IN DIFFERENT WORDS.

1.3 Paraphrasing Information

⇒ *Teacher Notes*

This exercise is quite difficult, and students should be given enough time to think about it. I would suggest that students attempt the paraphrase on their own, but that they be encouraged to work in pairs to compare their respective answers. Students could then be given an opportunity to make changes to their original responses. It might be interesting if you ask them to hand in both their original and revised versions and ask them to explain the changes they have made in the latter. Research indicates that consciously thinking about the language they have employed benefits students learning. You will have a chance to observe and comment on the way they have incorporated suggestions. It is important that they learn to differentiate between good and bad advice!

1.4 Paraphrasing information

Read the following short passage and then paraphrase it.

> If restaurants wish to give themselves a competitive edge in the market they must focus not only on their dine-in service but must also be mindful of how they do business online. To maximise the chances of online success restaurants must realise that online menus can significantly influence a customer's perception of a meal.
>
> (Adapted from Brewer & Sebby, 2021)

Brewer, P., & Sebby, A. (2021). The effect of online restaurant menus on consumers' purchase intentions. *International Journal of Hospitality Management, 94* 102777. https://doi.org/10.1016/j.ijhm.2020.102777

IF RESTAURANTS WISH TO BE SUCCESSFUL, THEY NEED TO PAY AS MUCH ATTENTION TO THEIR ONLINE CUSTOMERS AS THEY DO TO THOSE DINERS WHO EAT IN THE RESTAURANT. TO ENSURE THAT THEIR ONLINE SERVICE IS MEETING THEIR CUSTOMERS' NEEDS RESTAURANTS MUST BE AWARE OF THE IMPORTANCE OF THEIR ONLINE MENUS. IT IS ESSENTIAL TO APPRECIATE THE ROLE THAT THESE MENUS PLAY IN CUSTOMERS' IMPRESSIONS OF THEIR MEALS.

1.5 Linking words

⇒ *Teacher Notes*

In this exercise students are asked to locate linking words in the passage and identify their function.

1.6 Linking words

In the passage, there are a number of sequence and addition linking word/s. Find 5 of them and identify whether they are sequence or addition linking words. Make sure you have examples of both sequence and addition linking words. Then complete the table below. An example is provided.

Linking word	Type of linking word	Example
FIRSTLY	SEQUENCE	FIRSTLY, THE MENU MUST BE VISUALLY APPEALING – IN OTHER WORDS, IT MUST LOOK GOOD.
SECONDLY	SEQUENCE	SECONDLY, THE MENU MUST BE INFORMATIVE – IT MUST GIVE CUSTOMERS A LOT OF INFORMATION ABOUT THE FOOD THEY CAN ORDER.
FINALLY	SEQUENCE	FINALLY ORDERING THE FOOD MUST BE CONVENIENT – IN OTHER WORDS, IT MUST BE EASY TO ORDER AND PAY FOR THE FOOD.

(Continued)

Linking word	Type of linking word	Example
ALSO	ADDITION	IT IS ALSO IMPORTANT THAT THE FOOD THAT IS DELIVERED TO THE CONSUMER LOOKS LIKE THE PICTURE ON THE MENU.
ALSO	ADDITION	PEOPLE ARE ALSO INTERESTED IN THE HEALTH BENEFITS OF THE FOOD THEY ARE ORDERING.
LIKE	ADDITION	RESEARCH ALSO SHOWS THAT PEOPLE ARE MORE LIKELY TO BUY FOOD THAT IS DESCRIBED IN A WAY THAT MAKES IT SOUND TASTY SO WORDS LIKE CRISPY, TENDER AND CREAMY ARE USEFUL.
NEXT	SEQUENCE	NEXT THE PRICE OF THE ITEM MUST BE SHOWN CLEARLY. THIS SHOULD ALSO INDICATE WHAT IS INCLUDED.
ALSO	ADDITION	THEY LIKE THE FACT THAT THEY CAN ORDER FOOD QUICKLY AND EASILY AND ALSO NOT HAVE TO TRAVEL.
ALSO	ADDITION	THEY ALSO WANT TO BE SURE THAT THESE OPTIONS ARE SAFE.
FINALLY	SEQUENCE	FINALLY, THERE SHOULD BE FAST DELIVERY.

1.7 Categorising

⇒ *Teacher Notes*

This exercise tests students' understanding of the passage and their ability to place ideas in the correct category. Again, this might be a good exercise for students to do individually and then compare answers in pairs.

1.8 Categorising

Designing an online menu requires that you think carefully about a number of factors in three categories. Some of these factors have been filled in. Using the passage you have just read, fill in the gaps.

What to consider when designing an online menu

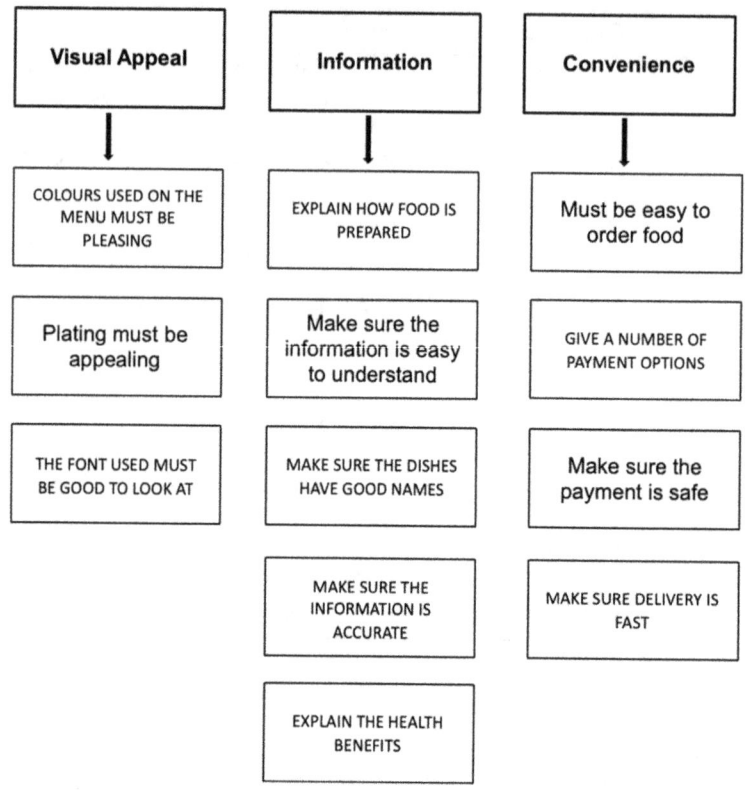

1.9 Analysing writing

⇒ *Teacher Notes*

In this exercise students are asked to apply the guidelines provided in the passage to ads for burgers. This exercise is probably open to different interpretations so once each student has formulated an answer ask them to get into groups and compare answers. If time allows, you might want to extend this exercise by asking students to reformulate the ads so that they better meet the criteria set down in the reading.

1.10 Analysing writing

Read the following ads for vegetarian burgers

A This scrumptious vegetarian burger is what you been waiting for. Sandwiched in a soft golden sesame bun is a succulent patty that oozes goodness. You can enjoy this mouthwatering mouthful without feeling guilty! Make your meal even better by including crisp fries cooked to perfection in avocado oil – the nutritionist's choice! Delivered to your doorstep in 15 minutes or you don't pay!

B   This vegetarian burger (350 calories) contains a soy patty. $9.00. Fries (220 calories) are an extra $5.00.

The reading will help you complete the tables.

What is done well in Ad A? What has not been done well?

What has been done well	What has not been done well
THE BLURB/CAPTION IS VERY APPEALING AND MAKES ONE WANT TO EAT THE BURGER.	NO PRICE IS GIVEN
THERE IS GOOD INFORMATION ABOUT THE FRIES.	WE DO NOT KNOW IF THE FRIES ARE INCLUDED WITH THE BURGER.
SOME OF THE HEALTH BENEFITS ARE EXPLAINED.	TOO LITTLE INFORMATION IS GIVEN ABOUT THE PATTY.
THERE IS INFORMATION ABOUT THE EXPECTED DELIVERY TIME.	MORE INFORMATION ABOUT WHAT IS IN THE REST OF THE BURGER WOULD BE A GOOD IDEA.

What is done well in Ad B? What has not been done well?

What has been done well	What has not been done well
WE KNOW THE FRIES ARE NOT INCLUDED WITH THE BURGER.	THE BLURB/CAPTION IS VERY DULL AND DOES NOT MAKE ONE WANT TO EAT THE BURGER.
THE PRICE IS GIVEN.	THERE IS NO INFORMATION ABOUT DELIVERY
WE ARE GIVEN INFORMATION ABOUT THE PATTY.	MORE INFORMATION ABOUT WHAT IS IN THE BURGER APART FROM THE PATTY WOULD BE A GOOD IDEA.
CALORIE COUNTS ARE GIVEN FOR THE HAMBURGER AND THE FRIES.	

Reference

Le, T.T., Bui Thi Tuyet, N., Le Anh, T., Dang Thi Kim, N., Trinh Thi Thai, N., & Nguyen Lan, A. (2023). The effects of online restaurant menus on consumer purchase intention: evidence from an emerging economy. *British Food Journal*, 125(7), 2663–2679. https://doi.org/10.1108/BFJ-10-2022-0916

Question 2

⇒ *Teacher Notes*

Question 2 is more academic than the first question. Students should now feel confident that they can manage the test items.
Read the passage and answer the questions that follow.

READING: INSECTS AS FOOD

Food supplies around the world are becoming increasingly uncertain partly because of population growth. Traditional agricultural methods will not be able to meet demand, particularly in a world that is facing growing environmental threats. Edible insects, which are widely distributed globally, can play an important role in helping to meet the demands of a hungry world. Over 1900 insect species are part of the diet of at least two billion people in 113 countries. On the North American continent Mexico appears to have the greatest variety of edible insects – 450 in total. A number of South American countries are also rich in edible insect life. Brazil has 140 edible species while Ecuador and Colombia have 93 and 62, respectively. Another continent rich in edible insects is Asia. China has 235 edible species, but Thailand with 272 and India with 262 species are even more richly endowed. Edible insects are an important part of the diet of many African countries. The Democratic Republic of the Congo has by far the most species – 255. The Cameroons is a distant second with 100 species followed by Zambia with 78, the Central African Republic with 62, South Africa with 56 and Zimbabwe with 52.

   Not everyone is prepared to make use of this food source. In many countries insects are regarded with distaste. Insects like cockroaches are regarded with aversion because they are associated with dirt and sickness. Yet mosquitoes, which are far more likely to spread deadly diseases, are not regarded with such dislike.

However, it appears that there are ways to overcome people's revulsion. A study of German people's willingness to eat insects found that Germans were more willing to eat processed insect-based foods (e.g. cookies made with cricket flour) compared to unprocessed foods. Consequently, the introduction of insects as a food source in those countries that do not typically eat insects is more likely to succeed if insects are incorporated into familiar food items.

REFERENCES

Deroy, O., Reade, B., & Spence, C. (2015). The insectivore's dilemma and how to take the West out of it. *Food Quality and Preference, 44*, 44–55. https://doi.org/10.1016/j.foodqual.2015.02.007

Hartman, C., Shi, J., Giusto, A., & Siegrist, M. (2015). The psychology of eating insects: A cross-cultural comparison between Germany and China. *Food Quality and Preference, 44*, 148–156. https://doi.org/10.1016/j.foodqual.2015.04.013

Omuse, E. R., Tonnang, H. E. Z., Yusuf, A. A., Machekano, H., Egonyu, J. P., Kimathi, E., Mohamed, S. F., Kassie, M., Subramanian, S., Onditi, J., Mwangi, S., Ekesi, S., & Niassy, S. (2024). The global atlas of edible insects: analysis of diversity and commonality contributing to food systems and sustainability. *Scientific reports, 14*(1). https://doi.org/10.1038/s41598-024-55603-7

Orkusz, A., & Orkusz, M. (2024). Edible insects in Slavic culture: Between tradition and disgust. *Insects*, 15, 306. https://doi.org/10.3390/insects15050306

Bar Chart

⇒ *Teacher Notes*

Students are familiar with this exercise. It requires careful reading and note taking but it is not particularly taxing. This is probably best done individually. Students could mark their own work.

2.1 Draw up a bar chart to show the 10 countries in the world with the largest number of edible insect species. Indicate approximately what those numbers are.
ANSWER

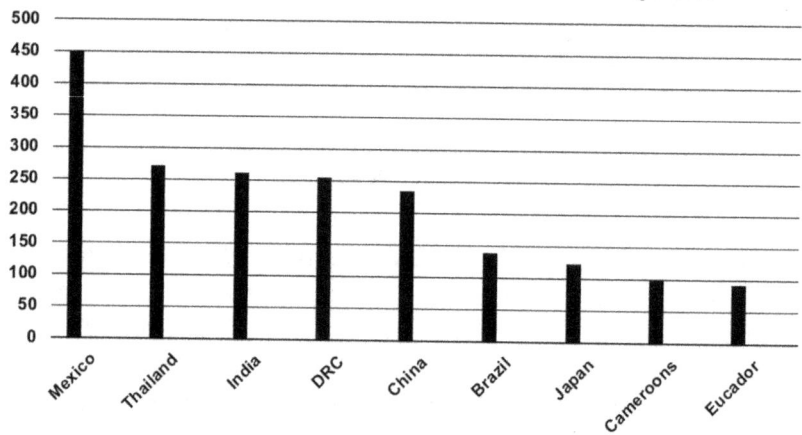

Vocabulary

⇒ *Teacher Notes*

This is a simple vocabulary exercise, highlighting the use of formal language.

2.2 Find four words in the reading that illustrate most people's feelings towards insects.
AVERSION, DISTASTE, DISLIKE, REVULSION

Expanding on Text

⇒ *Teacher Notes*

The following two questions ask students to use the material in the text and also to expand their answers. This could be turned into a brief class discussion which students could then use to help frame their answer to the final question.

2.3 Why do many people regard most insects with distaste? Is this feeling always logical?

>   INSECTS ARE OFTEN ASSOCIATED WITH DIRT AND DISEASE. PEOPLE'S FEELINGS ARE NOT ALWAYS LOGICAL AS INSECTS LIKE MOSQUITOES THAT SPREAD FAR MORE DANGEROUS DISEASES THAN COCKROACHES ARE NOT REGARDED WITH THE SAME LOATHING.

2.4 There are some insects which are well regarded – for example bees, ants and ladybirds. Why do you think this is so?

>   THESE INSECTS ARE OFTEN SEEN AS BENEFICIAL. BEES ARE ESSENTIAL FOR THE POLLINATION OF CROPS; ANTS HELP KEEP THE SOIL HEALTHY; AND LADYBIRDS KEEP APHIDS AND OTHER PLANT EATING PESTS IN CHECK.

My Attitude Towards Insects

⇒ *Teacher Notes*

In this final exercise students are asked to combine their own opinion with the information in the reading. It is a good exercise to monitor whether students follow instructions, an essential skill in future studies Many students are penalised simply because they do not do what was asked of them. In this exercise students need to indicate:

- Whether they would finish a drink if they found an insect in it.
- The insects (if any) that would not deter them from finishing the drink.
- The insects (if any) that would definitely deter them from finishing the drink.
- The categories that these two sets of insects fall into.
- The reasons for the categorisation.
- Circumstances that might cause them to finish the drink despite their reluctance.

I suggest you mark this exercise. Concentrate, in particular, on whether the students have done what they were asked to do. Give credit for original or appealing answers but the main point is to indicate to students whether they have followed the assessment brief or not.

> 2.5   My attitude towards insects
>
> If you found an insect in your drink, would you take it out and finish the drink anyway? Would your reaction differ according to the insect? For example, how would you react to a fly/beetle/wasp/bee/cockroach/spider/worm? Group the insects that would elicit the same reaction from you. Do you believe other people would react in the same way? Discuss your reasons for the categorisation. Are there any circumstances that could change your initial response? What would they be? Write approximately 150–200 words.
>
> FINDING AN INSECT IN ONE'S DRINK IS NOT A PLEASANT OCCURRENCE BUT IT IS BETTER THAN FINDING HALF AN INSECT. I WOULD PROBABLY TAKE OUT A BEE, A WASP OR A SPIDER AND FINISH MY DRINK. THIS IS BECAUSE I REGARD THESE AS CLEAN INSECTS. IT WOULD NOT BOTHER ME TO FINISH MY DRINK IF I HAD REMOVED THEM. HOWEVER, I WOULD NOT FEEL THE SAME ABOUT FLIES, COCKROACHES OR WORMS BECAUSE I REGARD THESE AS DIRTY INSECTS AND I FEEL THE DRINK WOULD NOT BE HYGIENIC. IF I WAS VERY THIRSTY OR WAS GREATLY ENJOYING THE DRINK I MIGHT FISH OUT A WORM AND CONTINUE DRINKING. I KNOW THAT THERE ARE SOME KINDS OF ALCOHOL THAT ARE BOTTLED WITH WORMS. I WOULD NOT FINISH THE DRINK IF A COCKROACH OR FLY HAD LANDED IN IT. I DETEST THESE INSECTS, AND NOTHING WOULD PERSUADE ME THAT THE DRINK WAS SAFE. I BELIEVE THAT OTHERS SHARE MY FEELING THAT THERE ARE CLEAN AND DIRTY INSECTS AND MOST PEOPLE WOULD ACT IN THE SAME WAY I WOULD. (175 words)

Alternative Assessments

Alternative assessment, according to Naraghizadeh et al. (2022), is "an ongoing process in which the students and teacher judge the success of the student using non-conventional methods" (p. 267). As far as academic writing is concerned, this means the different literacy skills are evaluated in circumstances similar to the situation in which these skills will be applied. Alternative assessment tests what students can *do* as opposed to what they know. For example, students are asked to demonstrate their understanding of intext citations by using citations in their writing. They are not asked to cite the relevant rules or to use citations in random sentences. In alternative assessments learners are required to demonstrate high-level thinking skills in real-life situations (Monib et al., 2020). These assessments are meant to focus on process and product, requiring students to evaluate and critique both the process and the product (Monib et al., 2020). Alternative assessments are increasingly being used in ESL/EFL classrooms around the world (Monib et al., 2020; Naraghizadeh et al., 2022).

An interesting article by Fraile et al. (2017) describes an exercise in which students co-created a rubric for marking essays with their teachers. This type of formative assessment is aimed at improving students' self-confidence and helping them reach a deeper understanding of what is required in their written assignments (Taylor et al., 2024). Chamcharatsri (2016) believes this approach is a democratic exercise that encourages students to take ownership of their work.

An Alternative Assessment in Essay Writing

This assessment has several steps and could take students some time to complete. Ideally it would be an activity that students could undertake when the course is finished. This alternative assessment would allow them to put into practice the skills they have acquired.

Step 1: Agreeing on a Rubric
A rubric is a list of assessment criteria and expected levels of performance for each part of an assignment. A rubric breaks down complex tasks into smaller, manageable parts and explains what is considered satisfactory or unsatisfactory work (Taylor et al., 2024). To simplify the task students could make use of the feedback form used in Cycle 4. I have provided a partial outline of how you might design a rubric with your students using the feedback form. You and your class could complete this rubric together or you could devise an entirely new one. There are numerous examples in the literature.

Rubric

	Excellent	Good	Satisfactory	Unsatisfactory
Structure	The introduction indicates very clearly what the essay will cover and how it will be covered. The essay follows the plan set out in the introduction and links between the different sections are carefully explained. The conclusion succinctly summarises the main points of the essay. It clearly indicates directions that could be taken in response to issues raised in the essay.		The introduction gives some indication of what the essay will cover and how it will be covered but the explanation could be clearer. The essay follows the plan to some extent. The links could be better developed. The summary in the conclusion does not adequately capture all the main points but gives a brief overview of what has been discussed. An attempt is made to suggest possible responses.	
Content				
Use of language	The vocabulary used is appropriate for the context. The sentences are well structured and the correct linking words are employed. It is an easy and pleasurable read. The mechanics of the writing (grammar, spelling, punctuation) are excellent.			
Referencing and in-text citations				

Step 2: Deciding on a Topic

It is motivating for students if they are allowed to write on a topic that appeals to them. You could let each student select their own topic, but I suggest that it might be more rewarding to encourage students to think about having one class topic or a few topics. This would allow them to pool resources and give peer reviewers deeper insight into the subject matter of essays they are reviewing. The class could select one topic or break into interest groups in which they negotiate a topic. If you have sufficient students from the same disciplines, they could work in an area of mutual interest. If the students have difficulty coming up with suggestions here are a few ideas:

- Social media platforms should be held accountable for the misinformation on their platforms.
- All citizens should be required to perform a year of community service once they have left school.
- Reality TV shows are a negative influence on society.
- Nuclear energy should never be used as a primary source of power.
- Human cloning should be allowed for medical purposes.
- Internet access should be a basic human right.
- Freedom of speech is more important than national security.

Step 3: Looking for Sources

If you are teaching in a tertiary institution your library might well offer sessions on locating data. If this is the case you could encourage your students to attend a session or one of the librarians might be happy to run a session for you. This short clip is a sensible introduction to finding credible sources that students might find helpful.

https://www.youtube.com/watch?v=esuRxK44d00

Remind them that once they have found a useful article the reference list of that article could well lead them to other informative sources. At this stage one of the reasons for working in interest groups or as a whole class becomes apparent. Students can share their sources. These sources can be uploaded to a shared workspace such as Teams. The groups (or the class) can decide if there is a minimum number of articles that each student should post – or possibly a maximum as well. Having duplicates will not be a problem as this will indicate that more than one student believes a certain source is valuable.

Step 4
Writing a plan – students can refer to the work done in the course to help them write a plan for their essay. At this stage students might want to discuss their plans with each other or consult the teacher.

Step 5
Using the plan as a guide students will write the first draft of their essay.

Step 6
Students will exchange the drafts for peer reviewing. Once the reviews have been completed, students will discuss the recommendations as writers and reviewers and decide which changes to implement.

Step 7
Students will revise the initial draft and submit this version to the teacher. The teacher will then have short interviews with each student to discuss the essay.

Step 8
Using teacher input the students will write a final version of their essay. After they have proofread the essay, it will be submitted for marking. The teacher will use the rubric designed in Step 1.

Conclusion

I hope this chapter has given you a few ideas as to how you can incorporate assessment as a learning tool in the academic writing classroom.

My goal in writing this book was to create something that could be of practical use to writing teachers. We know that in HE institutions "disciplinary knowledge and understanding are largely exhibited and valued through the medium of writing" (Coffin et al., 2003). Turner (2011) points out that policies such as widening participation have encouraged an increasing number of students from a wide range of backgrounds to enrol at tertiary institutions. Unfortunately, these same institutions often assume that "language is easily dealt with and easily fixed" (Turner, 2011, p. 18). We know that this is not so.

References

Boud, D. (2000). Sustainable assessment: Rethinking assessment for the learning society. *Studies in Continuing Education*, *22*(2), 151–167. https://doi.org/10.1080/713 695728

Boud, D., & Soler, R. (2016) Sustainable assessment revisited. *Assessment & Evaluation in Higher Education*, *41*(3), 400–413. https://doi.org/10.1080/02602938.2015.1018133

Chamcharatsri, B. (2016). Student-generated rubric assessment: A meaningful literacy practice. *Journal of Assessment & Teaching of English Language Learners*, *1*, 50–60.

Coffin, C., Curry, M.J., Goodman, S., Hewings, A., Lillis, T.M., & Swan, J. (2003). *Teaching Academic Writing: A toolkit for higher education*. Routledge.

Douglas, D. (2013). ESP and assessment. In B. Paltridge & S. Starfield (Eds.), *The Handbook of English for Specific Purposes*, pp. 367–383. Wiley-Blackwell.

Fraile, J., Panadero, E., & Pardo, R. (2017). Co-creating rubrics: The effects on self-regulated learning, self-efficacy and performance of establishing assessment criteria with students. *Studies in Educational Evaluation*, *53*, 69–76 https://doi.org/10.1016/j.stueduc.2017.03.003

Gibbs, G. 2006. How assessment frames student learning. In C. Bryan & K. Clegg (Eds.), *Innovative Assessment in Higher Education*, pp. 23–36. Routledge.

Kibble, J.D. (2017). Best practices in summative assessment. *Advances in Physiology Education*, *41*, 110–119. https://doi.org/10.1152/advan.00116.2016

Mahshanian, A., Shoghi, I. R., & Bahrami, I.M. (2019). Investigating the differential effects of formative and summative assessment on EFL learners' end-of-term achievement. *Journal of Language Teaching and Research,10*(5), 1055–1066. https://doi.org/10.17507/jltr.1005.19

Monib, W.K., Karimi, A.Q., & Nijat, N. (2020). Effects of alternative assessment in EFL classroom: A systematic review. *American International Journal of Education and Linguistics Research, 3*(2), 7–18.

Naraghizadeh, M., Azizmalayeri, F., & Khalaji, H. (2022). EFL teachers' perceptions and practices of alternative assessment Strategies and their relationship with teacher reflection. *The Journal of English Language Pedagogy and Practice, 15*(30), 266–290.

Rauff, M., & McCallum, L. (2020). Language assessment literacy: Task analysis in Saudi universities. In L. McCallum & C. Coombe (Eds.), *The Assessment of L2 Written English across the MENA Region: A Synthesis of Practice*, pp. 13–41. Palgrave Macmillan.

Sambell, K., L. McDowell, and C. Montgomery. (2012). *Assessment for Learning in Higher Education*. Routledge.

Seviour, M. (2015). Assessing academic writing on a pre-sessional EAP course: Designing assessment which supports learning. *Journal of English for Academic Purposes, 18*, 84–89. http://doi.org/10.1016/j.jeap.2015.03.007

Taylor, B., Kisby, F., & Reedy, A. (2024). Rubrics in higher education: an exploration of undergraduate students' understanding and perspectives. *Assessment & Evaluation in Higher Education, 49*(6), 799–809. https://doi.org/10.1080/02602938.2023.2299330

Turner, J. (2011). *Language in the Academy: Cultural Reflexivity and Intercultural Dynamics*. Multilingual Matters.

For Product Safety Concerns and Information please contact our EU
representative GPSR@taylorandfrancis.com
Taylor & Francis Verlag GmbH, Kaufingerstraße 24, 80331 München, Germany

www.ingramcontent.com/pod-product-compliance
Lightning Source LLC
Chambersburg PA
CBHW071359300426
44114CB00016B/2111